D1420561

# FILM REVIEW

1957 ★ 1958

YUL BRYNNER as the Pharaoh Rameses II orders his chariots to pursue and slay the slaves freed from his bondage by Moses. A scene from Cecil B. deMille's vastly spectacular *Paramount* picture THE TEN COMMANDMENTS.

# FILM REVIEW

*Compiled and edited by*

*F. MAURICE SPEED*

Yul Brynner as the Pharaoh in DeMille's
THE TEN COMMANDMENTS

*MACDONALD & CO. (Publishers) LTD.*

*1957-1958*

When you look at *M-G-M's* new glamour star BARBARA LANG it isn't easy to realise that she was once stricken with polio and told by her doctors she would never walk again. Miss Lang made her screen debut in THE HOUSE OF NUMBERS and has several more films lined up. Say *M-G-M* " Miss Lang falls into a definite category—she is definitely *not* the girl next door. "

# CONTENTS

*Universal-International's* popular young male star AUDIE MURPHY who though mainly seen in Westerns is now having a wider range of parts. His recent films have included JOE BUTTERFLY and NIGHT PASSAGE.

IF you saw the postman arriving early in the morning, and for many mornings, with a parcel of some 300 letters under his arm, and you knew that most of them would call for some sort of answer, how do you imagine you would feel ? I think I can guess ; you see, it happened to me last year.

When in the Introduction to the 1956–57 edition of FILM REVIEW I mentioned a demand —small, but still a demand—from some quarters for the dropping altogether, or at least a severe pruning, of those sections of the book devoted to covering in detail the film releases of the year and a greater concentration on the more general, or "fan" angles, I never for one moment imagined what I was letting myself in for. Typical of the many, and sometimes really abusive letters which I had as a result (and they came from literally all over the world, Australian readers in particular being most vituperative) was one which said, in so many words, that if I ever did adhere to such a scandalous plan and dropped the thumbnail reviews, with the other details of the year's films, they would make it their business to rub out the publisher, hamstring me personally and otherwise bring death and destruction to all concerned with this heretical theory.

Anyway, let me now assure this reader, and all others who wrote in similar if less violent vein, that no such revolution is considered. As I replied personally to all correspondents, the reaction provoked by even the hint was quite enough to convince all concerned that FILM REVIEW should be left as it is. To my intense joy, let me add. For I have always felt, as I think you know by now, that this volume does serve a real purpose and fills a gap that no other annual attempts. I always intended FILM REVIEW to be a record in word and picture of the year in the cinema, and it's the only one to give a complete list of the year's releases together with all such relevant details as the directors, producers and the casts of those films.

It would be, I assure you, a lot easier for me to fill these pages with articles by and about the stars ; with glamour pictures and all the rest of it. But even if the work involved would be considerably less, so would my satisfaction when the book went on sale.

All this means the present volume, the fourteenth in the series, will be found to be more or less strictly in line in style, contents and format with its predecessors. Its main object is again to give you a clear picture of the year in the cinema, the films and events of that year and a comprehensive idea of the films you'll be seeing in your local cinemas next year. Even the special features are designed with the same idea, to give you a better idea of all angles of film production and presentation.

A final point. I don't always mention it these days but I am still most consistently grateful to all the film companies for the very great assistance they give me ; nobody could ask for more co-operation than they supply. And I am grateful, too, to everyone else concerned with the production of the book, from my secretary to the printers, from my own family (who deal each year with the thousands of snapshots which have to be sent out at the rate of hundreds a day) to the publisher, who is so indulgent with my whims. Without this co-operation from all concerned there could, of course, be no FILM REVIEW annual.

It only remains for me to wish you all a happy twelve months of moviegoing and to express the hope that we'll all meet again next year—same time, same place.

NATALIE WOOD is *Warners'* busy and beautiful little star who made a hit in REBEL WITHOUT A CAUSE and has since appeared in THE SEARCHERS and THE BURNING HILLS. Latest film is THE GIRL HE LEFT BEHIND and her next is BOMBERS B 25

*J. Arthur Rank* star ANTHONY STEEL, whose more recent films have included CHECKPOINT, Betty Box's exciting motor racing film in which he played a driver mixed up in a plot to smuggle a murderer across the border.

FOR the cinemas this has been a year of constant battle. With something like desperation they have been forced into fighting on several fronts. On the one hand they have been seeking overdue relief from the crippling high rate of taxation, and on the other they have been objecting to the forced levy by which a portion of every admission fee goes towards a fund for further British production.

It was obviously becoming an impossible situation when, with large numbers of cinemas closing down because they were losing money, the rest were paying out to the Chancellor of the Exchequer 6*s*. 4*d*. in every pound taken at the box office with another 6*s*. going out in wages. The balance had to cover everything from film hire to overheads !

On top of these twin battles the cinema was also, of course, engaged in a struggle with the counter attractions of TV, and though I think that now, as in the past, too much is made of the opposition afforded in the long run by the small screens, it is quite obvious that TV must have had some effect on the falling cinema attendances.

However, in the case of TV, the cinema's counter attack with the new large-screen techniques, the fuller use of colour and spectacle, and the concentration on fewer and better films, has already had some effect, and not only was the recent several-year trend of falling audiences halted, but actually some ground was won back.

Ultimately anything can happen. It is quite certain that before many years have passed TV will also be generally projected and received in colour and larger screens than anything now used are also a probability. But there is no need for the cinema to feel despondent about this, for personally I've no doubt that the film-makers with further innovations and advances will be able to hold the long technical, artistic and entertainment lead they already hold over TV.

Turning now to the films themselves, production has been running pretty steadily at the rate of the previous year. I understand something like 130 British films will have been available to British exhibitors for 1957 as against 120 during 1955 and 130 last year (these figures are approximate).

The corresponding numbers of American films available here have been 300 (1957), 310 (1956) and 330 (1955). The total of foreign films available, that is films from countries other than America, have stayed pretty steady at around the 80 mark.

It is, incidentally, extremely interesting to note that according to one poll taken in this country, seven out of the top ten money makers of 1956 were British productions, with *Reach For the Sky*, *Private's Progress*, *A Town Like Alice*, *The Baby and the Battleship*, *Cockleshell Heroes*, *It's Great to be Young* and *Sailor Beware* named, along with America's *Trapeze*, *The Bad Seed* and *The Searchers*.

British films however, high as their standard now is, still don't get the wide and general showing in America which British producers feel they deserve, and it was stated last winter by John Davis, boss of the J. Arthur Rank empire, that he was doing something positive about this situation. He announced that the Rank Organisation was setting up a new and specialised distribution organisation in America to sell our pictures to the New World. And part and parcel of this operation was to be the purchase of a number of American cinemas to ensure an outlet for them. As the first step in this direction, in May last the 600-seat Sutton cinema in New York was bought on a long lease. This was promised to be just the start and more purchases of a similar nature would follow.

In the past several brave attempts have been made to get British pictures a wider showing in America, but they have all failed. This time, owing to the way in which the matter is being dealt with, allied to the present definite film shortage in America, there seem greater possibilities than ever previously that the job may be pulled off.

British production has been flourishing and most of the studios still operating have been pretty busy. The Rank group has been pouring out a steady stream of movies and they have maintained a pretty high standard. Likewise have the Associated British productions. Though these films may not all have been what might be termed " critics' pictures " they have made money and from the film industry point of view that is what really matters. Prestige is fine, as one producer put it, but prestige and penury have an unhappy knack of going hand in hand !

Of course, it would be wrong to sound a too optimistic note. Everything in the cinematic garden isn't lovely and it would be idle to pretend it is. Very sobering to all concerned was the Rank announcement last autumn that because of high costs and the throttling effects of the Entertainments Tax they had decided to close down some 79 Odeon and Gaumont cinemas that were no longer paying their way. They explained that though these cinemas were losing money they had between them contributed something over £455,000 in tax ! At the same time it was

21-year-old *M-G-M* star MARJORIE HELLEN, former waitress, model and " bit " part actress who became " Miss Colour Television of New York ". Her first important screen part was in *M-G-M's* HOT SUMMER NIGHT.

*REVIVALS. With the new screen sizes and with many companies selling or leasing their old films in blocks to TV in America, we may see less re-issues of the old screen classics in the cinemas in the years to come, though let's hope that the now flourishing repertory cinemas will continue to provide us with an opportunity of seeing the great, and otherwise specially interesting, films of yesteryear not otherwise available. Meanwhile this past year has seen the re-issue on quite a large scale of two of the great films of the past. M-G-M's* Camille, *a wonderful Garbo movie in which she co-starred with Robert Taylor, and Chaplin's classical comedy* The Gold Rush, *which after a season at the London Pavilion had quite a wide showing. And Disney's wonderful* Fantasia *was also re-presented, to prove just how far ahead of its time it was when originally shown.*

suggested that unless there was some sort of relief in the next budget many more hundreds of cinemas would have to close down within the next year or so.

Well, relief there was, and to the tune of £6,500,000. But if the Chancellor expected beaming smiles he was sadly disappointed for immediately the cry went up "Totally inadequate". It was claimed that even this amount would not stay for long the closing of smaller cinemas.

The full terms of the relief are too complicated to give here and, indeed, with the Finance Bill still going through nothing has been yet finalised. But it is doubtful if the relief will be increased this year.

Another somewhat unhappy signpost was the announcement at the beginning of this year that the Paramount newsreel would suspend operation in the middle of February. This came less than six months after the Warner-Pathe newsreel had folded. Newsreels, in fact, have probably been hit harder than any other form of film by TV, which with its twice-or-more nightly newsreel bulletin including newsreel footage has a great advantage over the cinema which changes only bi-weekly. One wonders if, however, good might not come out of even this unfortunate trend, for many people have for long thought that the film newsreel as now constituted has been over-taken and outdated by progress and that it should now be completely reshaped and presented in a new and more virile form.

Technically there have been no great strides forward during the year under review. The greatest novelty promised was the showing of the Todd-AO film *Around the World in Eighty Days*.

Finding no cinemas willing to pay out the considerable sums needed for conversion to this new giant-size method of presentation, the fabulous showman Michael Todd himself came over here on a flying visit to fix things. It was subsequently announced he had taken a lease of the Palace theatre with the idea of having it converted, but a later announcement told of an arrangement whereby the film would be shown at the converted Astoria (Rank Group) cinema—where indeed it actually had its British premiere in July.

One of the most significant features of the year has been the various shake-ups, prunings and reorganisations that have been carried out by the various American film companies. Republic's decision, for instance, to put future releases of their films through British Lion in this country, and RKO-Radio's subsequent announcement that they would release their productions through Universal in America—though maintaining their own release organisation in this country as before.

Another milestone was the re-organisation of Warner Brothers, though eventually Jack L. Warner emerged as the leading figure in the new company; and the changes at the top of the M-G-M hierarchy, which involved the departure of studio chief Dore Schary and the retirement of Nicholas Schenck, president of Loew's-M-G-M and "elder statesman" of the American industry for decades.

One of the less happy aspects of the new methods of presentation has been the selling by many of the larger American companies of great blocks of their older, conventionally shaped films to the television companies. This may well mean that we shall be less likely in the future to see in our cinemas revivals of the great films of the past, though it is sincerely to be hoped that enough of these will remain available to the repertory cinemas who

GREGORY PECK's several films during recent months have shown again his great versatility, ranging from the heavily dramatic role in the John Huston film MOBY DICK to his delightful light comedy performance in *Metro's* DESIGNING WOMAN.

*IN MEMORIAM. Death has robbed the screen of a number of famous personalities during the last year, some of the most tragic cases being the early and sudden deaths of our own Anne Crawford and Sweden's charming star, Marta Toren. And, of course, there was the fatal illness of one of the screen's greatest and best-loved tough men, Humphrey Bogart, who faced a painful end with all the courage he ever showed on the screen.*

do such fine work in this direction.

In this connection one of the most significant announcements of the year, I think, was Loew's autumn decision to lease no less than 725 pre-1949 M-G-M films to a TV station and at the same time to take up 25 per cent of that station's stock. I think we shall be seeing more deals like this in the future so that the film industry, which has always regarded TV with suspicion and distrust, may in the end do the old about-face trick and buy themselves into the business in a big way. Such arrangements have many great and obvious advantages.

Now, as to the actual films of the year. Well, the first thing that strikes you, I think, when you start to compile any sort of list, is the number of really excellent movies that we've been offered this past twelvemonth and the general high standard which has been, and still is prevailing.

Especially do these remarks apply to our own British productions. Think, for instance, of comedy and immediately the Boulting Brothers' *Brothers in Law* comes to mind: as well as the uproariously funny *The Baby and the Battleship* (in which John Mills—and, of course, the "baby"—gave such a brilliant comedy performance). Then, jostling for a place, the third and extremely successful Betty Box "Doctor" film, *Doctor at Large*. And, perhaps a little less forcefully, will come such entertaining pictures as *Three Men in a Boat*, Betty Box's original *The Passionate Stranger* and that delightful Alastair Sim vehicle *The Green Man*. And though not, I suppose, comedy in the strictest sense, the Australian-made *Smiley* has as much comedy as charm—of which it had plenty.

War films continued to considerably occupy the attentions of our producers, quite understandably in view of their high percentage of success at the box-office. Powell and Pressburger used an exciting cloak-and-dagger incident on Crete as the basis of their *Ill Met by Moonlight*—which I personally preferred to their considerably more lavish *The Battle of the River Plate*, again based on fact.

From Herbert Wilcox came the fine, documentary-style relation of the exciting story of H.M.S. frigate "Amethyst" in *The Yangtse Incident*. But most successful of all, of course, both with critics and moviegoing public alike, was Daniel Angel's finely made story of the exploits of Britain's amazing, legless fighter ace, Douglas Bader, *Reach For the Sky*, in which actor Kenneth More in the main role achieved a new status as an actor.

Another, though very different, story set in the skies was Ealing's modest but consistently exciting *Man in the Sky*, in which Jack Hawkins played the somewhat elderly (by purely aerial standards) test pilot who finds himself alone in the air with a prototype air freighter which he has little hope of landing safely. Hawkins was good, too, in another British picture, *The Long Arm*, which with fidelity showed something of the real manner in which Scotland Yard works to beat crime.

While on the subject of British pictures it should be noted with general satisfaction, I think, that though Ealing Film Studios as such are now no more, Ealing's trade mark continues to be seen on the screen, as many members of that grand team of moviemakers under the Sir Michael Balcon banner have now moved over to M-G-M's studios at Elstree, and there continue making those pictures which have in the past included some of the best ever produced in this country.

Some of the other films which I recall with pleasure are *The Good Companions*, the Nova Scotian Rank production *High Tide at Noon* (which revealed a whole crowd of most exciting, promising young players) and *Yield to the Night*, the Associated British film in which glamorous Diana Dors threw off her war paint and, as the girl doomed to be hanged for murder, gave a most moving performance.

All these, and I still haven't mentioned many of the films worth discussing. For instance, *The Spanish Gardener* (in

*PERSONALITY. One of the larger screen personalities of the year has been Michael Todd, that maker and loser of fortunes who kept on making news with his film,* Around the World in Eighty Days, *and its special giant-screen system of projection (Todd-AO) and with his wooing, winning and marrying ex-Mrs. Michael Wilding, the lovely Elizabeth Taylor.*

Lovely KIM NOVAK, the *Columbia* star whose rise to top screen fame in 1956 has been maintained with a series of films including THE EDDIE DUCHIN STORY, PICNIC and—her latest—JEANNE EAGLES.

which Dirk Bogarde gave such a charming performance), the Anglo-American *Trapeze* (directed by Sir Carol Reed and starring Lollobrigida—who incidentally, also had the less pleasing distinction of starring in one of the year's most easily and best forgotten productions, the re-make of *The Hunchback of Notre Dame*), and the East End thriller *The Secret Place.*

What did Hollywood offer in comparison? Quite a lot. *Designing Woman*, for instance, that highly amusing, witty M-G-M comedy co-starring Gregory Peck and Lauren Bacall—a real vintage quality movie. *Anastasia*, Fox's polished drama in which Ingrid Bergman gave the shining performance which deservedly won for her this year's "Oscar." Those several, large, lavish and brilliant musicals, including *Oklahoma*, *Funny Face*, *The King and I*, *Guys and Dolls* and *High Society*, etc. The vast, sprawling but always impressive *Giant* (notable for Rock Hudson's splendid performance and the last screen appearance of the late, phenomenal James Dean), *Baby Doll*, which, based on the Tennessee Williams play, was as impressive as it was unpleasant (it also included two notable performances from newcomers in Eli Wallach and Carrol Baker). John Huston's gargantuan *Moby Dick* (impressive though not the best film he has made), *Bus Stop* (which proved Marilyn Monroe's worth as a comedienne), *The Girl Can't Help It* (which equally certainly proved Jayne Mansfield's prowess in this direction) and a number of grand Westerns for which, of course, Hollywood has no rival. Here Ford's *The Searchers* headed an impressive line-up which included *The Fastest Gun Alive*, *The Proud Ones*, *Tension at Table Rock*, *The James Brothers*, *The Last Wagon* and a number of others.

Well out-of-the-rut, thoughtful movies were *The Bad Seed* (a good film based on what appeared to be a bad premise), Jose Ferrer's ironic *The Great Man*, Fox's *The Man in the Grey Flannel Suit*, and James Mason's controversial "cortisone" picture *Bigger Than Life*.

What else? Well, I loved M-G-M's charming Quaker family period piece *Friendly Persuasion* (which, rather astonishingly, went on to win the premier award at this year's Cannes Film Festival). I rated *D-Day, the Sixth of June* as the most moving love story filmed during the year. I was vastly entertained by Disney's *Great Locomotive Chase* and *Davy Crockett and the River Pirates*. I was duly impressed by *War and Peace*, especially the magnificently handled spectacle of the latter half. I was also impressed with the artistic integrity of M-G-M's story of Van Gogh, *Lust for Life*; equally impressed by Kirk Douglas's performance as the artist. I noted *The Killing* as an outstanding thriller. I thought Hitchcock's *The Wrong Man* one of his least successful films—though I appeared to be in a small minority about this. And I thought Gene Kelly's *Invitation to the Dance* one of the most brilliantly conceived, original and worthwhile movies of the period—and again I appeared to be in a minority.

In this brief survey I have, I know, omitted many movies worthy of mention. Possibly I have left out several of your own special favourites? But, in any case, you'll find them all commented upon even if only in thumbnail fashion later in other sections of the book. But I think I have at least done what I intended, to prove my opening contention: that this has been a generally good year for us moviegoers, a far better year than average. Don't you agree?

*MUSEUM. You never saw this scene in the final print of M-G-M's* Bhowani Junction, *for it was taken during the early shooting of the film and subsequently the actor sharing this scene with Ava Gardner, Joseph Tomelty, was badly injured in a car crash and all his scenes had to be re-shot. It is good, incidentally, to learn that this very talented and delightful Irish actor-playwright-author is now making a complete recovery. Another film scene you've never seen is this one with that delightful new British comedian Ian Carmichael. This film is called* The Big Money *and it was for some reason withheld when completed. It joins the puppet film,* Alice in Wonderland, *on the shelf from where (it is greatly to be hoped) they will one day be taken, dusted-off and shown.*

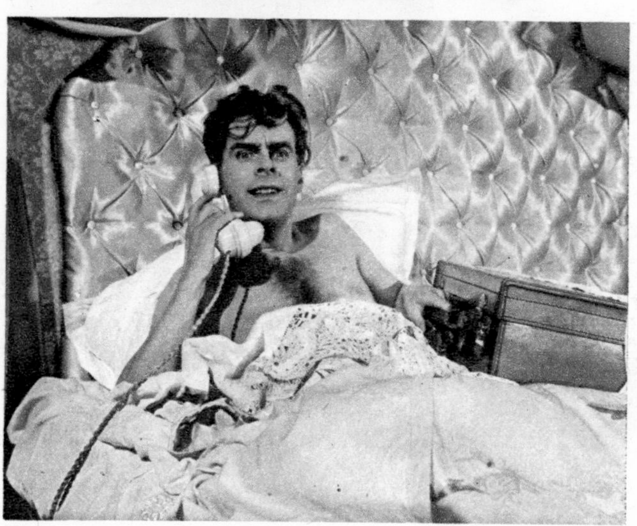

# The History of the Film Musical

by William K. Everson

Varsity Show—*a typical mid-thirties musical number.*

WHILE undoubtedly the film musical—as a genre—could not be born until the wholesale changeover to sound in the late twenties—it would be both unfair and inaccurate to pretend that it did not exist *until* that time. As early as 1910, Thomas Edison was turning out musicals in his West Orange studios—and charming, if simple, affairs they were too. Each film ran about six minutes and was nothing more than a photographed variety act : the singers (The Edison Quartette, and the Edison Minstrels) went through their paces on a single set, and the camera, from a fixed position, ground out the whole film in a *single* take. Some of the films, like *Nursery Favorites*, showed a pronounced Gilbert and Sullivan influence. The songs were both witty and tuneful. Others, like *Five Bachelors*, used music to tell a comic story.

The sound of course was recorded on cylinders which had to be kept in perfect synchronisation with the film ; the novelty value in those early days must have been exceptional, but presumably the process was killed by the same inept projectionists who, through their failure to maintain synchronisation, brought about the untimely demise of 3-D. Having screened some of these Edison musicals recently, I can assure you that they remain delightful little items, with sound and clarity of a remarkably high degree.

Even without the benefit of actual sound, the silent era produced many films which rightly deserve to come under the " musical " classification. Ernst Lubitsch's charming *The Student Prince* of 1927 was such a film ; it had a lyric beauty which created its own music—and Norma Shearer was never lovelier.

The importance of *The Jazz Singer*, also of 1927, in establishing the film musical is probably vastly over-rated. Actually, Vitaphone musical shorts had preceded it, and the wonder is that the industry was so slow in realising that sound was something far more than a mere novelty. In any event, *The Jazz Singer*—*under*-rated as a film, and

Varsity Show *again—Dick Powell leading a typical collegiate number.*

*over*-rated as a musical—did both boost Al Jolson's stock, and indicate that film musicals could be mighty box-office. Unusually slow in jumping on the bandwagon, however, Hollywood struggled for a while with technical problems, and not until 1929 was the big musical boom really on.

This was a fabulous, wonderful, and awful, period in Hollywood. Filmically, the perfected artistry of silent technique was being jettisoned in favour of talk and noise for its own sake. The roaring jazz era was fading into a depression that was just around the corner. Prohibition and gangsterism were still important plot factors, and were frequently allied with musical extravaganzas. Out of this hectic, frenzied Hollywood came, at first, two types of musicals. There were the multi-starred revue films, big, escapist, somewhat overpowering. M-G-M's *Broadway Melody* starred Bessie Love and Anita Page ; the story was slight, and the film (which, incidentally, won an Academy Award) included a Technicolor number. It was followed by *The Hollywood Revue*, which eliminated plot entirely in favour of a series of acts featuring all the top M-G-M stars. One would give much to see this film today, for M-G-M's star roster at that time was most impressive, and the music, by Gus Edwards, earned itself quite a reputation. Warners' equivalent revue—*The Show of Shows*—does not stand up at all well today. Fine moments were provided by John Barrymore and by Noah Beery, singing a fruity pirate ditty, but too many of the stars were sadly wasted on inferior material.

Contrasted with the elaborate but empty revues were the more solidly constructed " dramatic musicals," of which Universal's *Broadway* is typical. Under the leadership of Carl Laemmle, who was wont to fill his lot with imported talent, the studio marched along to the tune of Germanic

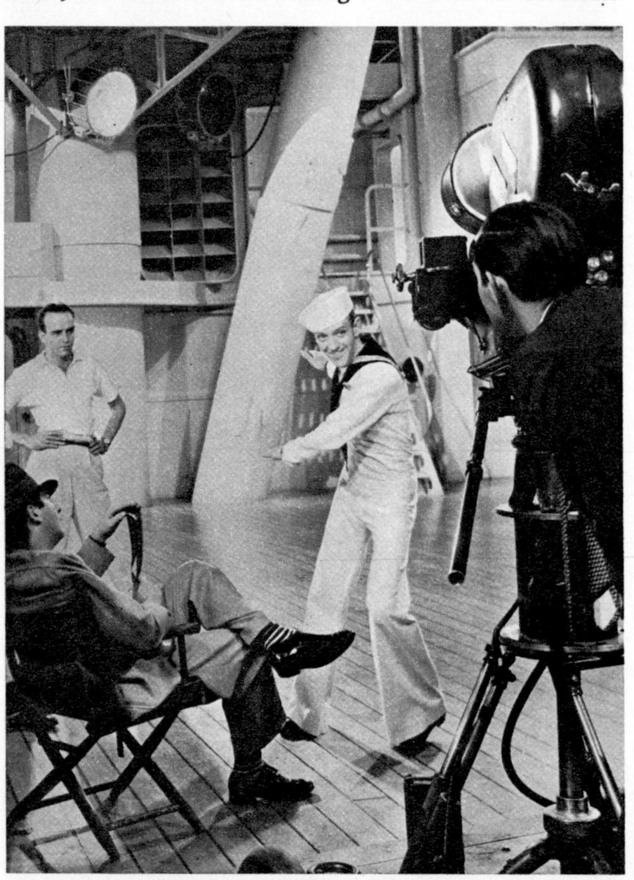

*Fred Astaire*—Follow the Fleet

brass bands and mass stoppages of work to welcome the arrival of each new German or Hungarian star or director. Paul Fejos, a fine European director with, naturally, a Continental outlook, was signed to direct the very American *Broadway*, dealing with babes, booze racketeers and jazzy production numbers. The nightclub set was a huge surrealist nightmare approximately the size of Grand Central Station ; people at Universal neither knew or cared that New York boasted not one nightclub a tenth of its size. All that mattered was that it be the biggest in Hollywood—and it certainly was ! A special camera crane was evolved to photograph the enormous set, and *Broadway* emerged as a fascinating production. The musical numbers, in Technicolor, were lavish, and dramatically the film was so strong that it was released, quite successfully, in a silent version. Its success spurred Carl Laemmle to sign Paul Whiteman's orchestra for *The King of Jazz*—which turned out to be unquestionably the most expensive musical in Hollywood history. To start with, no script awaited Mr. Whiteman on his arrival—and he was paid a fabulous salary while cooling his heels for many weeks (and picking up money on the side by playing in California nightclubs !). Then Johnny Murray Anderson was brought in from New York to design and direct the production, and he promptly went to work with a squad of workmen digging massive holes in the old " Broadway " stage. Several weeks later he was able to unveil for Mr. Laemmle's admiring eyes a number of gigantic revolving stages—and admire them he did, until he innocently enquired why they were to revolve. Mr. Anderson replied that it was so the audience could see everybody on the stage—apparently he didn't know that the cameras could move around the stages, so he had spent several hundred thousand dollars enabling the stages to move around the cameras ! But this was only the beginning—later in the day, the negative of the nearly completed film was totally destroyed, and it *all* had to be re-shot. Yet, despite all the set-backs, *The King of Jazz* emerged as quite a picture.

Another interesting musical of this early period was *The Great Gabbo*, a strange collaboration between star Erich von Stroheim and director James Cruze—both on somewhat unfamiliar ground. The dramatic and musical elements somehow never quite fused, and it was rather like watching two quite separate films at the same time ! The musical numbers were bizarre and somewhat disorganised, but loads of fun. " I'm in Love With You " was repeated *ad nauseum*, and especially delightful was a number entitled " Caught in the Web of Love " in which the players, costumed as spiders and butterflies, performed on a gigantic spider's web. The floorboards reacted with a thunderous clatter when the bulky Don Douglas—supposedly a light-on-his-feet dancer—pranced about the stage. Again the musical sequences were in colour. Far outstripping *The Great Gabbo* in 1929 was *The Love Parade*, first of the delightful Maurice Chevalier-Jeanette MacDonald risque musical comedies. Directed by Lubitsch—and also featuring Lupino Lane and Lillian Roth—it was a deliberately artificial quasi-operetta, and still sparkles today. The wonder is that Paramount didn't re-issue it to cash in on the Grace Kelly wedding—although possibly Lubitsch's delightful satire of a royal wedding might raise a few eyebrows today. Chevalier and MacDonald went on to make three more musical comedies together—*One Hour With You*, *The Merry Widow* and, best of all, *Love Me Tonight*—directed by Rouben Mamoulian (the others were all made by Lubitsch) and with a fine score by Rodgers and Hart.

The first big flurry of musical extravaganzas over—the charming operettas like *Viennese Nights* considered out of date in an era more concerned with overcoming the depression and prohibition—the musical film went into a sudden nose-dive in the early thirties. Several films even had elaborate production numbers removed and were released as straight dramas. But the tabu on musicals didn't last. In early 1933 Warner Brothers made *42nd Street*, not with any thought of starting a fresh cycle, but principally to combat depression gloom by offering a cheerful, optimistic musical in a contemporary setting. For all its musical extravagance and its simple plot, *42nd Street* was a realistic affair which did capture the spirit of those unhappy times, and presented show business as a dog-eat-dog business, devoid of glamour. Bebe Daniels, Ruby Keeler, Dick Powell, Ginger Rogers and George Brent were official stars of this remarkable production, which retains its punch, but perhaps the *real* star, from a musical standpoint, was Busby Berkeley, who staged the numbers. Berkeley was the Griffith of the musical world : he worked on the epic scale, used chorines (unusually lovely ones) by the score and sometimes by the hundred, and was a great believer in using camera tricks to supplement the music. It was Berkeley who developed those wonderful overhead shots, with the camera looking down on groups of chorines weaving intricate patterns—patterns, incidentally, that were of course quite wasted on the audiences supposedly watching them ! Such logic never worried Berkeley. One number in *42nd Street* starts with a simple set on a theatre stage. The camera zooms forward to a window of a house—through it—and behind the window is a fantastic set that covers acres. Here the bulk of the number is performed, and at its conclusion, the camera again zooms out through the window and back to the theatre stage—where an audience, who at best could only have heard distant strains of the number coming from afar, is applauding enthusiastically ! Such musical numbers, despite their patent absurdity, had tremendous vitality and rhythm ; they were almost mathematically constructed, and edited with a precision which would have delighted even Einstein ! Dancers were photographed from left, right, above and below—and the shows grew bigger and bigger. The " By a Waterfall " number from *Footlight Parade* stands out as one of the most monumental of them all. Berkeley, giving of his best for Warners, also had time to handle the Eddie Cantor musicals for Samuel Goldwyn too. The opening production number in *The Kid from Spain* is set in a girl's dormitory designed with all the splendour of ancient Babylon. Paulette Goddard and Betty Grable were among the girls cavorting on marble staircases and in a huge swimming pool—and photographed largely from dizzy heights.

But if 1932 and '33 gave a fresh start to the monster musicals, they also produced some unusually refreshing minor ones. One of the best—and most under-rated—was *Hallelujah I'm a Bum* (recently re-issued in England as *Lazy Bones*). A lovely, fragile little romance, it used the depression as its background, and told much of its story in musical dialogue written by Rodgers and Hart. The late Al Jolson (who has gone on record as considering it his worst film !) was never better, and director Lewis Milestone even managed to subdue a lot of the Jolson bombast that annoyed so many. Lovely Madge Evans, lovable Harry Langdon and Frank Morgan—*really*, moving in a straight performance before M-G-M made him a buffoon—all helped to make this such an interesting film that it is sad it was both unsuccessful and unappreciated.

As the thirties progressed, the monster musicals gradually began to disappear from Warners and to re-appear, less successfully, at M-G-M. *The Great Ziegfeld* had some of the biggest production numbers of them all—but the film was a ponderous bore for the most part, with the music occupying only a couple of its twenty-one reels ! The Eleanor Powell films, such as *Rosalie*, were certainly *big*—but somehow they lacked zip. More successful were the Nelson Eddy-Jeanette MacDonald operettas (1935–40)—old-fashioned, nostalgic, corny if you like, but well done and thoroughly appealing. Films like *Rose Marie* exploited Jeanette MacDonald's voice far more than her earlier Lubitsch muscials had done. There her sex-appeal had been given almost equal prominence. Although Jeanette had made earlier filmic operettas (the almost

*Jolson in* The Singing Kid.

*A very typical Eddie Cantor routine—from* Roman Scandals.

*A near-surrealistic number from* Paramount on Parade.

*Maurice Chevalier in* Paramount on Parade.

laughable *The Lottery Bride* for example—in which stagey songs of the " With a Slap on the Back and a Clasp of the Hand " type seemed almost like parodies) it was the teaming with Nelson Eddy that finally brought her real stature.

While Warners (moving away from revues to musicals with radio or collegiate backgrounds) and M-G-M continued to dominate musical production in the thirties, there was activity on other fronts. Paramount was putting Bing Crosby and Betty Grable into endless collegiate musicals—unpretentious affairs, but films with lots of life and sparkle. R.K.O. had developed the fabulously successful team of Fred Astaire and Ginger Rogers, whose films combined simple comedy and romance with only occasional hints of spectacle. *Top Hat* certainly had an elaborately staged dance finale, but individual dances against naturalistic backgrounds tended to predominate in all their films. Actually, the personalities of the stars were the only really notable aspects of these films ; the plots were inane often to the point of insulting the intelligence (*Swing Time* in particular) and the films had a curiously cold, calculating and condescending atmosphere to them. They were filled with little bits of " sure-fire business "—but they had none of the genuine warmth and friendliness of, for example, the early Shirley Temple films, or more especially the gay, charming Deanna Durbin vehicles of which *Mad About Music* remains an especially enchanting specimen.

Incidentally, in Dick Powell and Joan Blondell, Warners had a team that quite equalled R.K.O.'s Astaire and Rogers. A singing, rather than a dancing duo, they were backed by the usual Warner production numbers and admittedly exuded more of a smart Broadway flavour than did Astaire and Rogers. Perhaps because they were thus not quite as unique as the R.K.O. team, they were somewhat lost in the shuffle—but films like *The Broadway Gondolier* were first-class musicals, and it is unfortunate that they have never been revived.

Of course, America did not monopolise musicals in the thirties. Britain was turning out the more intimate but no less entertaining Jessie Mathews films—and the thoroughly enjoyable musical comedies with the Jacks Hulbert and Buchanan. Germany and Austria both produced monster revues and those delightfully old-hat stories in which buxom village girls (always Martha or Maria) sang as they scrubbed shirts in the river—or danced happily in flower-bedecked beer gardens. Mexico too, turned out plenty of slick, jazzy musicals. One day, perhaps, historians will recognise the attributes of their current top-liner, Maria Antonietta Pons, who shakes, wiggles, twitches her nostrils, and is a Mexican composite of Gina Lollobrigida and Greer Garson ! And some of the most enjoyable musicals of all come from India—completely undisciplined, outrageously plagiaristic, combining Eastern and Western music—and yet so full of verve and rhythm that aesthetic criticism seems quite pointless.

By the forties, dominance of the musical field had passed to 20th Century-Fox, who, following the pattern of earlier successes (*Alexander's Ragtime Band*, *Rose of Washington Square*) concentrated on hoked-up biographies, and star vehicles. Somehow there was a sameness to them all, and none of the Betty Grable subjects (*Song of the Islands*, *Sweet Rosie O'Grady* and others) had any real merit, although all were tremendously successful—thanks mainly to the wartime mania for pin-up queens, and the successful merchandising of Grable along these lines with the Forces. June Haver and Rita Hayworth, whose films were less assembly-line produced and thus correspondingly slightly better, also failed to appear in any really noteworthy musicals, although Hayworth's *Cover Girl* did have some tuneful melodies. The Bing Crosby vehicles at Paramount (*Dixie*, *Holiday Inn*) were likewise uninspired. Musicals during the war years, often inflicted with patriotic ditties and near-nauseous propaganda content, were generally of little interest. The best were usually those which had more dramatic than musical content—*Yankee Doodle Dandy*, James Cagney's Oscar-winning George Cohan biopic ; *Syncopation*, an interesting story of jazz, and an almost forgotten but extremely well-made melodrama from Warners entitled *Blues in the Night*. The monster musical was no more, replaced by the straightforward " A " musicals a la Grable and Hayworth, and scores of " B's ", principally from Universal, featuring the Andrews Sisters, Grace MacDonald, Dick Foran and Jane Frazee. The hep-cat dialogue and musical gibberish of these patriotic wartime " B's " seems quite incredible today ; seldom has any group of pictures dated so much—so soon.

The post-war era saw very much of an improvement, although still hardly a return to the " golden age " of the early thirties. Films like *The Pirate* and *One Touch of Venus* (as overlooked a film as was *Hallelujah I'm a Bum*) had both charm and individuality. Younger players of the calibre of Donald O'Connor and Debbie Reynolds could hardly replace the Dick Powells and Ginger Rogerses but they did bring a freshness and a likeability that was refreshing in the wake of stale Grable and Hayworth films. If there was any one dominating trend in the new musicals, it was towards biographies of show business personalities—doubtless touched off by the fabulous success of *The Jolson Story*. Some were quite well made, but far too many had no kind of regard for established fact. The story of Eva Tanguay, told in *The I Don't Care Girl*, became one of the most monumental filmic messes of all time. *The One-Piece Bathing Suit*, re-telling the Annette Kellerman story, showed that old maestro Busby Berkeley could still play around effectively with musical spectacle and overhead cameras, but otherwise it was blatantly false—even giving Miss Kellerman a big Hollywood career when all of her films were made in Bermuda ! Most disturbing of all, perhaps, has been the inaccuracy of music itself in these show business biographies. *I'll Cry Tomorrow*, an otherwise creditable screen biography of Lillian Roth fell down badly on its musical and other background detail. Apart from the fact that the film created no sense of time or period (its fashions, cars, decor remained strictly 1955 during the thirty-odd years it covered), its music throughout was essentially modern. Thus, while belting out " Sing You Sinners " in a film studio at a period presumed to be 1929, Miss Hayward is accompanied by the neurotic and sexually suggestive pseudo-ballet prancings that are strictly a product of the fifties—and which, in an attempt to add " tone " to musicals, have ruined so many of them. Another M-G-M biopic, *Love Me or Leave Me*, equally amiss in its sense of period, was far more satisfactory in its musical department. Both films were made by M-G-M, who now seem to have taken over the *quantity* lead in musicals held by Fox in the forties, as well as the *quality* lead. Most of the original and worthwhile musicals of recent years have come from this stable—the minor but pleasing *Give a Girl a Break*, *The Band Wagon* and especially *Singin' in the Rain*, one of the best musicals since the grand old days. And perhaps there is a lesson in this. *Singin' in the Rain* is set in the days of the switchover from silent to sound movies. Its highlight was a brilliantly staged reconstruction of the old-style extravaganza numbers—weaving chorines, sweeping camerawork, overhead shots. It was done—of course—by Busby Berkeley, and though in a satirical vein, remained the highlight of the whole production. 1953's *Band Wagon*, apart from starring old-timers Fred Astaire and Jack Buchanan, drew most of its numbers from the 1931 Broadway revue on which it was based. In view of these successes, any claims that musical tastes have changed seem quite futile. They are, in fact, a lame excuse to cover the fact that productions of the calibre of *Wonderbar* or *Footlight Parade* would today cost more than the average producer cares to spend. And yet the perennial sales-argument that the motion picture screen can provide so much more than television seems in itself a plug for a return of the older style film musical. Certainly home viewers have a plethora of " intimate " and " naturalistic " musical entertainment—which is undoubtedly why so many " in-between " screen musicals—*My Sister Eileen*, for example—die the death of a dog at the box-office. Producers, realising that Hollywood musicals need an extra something to combat the competition of TV, have found that " something " in overdoses of sex—but a harsh, aggressive sex (as in the woefully re-arranged *Desert Song* number in the recent biopic where Jose Ferrer played Sigmund Romberg). Certainly the Goldwyn Girls of old exuded sex—and how !—but it was a Ziegfeld Follies type of sex, all showmanship and nothing else. And some of the old-time showmanship is really what musicals need again today. M-G-M have realised that, and *Singin' in the Rain* and *The Band Wagon* have resulted. How about some more of the same from Warners, Universal, Fox and Paramount ?

*Betty Grable in her early Paramount period—the perennial campus queen.*

# Film Festivals

**PETER NOBLE explains what Film Festivals are, who started them and what they do.**

FILM FESTIVAL. A festival of movies. What delightful vistas these words conjure up. Excitement, stars, parties, publicity, premieres, photographers; the glitter and glamour of international film stars on holiday. Film festivals are indeed all these things. A great deal of work goes on behind the scenes, however. Back-room boys spend a whole year organising an event which takes place for only two weeks. And the amount of behind-the-scenes conniving, scheming and jockeying-for-position that goes on among the officials representing the various competing nations is quite fantastic.

It has now become quite an honour to carry off an award at a film festival, an honour which may well turn into great financial benefit. Hence the fierce rivalry between competing countries to show their very best films at what they consider to be the very best showing times. Hence also the publicity which starts being pumped out months before the event. Not that the eminent people who act on the juries at these festivals are likely to be actually influenced in a direct fashion. The hope of the various contestants is that the blast of publicity about a particular movie may have an indirect (or even unconscious) effect on some of the judges. And no doubt they are right!

Over the years film festivals have indeed become big business, but this is not to say that they are bad in themselves. On the contrary. Cinematic purists have recently contended that the whole spirit of film festivals has disappeared in the past few years and that they have become commercial ramps, gigantic selling campaigns for mediocre films. This is unfair. Granted, the character of film festivals has changed somewhat in recent years. No doubt they have become more "commercialised," but they certainly do a great deal more good than harm. Like the Olympic Games, they bring together people of all nations in friendly rivalry. They provide a platform on which various countries are able to demonstrate cinematically their way of life. From greater knowledge comes greater understanding. On a political basis film festivals have certainly been of great benefit in the post-war years.

That aesthetic values have been lowered, as some serious film critics have asserted, is possibly true. With the growing popularity of these annual affairs and the participation of more and more countries showing more and more films, it is quite logical that standards may have dropped and that less and less "arty" films tend to be shown.

Even so, I am all for more and more film festivals. For one thing, in my view any excuse for a party is a good excuse. And a party held in Cannes or Venice or Berlin or Uruguay, with lots of exciting motion picture personalities attending, is the kind of party I rate at the top of my list!

How did film festivals start? Credit for the first one ever held must go to Italy. It was in 1932 that a group of Italian film critics and directors got together to plan an annual festival of motion pictures from all over the world, to be held in Venice, one of the most beautiful cities in Italy. Invitations went out to Hollywood, Britain, France and other European and Asian countries. The response was enthusiastic. Many countries offered to compete and also volunteered to send some of their leading picture personalities to attend.

Thus in September, 1932, in the incredibly beautiful Venice, the very first film festival in the world was held. The American picture *Grand Hotel*, starring Greta Garbo, John and Lionel Barrymore, Wallace Beery, Joan Crawford

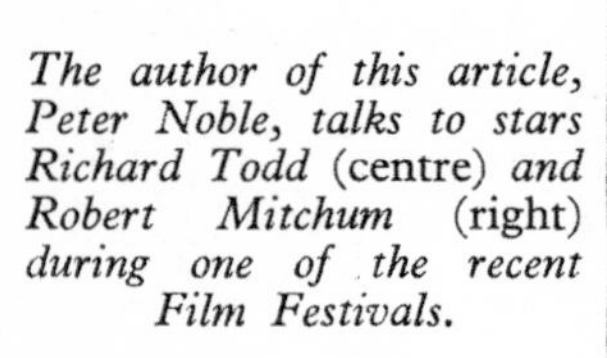

*The author of this article, Peter Noble, talks to stars Richard Todd (centre) and Robert Mitchum (right) during one of the recent Film Festivals.*

and other famous stars, was just beaten for first place by the German film *Children in Uniform*. It was all very exciting. Many celebrities attended from all over the world and newspaper interest in the art of the cinema was undoubtedly heightened by the success of the event.

It is interesting, on looking back, to see that the British film *Man of Aran* won the first prize in 1937 as the best foreign film. In 1935 Hollywood won this award with *Becky Sharp*. In the following year that great French film *Le Grand Illusion* was the winner, and in 1938 Hollywood again carried off the prize for the best foreign film with William Wyler's *Jezebel*.

By 1938 France had begun to envy Italy's success with its Venice Festival, and French film producers decided to initiate their own annual event, to be held every Spring in the delightful setting of Cannes on the sun-kissed Riviera. Everything was all settled for the Cannes Festival to commence in the early summer of 1939. Norma Shearer, then one of Hollywood's biggest stars, flew over to Paris in preparation for the event. She was to officiate at the grand opening ceremony. But by this time war clouds had begun to hang heavily over the face of Europe and it seemed inevitable that Hitler was planning to annex Poland just as he had taken over Austria and Czechoslovakia. Reluctantly the French decided to abandon their plans for inaugurating the Cannes Festival, and Norma Shearer flew home to Hollywood. The Italian authorities similarly decided to cancel the Venice Festival of 1939. So, for the duration of the war, the festival idea was put into cold storage.

Cannes started up in 1946, but it took the Italians a further year before they could re-commence the Venice Festival. Since that year both festivals have run neck and neck in popularity and prestige, and they still lead the world. There are many other film festivals, of course. They are held in Edinburgh, Berlin, Uruguay, Locarno, Knocke and Brazil. Each has functioned with varying success. Each one has its own particular flavour.

At Edinburgh, for example, it is the documentary film producer who gets the spotlight. Although some full-length feature films have been entered for the festival from time to time, the particular emphasis here is on documentaries, cartoons, travel films, sponsored films, educational pictures, shorts and unusual *avant garde* entries.

It is at Edinburgh that the younger film-maker gets the opportunity to show movies which often get lost in an ordinary cinema programme and are used as "fill-up" material to support the feature film. The film director who makes a little picture on a shoe-string gets his opportunity at Edinburgh, if the picture has artistic merit, to bring his brain-child to the notice of assembled press-men and film critics from all over the world. No prizes are awarded at Edinburgh. For a film to be accepted for showing at this Festival is considered an honour in itself.

This question of prizes has been the most vexed one since film festivals became front-page news. There is a strong feeling of opinion that the giving of awards negates the whole spirit of the festival. The main object, say these critics, should be for all writers, directors and actors to be able to show their latest efforts to each other, to learn from each other and to utilise the festival as a means of emphasising the friendliness and comradeship of film-makers, no matter where they come from. Awards, these critics contend, bring the wrong spirit of rivalry into the festivals.

This is all true enough and the sentiments are admirable. The various festival authorities, however, differ from this view by asserting that the whole point of film festivals is to draw attention to the great pictures which are being made by various countries and to emphasise the great artistic contributions made each year in the field of the cinema. Only by presenting awards, which make newspaper headlines everywhere, can due prominence be given to the films which deserve the prizes and to the countries which made them.

There is, of course, something to be said for both views. I favour the giving of awards. They act as incentives and

*In the evenings are the inevitable premieres : in this case Irene Ganna and Janette Scott are escorted into the cinema by Vernon Gray.*

*Between the films and the publicity and all the rest of it the stars do manage to squeeze in a little relaxation. Bound for their morning dip during the Venice Film Festival last year are a trio of Associated British stars : Vernon Gray, Janette Scott, and Richard Todd with Italy's Irene Ganna.*

they certainly help to rivet public attention to a picture which otherwise might be completely neglected. Take the Japanese film *Rashomon*, for example. In winning the First Prize at Venice in 1951 this picture not only drew attention to its great acting and direction, but it gave an unprecedented boost to Japanese films. Since that time several other Japanese pictures have been shown with success in countries (Britain included) which had previously neglected to show any of the vast number of good pictures made in Tokyo.

Similarly the remarkable popularity of French and Italian films in Britain during the past few years is directly attributable to the success which these movies have had at the various film festivals, particularly at Cannes and Venice. I will, of course, admit that the charms of Gina Lollobrigida and Brigitte Bardot account in some part for the new popularity of Italian and French productions here! Nevertheless international film festivals have done a great deal to spotlight foreign films and to ensure that these pictures get a showing in countries which had ignored them. Which certainly means that filmgoers everywhere owe a debt of gratitude to Cannes, Venice and the other festivals.

Apart from the aesthetic aspect and the betterment of international relations which derives from these festive gatherings of many different countries, film festivals are, of course, very enjoyable as social events.

I have been going regularly to festivals for many years. I look forward to them. I always have a wonderful time. I see lots of new movies, many of which I might otherwise not have a chance of enjoying. I meet many well-known movie-makers, have meals and drinks with screen celebrities from all countries, meet fellow-journalists and critics and attend dozens of press shows, cocktail parties, dances, midnight galas and costume balls.

Into two weeks are crammed dozens of meetings and events. Time flies by. Something different and exciting is happening every hour of every day. Sometimes there is a squabble between the Russians and the Americans about a particular movie which throws discredit on one or another. Occasionally the Japanese or the German delegates walk out to express some kind of protest. Last year at Cannes, for example, the Japanese protested against the inclusion of that fine British picture *A Town Like Alice,* which dealt with the Japanese invasion of Singapore. The picture was withdrawn from the contest, and shown at a different cinema "out of the competition". It was quite a *cause celebre.*

Stars have feuds, and make up again. Starlets pose prettily on the beaches all day long, trying to cash in on the world-wide publicity which surrounds a film festival. Outstanding new films are shown. Sometimes we have to sit through a bad film, though not often. Many times I have seen a Japanese film with Italian sub-titles or a Soviet film with French sub-titles! Confusing? Yes. But highly diverting. Meat and drink to the enthusiastic filmgoer.

*Mostly Film Festivals are held in a hot and sunny climate but in the case of the Helsinki one it is snow which provides a backdrop, and taking advantage of this to get a little ski-ing practice is Sylvia Syms.*

And then, of course, there are the ballyhoo sidelights of all festivals. Dozens of publicity men arrive with dozens of photographers. All are equally determined to get their particular country's stars in the newspapers of the world. There is fierce, often funny, competition for the posing of little-known starlets with renowned stars. "Stunts" are organised. Many of them misfire. But some of them make front-page news everywhere. There was the well-known incident at Venice two years ago when Associated British star Janette Scott fell into the lagoon and was rescued by Associated British star Vernon Gray, while an Associated British cameraman (who happened to be conveniently nearby!) took dozens of shots of the hair-raising rescue operations.

Photographs of Janette being rescued by Vernon appeared all over the world. There were those sceptics who asserted that Janette was rescued from only three feet of water! Others were quite sure that it was just another of the many festival publicity stunts. Associated British publicity chief Leslie Frewin (who now has his own independent public relations organisation in Berkeley Square) just grinned and said nothing. If you persisted in questioning him about the incident he merely pointed delightedly to a huge pile of press cuttings from all over the world relating to the famous rescue!

"Did Janette fall or was she pushed?" was quite a popular question asked at Venice that year.

Last year, at the Cannes Festival, the question was: "Will Diana Dors go home, or stay and pay her own expenses?"

In a fantastic blaze of publicity Diana arrived at the Carlton Hotel, Cannes, complete with husband Dennis Hamilton, a huge ice-blue Cadillac, a personal manager and the ubiquitous Mr. Leslie Frewin.

Diana's latest film, *The Weak and the Wicked*, was entered for the 1956 Cannes Festival, and Diana was there to give the picture a send-off. "Send-off" is perhaps an understatement! La Dors, with her bubbling personality, ready wit and friendliness allied to her fabulous figure and long blonde hair, was the favourite of the *Croisette*. She stole all the headlines from Hollywood stars, French stars and Italian stars. Many a top movie name flew off home in a huff after Diana had taken over Cannes! It was indeed a famous victory.

Then came the hullabaloo over whether or not Associated British Studios should pay all her husband's hotel and living expenses as well as her own. The rights and wrongs of the argument were hotly debated in every newspaper, finishing up with Diana's statement that she was "going home to London as a protest."

Needless to say, it was all smoothed over, after La Dors made her famous statement that she was going to throw her "measly expense allowance" out of her hotel bedroom window on to the beach below, as a gesture of defiance.

Robert Clark, genial head of Associated British and a man with a delightful Scots sense of humour, averred that he waited underneath Diana's bedroom window for hours hoping to catch some of the money she had announced she was going to throw away!

Everyone finished up firm friends. *The Weak and the Wicked* was a success and Diana's acting surprised everyone at the Festival, so assured and sensitive was it. Out of it all Britain had gained hundreds of inches of newspaper space, drawing attention not only to Diana Dors and Robert Clark but to British pictures generally.

Each Festival has its quota of incidents, its publicity "stunts," its quarrels and its scandals. But these are just a by-product of almost any film function.

They cannot hope to spoil the essential goodwill of film festivals, the warm spirit of friendly competition and the overall benefits to motion picture art which arise out of them. Long may we have them. And may *I* continue to be invited to *all* of them!

# SO YOU TOO WANT TO BE IN PICTURES

**OSWELL BLAKESTON**
**describes how one becomes a film " Extra "**

HAVE you ever looked analytically at the people jostling along some street in a film and tried to work out how many young folk there are compared to old ones ? Most likely, unless you're examining some very highbrow film, you'll find that screen statistics are more optimistic than real-life proportions. Its nice out there in film land, for there are more young people, and better looking !

So if you want to get among them—and thousands of fans do dream of being "film extras" and appearing on the screen in crowds—you can take it that you stand a better chance if you're young and good looking. For the plain fact is that many directors don't think of extras as " artistes " but as " decorations." They want them around to give the shot " a bit of life and movement." They don't want it to look " real " but to look " good " and " animated." They're convinced that audiences prefer the bias towards idealism, and get more kick out of looking at a young and attractive crowd rather than a correctly balanced sample of the population.

Yes, alas, the older an extra grows, the harder it is for him or her to find work. The extra doesn't become more in demand with experience. His job isn't considered all that difficult. So youth is what he really has to sell.

What else do film directors want from extras ?

MEN. Tall men are in demand, about five foot ten or six foot. English directors prefer genuine standard English types. Male extras should be manly-looking, and they should not favour crew cuts or fancy trimmings as a rule.

GIRLS. Some modicum of glamour is basic. No one expects star-quality from film extras, but some ration of " it " is a must. There's no getting around " it." The " interesting " and " unusual " types may make rewarding successes as small part character actresses, but not as extras. They'd be up against " the way things work out."

Well, then, how do the rules and regulations get classified ?

The first thing to do, if you want to be an extra, is to put yourself in contact with the union which looks after the interests of crowd artistes and knows all " the ropes " : The Film Artistes Association, 50 Manchester Street, W.1. No one can become a film extra without union membership. You can write to begin with, submitting details of your appearance and your wardrobe ; and *don't forget to enclose a stamped and addressed envelope*. But now, even if you've written a good letter and sent an attractive photo and been careful to slip in the required stamped and addressed envelope, you may not get an answer by return. You may have to wait some time before the union is sanctioning a fresh intake of members into the ranks. It is not until this happens that you are likely to get an answer to your enquiry.

The intake of new members is controlled in the interests of those who are already members. As long as things are slack and there is not enough work for the some thousand existing members, the union is not keen on enrolling more names. In boom periods, of course, things are different, and agreeable applicants may be beckoned forward.

Alas, the present moment cannot be called a boom time for the extra market. So many television films are occupying studio space, and these films generally do not call for big crowd scenes. The well populated scene has proved confusing and ineffective on the small television screen ; and so producers of this genre of TV feature can economise on crowd scenes with clear consciences.

But, inevitably, there are some intakes into the union even in years which are not planned entirely for film extras to live in. Union members do drift away from extra work or retire, and then the ban is lifted and some new applicants are accepted into the fold. But note again that old people who retire will probably be replaced with young members. There are always sufficient elderly people, who have matured as extras, on the books to supply the small demand for their services.

One cannot say that it is over-encouraging, can one? So before you trade in your youth, you'd better ask yourself just why you want to become an extra. Is it, by any chance, that you think of it as a first step to "getting your name in lights"? You are making a sad mistake if you do, for film extras don't. Occasionally an alluring extra girl in the crowd may be asked if she can speak a line; and if she can, she may say it in the film. But even if she is chosen more than once for such distinction, the occasions won't add up to "something better." Film people just don't think of extras as budding actors and actresses. Film people think that if a man or a girl is an extra it means that he or she has no ambition to be anything else.

If you want to be an actor or an actress on the screen, the way to fame and fortune is through theatre work in a provincial repertory company—until you've learnt your job. Then you can try breaking in to the studio as a small part player. And then the executives will be expecting you to have ambition. Your opportunities will now "add up." If you show talent and aptitude, you will slowly build up "a name." This is something an extra can never do, because the fact of becoming an extra means one does not want to do it.

I think, perhaps, that a great many people who dream of becoming extras have *not* realised this, the fact that extras are in a special compartment. You see, it can't even happen the other way round—actors can't become extras when they are out of work and jobs as extras are going. Actor and extra are watertight occupations and managed by different unions. "If a girl has failed to make the grade as an actress," an executive of the Film Artistes Association said to me in a burst of confidence, "she may become a film extra if she has the physical attributes; but if she wants to get on in films, she won't dream of starting as an extra. It's a start—and a finish."

Definitely, the job of being a film extra is and isn't a way into films. It's a way of becoming a blur in the background. And that's that, if one cares to make a career of being a mere glimpse at a ball and a passing face on a sidewalk. Will this content you? Clearly it is sufficient for some; but authorities suggest that people become extras because they don't want the responsibility of anything more difficult. In a sense, it is a lack of ambition rather than an ambition.

It is, maybe, a way of picking up some pocket money: but please don't imagine that you can rely on extra work for support. Months may go by without there being a day's work at the studios. Extras who rely on film work live in real insecurity. Then, when a call comes, it's a basic £3 a day plus overtime of 10*s.* 6*d.* an hour, plus small additional fees like "danger money" or compensation for standing in the artificial rain and catching real pneumonia. It's true enough that during a sequence of working days, an extra can knock up quite a good sum; but there is no guarantee that such a sequence will come even once a year. It must be taken into consideration, too, that film extras have to cover their own travelling expenses to the studios, which often are in remote places.

And thinking of remote studios reminds one that extras have to get up fiendishly early in the morning to give the make-up departments time to get all the crowd ready for the day's shooting. So . . . all in all . . . are you sure you can take it?

And have you a wardrobe?

Extras have to supply their own wardrobe except in costume pictures. A male extra, for example, must possess about four lounge suits, morning coat and pinstripes, dinner jacket, tails and perhaps riding kit. He'll get a bit more for wearing "special clothes" like breeches or tails, but he'll simply miss the job if he hasn't got them. (All the same, it must be put on record that it's no use having the clothes if you can't look natural in what you've got!)

But by this time I expect you're beginning to wonder who on earth can afford to be a film extra, someone with a substantial wardrobe and a very insecure return from the film studio. Well, the official answer includes young girls who model for photographers and can fit that in with assignments as extras; and young men who find they can spare a day or two off from sales patter when a "call" comes from the studio. But you see how it is?

If you can't be shaken, if you still want to go on, then one day you'll get an answer to that letter you sent to the Film Artistes Association and you'll be summoned to union headquarters. A selection committee will decide if you "pass the test". If you are admitted to the union, you will pay a guinea entrance fee, and a subscription of £3 12*s.* 0*d.* a year.

Your friends will then start to search for you on the screen—your feet in the mob scene or the back of your head in that flash of a party on Brighton Beach! You'll be in! And I hope you'll enjoy every split-second of your triumph. For honestly, sir or madam, it remains true that the film wouldn't be the same without you!

# star snapshot album

IN spite of the extremely detailed instructions outlined in the introductory notes to this feature each year, quite a few readers do not carry them out, with the result that either their snapshots are greatly delayed or, in some cases, they do not get them at all! The offer, as old readers will now be aware, is that providing you fulfil a few simple conditions you may obtain copies (suitable for insertion in your own album) of any **three** of the authentic film star snapshots illustrated in the next few pages. **But to receive these snapshots you MUST—and all this is very important :—**

1. **Send a note of the numbers of the three snapshots you select, together with**
2. **a stamped and addressed envelope for reply and**
3. **the coupon you'll find on the inside flap of the back cover of the dust jacket.**

**Too many readers last year either forgot to enclose the coupon, or omitted the stamped and addressed envelope, or asked for photographs other than those illustrated. All such applications cannot for obvious reasons be considered.**

So, to get things quite straight, if you would like copies of any three of the snapshots in this feature, send me a note of the numbers of your choice, together with the coupon and a stamped addressed envelope for the reply. Address your applications to The Editor FILM REVIEW, c/o The Londoner Ltd., 41-45 Beak Street, W.1.

No applications can be considered from United Kingdom readers if received after the end of the second week in March. In the case of foreign and Dominion readers, this closing date is extended to the end of the second week in May.

And there's a special note for these latter applicants. Obviously it's no good sending a stamped and addressed envelope in your case as foreign stamps are not valid for posting from this country, so please instead of sending stamps, obtain and enclose a coupon to the value of the stamps instead.

---

* As it happens that towards the latter part of the period certain numbers sometimes run out and replacements are unobtainable, please in each case send an alternative choice.

*Happening to come upon this starry trio visiting each other in the Universal-International studios, our photographers whipped out their camera and this snap was the result. All three stars were at the time making films for U.I. James Cagney, centre, was making* Man of a Thousand Faces, *playing the late, fabulous Lon Chaney : James Stewart had hopped across from the set of his new Western* Night Passage *and Orson Welles* (right) *was filling in the time between takes of his* Pay the Devil.

*One of the biggest personal successes of the year was that scored by the curvaceous 20th Century-Fox star Jayne Mansfield in* The Girl Can't Help It. *This home snap shows Jayne in another role, that of mother. Six-year-old Jaynie Marie tries to listen in to the phone call that has interrupted mummy's good-night kiss.*

*Two nice young people. Snapped on the way back to the set from the studio restaurant during the shooting of* The Good Companions, *Associated-British co-stars Janette Scott and John Fraser.*

*Caught in playful mood with his poodle pet is that rapidly rising British star George Baker. This picture was actually taken in the brief interval between his two* 1957 *films for Associated-British,* No Time for Tears *and* These Dangerous Years.

*A quick-witted camera-hawk got this picture of a " take " that went wrong. It happened during the filming near Paris of the picnic scenes for the Associated-British picture* Love in the Afternoon. *Gary Cooper, supposed to lean lovingly over co-star Audrey Hepburn, leaned a little too heavily and slipped . . . .*

*The lovely young lady with the Siamese cat—a newly presented pet, named " Bobo "—is one of Mr. Rank's brightest young starlets, Maureen Swanson, who was given her biggest role in the 1956 Wisdom film* Up in the World.

*One of Britain's younger male hopes is Michael Craig, whom you may have first noticed as the hero of the J. Arthur Rank film* House of Secrets. *This thriller was shot partly in France and during an interval between shots along the Marseilles waterfront Michael gallantly posed for this picture for a British visitor.*

*Much fancied by U.I. for future stardom, and now under long term contract to them, is tall, dark and handsome John Saxon. 21-years-old John came to the screen by way of modelling, and he made his screen debut in Universal-International's* The Unguarded Moment, *subsequently scoring something of a hit in their musical* Rock Pretty Baby.

*Even lens-shy James Mason gets caught by the candid camera sometimes, as this off-duty shot of Joan Collins and him sampling some of the exotic fruit of the West Indies testifies. Both stars were in Barbados on location for the 20th Century-Fox British film* Island in the Sun, *based on the best-selling Evelyn Waugh novel.*

# Rising Stars and New Faces

A little plump in the face, blonde, smiling and charming **Shirley Jones** made a great impact on cinemagoers in her first film, RKO's *Oklahoma*, and confirmed the impression that we had a new kind of screen star by her work in her next movie, Fox's *Carousel*. Shirley lacks the factory glamour of Hollywood, but she has a real, fresh beauty, a most pleasant personality and, of course, a fine singing voice.

She comes from the small Pennsylvania coal-mining town Smithton (pop. 800). Her parents, soon becoming aware of their daughter's fine voice, began giving her singing lessons when she was 12. In 1952 Miss Jones represented the nearby Pittsburgh in a Miss America beauty contest. And by the following year she was singing in the local Light Opera Company's productions. In August, 1953, she went to New York intending to carry on her education, but her singing teacher advised her to call on a Broadway theatrical agent there. He was so impressed with young Miss Jones that he took her to the Rodgers and Hammerstein offices. The company's casting director arranged an audition with a full-scale orchestra and she was promptly signed to a seven-year contract ! Shirley was put into training—in the chorus of " South Pacific " and understudying a lead in " Me and Juliet ". At 21, when the slender, hazel-eyed girl tested for the role of Laurey in the film of *Oklahoma*, the judges immediately recognised her as ideal for the part, and Miss Jones's film career was launched.

Though it was during recent months, in big Westerns like John Ford's Warner film *The Searchers* and Fox's *The Proud Ones*, that **Jeffrey Hunter** has made his biggest impact, he is actually a star of long standing, with more than a dozen films to his credit, the first three of these having been made as far back as 1950.

Born in New Orleans in 1932, Jeffrey (whose real name is Henry H. McKinnies, Junior) was " spotted " by talent scouts while still at college and playing there in amateur dramatics. Fox beat Paramount to the draw—and his appearance in the former company's *Fourteen Hours* was the result. Incidentally, for his college theatre Jeffrey made his debut as a 60-year-old man in a production of " Goldilocks and the Three Bears " ! Until he signed his film contract however, Hunter was a sportsman first and an actor (a long way) after. Now he's had to reverse that.

Though the Fox test led to his contract and his film career, the Paramount test around the same time led to almost as important, though different, consequences, for playing with him before the Paramount cameras on this occasion was starlet Barbara Rush. Miss Rush was subsequently, and soon, to become Mrs. McKinnies. For the record, Mr. Hunter tips the scales at 180 lbs., is one inch above six feet tall and has dark brown hair and blue eyes.

Last November one of the film fan magazines published the startling news that No. 1 star with the youngsters was **Jeremy Spenser.** Not only were the fans demanding more news and photos of him than of older top-liners like Tony Curtis and Rock Hudson, but their interest revealed in this fashion was double that shown in the late and fabulous James Dean.

Jeremy, even now only around nineteen, was born at Thames-side Richmond and educated at Downside School. It was by accident that he made his film debut in 1940. Elder brother David (four years Jeremy's senior) was turned down for a part in *Anna Karenina* because he was thought to be too adult. Casually he mentioned brother Jeremy ; the producer, interested, asked the boy to come along. He did—and got the part.

Since that moment Jeremy has never had to look for a job —his problem has been which to accept and which to refuse. His films have included *The Dancing Years, The Spider and the Fly, Appointment with Venus, Escapade, It's Great to be Young* and *The Sleeping Prince*, for which he had ten weeks' leave from the Army. On the stage he impressed in such West End successes as " The Winslow Boy ", " His House in Order " and " The Innocents ". And in TV, too, there's been no lack of work, with such productions as " The Reluctant Dragon ", " Huckleberry Finn " and " Ann of Green Gables ". His ambition ? To play the really passionate lover—if the scriptwriter and the censor will let him !

**Maureen Swanson** is another lovely young film actress who started out as a dancer, for she spent the first three years of her professional career dancing with the Sadler's Wells Ballet Company. Raven-haired, green-eyed Maureen was born in Glasgow on November 25th, 1932. There was, it seems, no " theatre " in the family ; her father was a business man. She was educated at school and convent in Scotland before going to Paris to study the ballet. In 1951, having left the Wells the previous year, she played juvenile lead and leading dancer in the Drury Lane production of " Carousel " but it wasn't until three years later that she really embarked on a straight-acting career, playing and studying with repertory companies at Hornchurch and Windsor and at the " Q " theatre.

In 1953 she made her screen debut in *Moulin Rouge* and the following year she was Robert Taylor's bride in *Knights of the Round Table*. In 1953, incidentally, she was placed by the late photographer Baron in a list of the world's ten most beautiful women.

In 1955 Maureen made her TV debut in this country—though she had already acted and danced in a series of six TV films made for American TV. The same year her screen career took a sudden upward trend with her appearance in *A Town Like Alice*, to be followed by *Jacqueline*. Then came *The Spanish Gardener* and *Up in the World*, in which she played leading lady to Norman Wisdom. Under contract to the Rank group, she has many more films lined up for her and we're likely to be seeing her on our screens quite a lot in the future.

28-year-old **Stephen Boyd** has been hailed as " the greatest screen find since James Mason ", with whom, indeed, he has several things in common, including a habit of speaking his mind.

Born in Belfast (in 1928), Stephen is the son of an Irish mother and a Canadian father. From early childhood he wanted to act. He began with the Ulster Theatre Group. He went to Canada at the age of 18 and there joined the summer stock companies and did a lot of broadcasting, before moving to the U.S.A. There he made a coast-to-coast tour in 1950, playing leads in " Streetcar Named Desire " and other plays.

At the end of 1950 he came to Britain, but met little success. All sorts of jobs had to be taken, including serving in a cafeteria. Now, he will tell you ruefully, " I never want to pour another cup of coffee." This long period of theatrical unemployment culminated in a severe illness. For days he practically starved and on recovering found himself broke and hungry. He took his guitar and played to cinema queues in London's Leicester Square. Later he found a job of another kind in Leicester Square—as a cinema commissionaire. Michael Redgrave happened to speak to Boyd one day, and guessing he was an out-of-work actor, introduced him to the well-known Windsor Repertory Company. Within a fortnight Boyd was rehearsing the lead in a play.

Several months later he joined the Arts Council's Midland Theatre Company and played leading roles in plays like " The River Line", "To Dorothy A Son" and "Winter's Journey". Returning to London in the middle of 1954, Stephen was cast for several small film parts, and appeared in four television plays. One of them, "Barnett's Folly", was the turning-point in his career. His performance was a triumph which had film companies bidding for him, and a screen test for London Films in March, 1955, led to a seven-year contract.

After another small film part, producer Andre Hakim of Sumar Film Productions gave Boyd his major screen role as the Irish agent in *The Man Who Never Was*, to be followed by his part in *Island in the Sun*.

Over six feet tall and well-built, Boyd has dark wavy hair, an Irish-Canadian accent, and a strong face that can switch from an engaging smile to sinister menace.

Three years ago **George Baker** was an unknown actor with an unswerving ambition to get to the top—both on stage and screen. This year he achieved his goal—starring simultaneously in the Wessex film *A Hill in Korea* and the Agatha Christie play "Towards Zero" (his first West End leading role).

Baker was born in Bulgaria, twenty-five years ago, second of the five children of the Yorkshire born British Consul and his Irish wife. At school in Sussex George decided—at fifteen—to run away, with the vague idea that his future lay in the theatrical world. He arrived in London with a great deal of ambition and no money, but succeeded in finding his keep by doing a variety of odd jobs. Then he heard that the Deal Repertory Company were on the look-out for people and managed to persuade them to employ him. He stayed at Deal for eight months, graduating from walk-on parts to leading roles. Then he landed a job as assistant stage manager at the Richmond Theatre. He was just seventeen. After periods of unemployment—during which he worked in the Regent Palace kitchen and a carpet warehouse—he was forced to forego his first West End opportunity owing to the imminence of his National Service call-up. During embarkation leave he married Julia Squire, one of Britain's leading film costume designers.

On his return from Army Service in Hong Kong, George got started again in repertory—this time at Salisbury, Croydon and Walthamstow. Then he got his first real break with a small part in *The Intruders*. This led to a bigger part in *The Dam Busters* and, within months, to his first major role in *The Ship That Died of Shame*, followed by star billing in *A Woman for Joe*, *The Feminine Touch*, and *The Extra Day*. Even now, George Baker still feels it is only just the beginning!

One of the newcomers making the biggest impact during the year has been **Rod Steiger.** Long Island born (April, 1925) Steiger entered dramatics in a rather odd way. Having joined the U.S. Navy at the age of 16 and gone to war, at 21 he was given an office job with the U.S. Veterans Administration. Now it happened that every time he tried to date one of the girls in the office he failed because they were busy with local theatricals. So Steiger, more or less in desperation, joined the company himself—and it wasn't until that year that he saw his first professional play !

Steiger soon proved a success as an actor, so much so that he left his office job and began training first with the Dramatic Workshop, and then with Elia Kazan's group. His first professional appearance was in " The Trial of Mary Dugan ", and while still in his twenties he appeared on Broadway—as the 55-year-old detective in a revival of Odets' " Night Music " ! In 1953, Steiger won the Sylvania Award as the most outstanding TV actor of the year. He made his screen debut in *Teresa* for Fred Zinnemann—so much to the director's satisfaction that, when casting was under way on *Oklahoma*, he insisted that Steiger be cast as " Jud Fry ". In between these assignments, Kazan commissioned him for the role of Marlon Brando's brother in *On the Waterfront*, in which he gave a most impressive performance. " Heavy " roles followed in *The Big Knife*, *One Man Mutiny*, *The Harder They Fall*, *Jubal* and *Back From Eternity*.

" The most exciting discovery since Marilyn Monroe," is what they call blonde, shapely **Sheree North** at 20th Century-Fox, where she was put under long-term contract for grooming for stardom only a month after she turned 21. She dances, she sings, she acts. And she has one of the most voluptuous figures and sultry faces the screen has seen for years.

Two years ago Sheree decided to give up dancing because she had been doing it since she was six and was tired of the travel it involved. With money earned in a picture she began taking business courses at Santa Monica City College to qualify for a job as a secretary-receptionist offered her at an aircraft factory.

Choreographer friend Bob Alton heard of her plans and went to see her to talk her out of quitting. He found her dyeing her platinum-blonde hair brown and talking of changing her show-girl name. Alton insisted that she go to New York. She did, and through him landed a small dance number in "Hazel Flagg ". When the reviews came out the producer saw she was a hit and built up her number. She danced in the show for a year and returned to Hollywood in January, 1954, to do a dance number with Jerry Lewis in Paramount's *Living It Up*. It was a hectic Betty Hutton sort of stomp and she was a sensation. Bing Crosby saw it and put her on his TV show as Jack Benny's girl friend. Millions of TV viewers saw her at her best (in tights which showed off her 35½—23½—35½ form !) and she became one of the most talked about personalities in Hollywood.

Then began her long series of tests at 20th Century-

Fox and her long-term contract. The prospect of becoming a big star did not ruffle her because she was accustomed to seeing her name in lights. Instead, she thought of it more as a steady job which would permit her to settle down and make a stable, secure home for her five-year-old daughter, Dawn, born when she was sixteen, of a marriage that lasted only 18 months. Sheree was born in Los Angeles, is of Scottish blood on her mother's side and German-French on her father's. Her real name is Dawn Bethel.

A new star of promise on the Hollywood horizon this year has been **Paul Newman,** the Ohio lad who, after scoring a hit in M-G-M's *The Rack*, was given the important central role of world boxing champion Rocky Graziano in *Somebody Up There Likes Me*.

Newman is no tyro. At 12 he was playing in " St. George and the Dragon ", but it wasn't until much later, after he had become known for his sporting prowess and served three years with the Naval Air Arm during the war, that he turned seriously to dramatics as a career.

A short period with summer repertory companies was followed by the death of his father, who left to Paul his Cleveland sports goods store. But the actor struggled with the storekeeper, and eventually won the day. Soon, Paul had enrolled with the Yale Drama School. His first professional engagement came in New York where he was immediately engaged for several shows on TV including " The Web ", " You Are There " and " Danger ". He was selected for a featured role in " Picnic ", and he appeared in this Broadway hit for 14 months.

His first New York production brought him a screen contract with Warner Brothers, the romantic lead in *The Silver Chalice*, and the praise of producer-director Victor Saville. It was on the completion of this picture that he returned to Broadway to star in " The Desperate Hours " and to make several TV appearances. He was then loaned to M-G-M by Warners for *The Rack* and *Somebody Up There Likes Me*.

Newman makes his home on Long Island, New York. He still enjoys all outdoor sports, particularly riding, swimming and diving. When he first arrived in New York, he began studying at the well-known Actors' Studio. He declares it has exerted the greatest influence on his acting development, and still attends classes two nights a week whenever he is in New York.

*Universal-International* star ROCK HUDSON achieved a new status this year. Not only did his own company keep him busy with a series of important roles in major films like BATTLE HYMN but, loaned to *Warner*, he gave his best performance to date in GIANT.

# THE GENERAL RELEASES OF THE YEAR IN PICTURES 1956-7

Glamour girl DIANA DORS gave her first real dramatic screen performance—and considerably impressed us with it—in the grim *Associated British* film YIELD TO THE NIGHT, a detailed, moving and balanced—and certainly surprisingly unmelodramatic—account of the last weeks of a girl condemned to hang for murder. With prisoner Miss Dors in this scene, wardress JOAN MILLER.

GORDON MACRAE, the virile singing star who has had successes in several big musicals this year, notably in *R.K.O. Radio's* OKLAHOMA and *20th Century-Fox's* THE BEST THINGS IN LIFE ARE FREE.

BURT LANCASTER as the Man on the Flying Trapeze and TONY CURTIS as the youngster he takes under his wing and, literally, to the Top. Ungrateful Tony is just about to strike his tutor. And the cause of it? GINA LOLLOBRIGIDA (*inset*) who comes between the two men and almost brings about tragedy. The film is Carol Reed's circus story for *United Artists*, TRAPEZE.

One of the best and deservedly most successful British films of the year was Daniel Angel's production for the *Rank Organisation* REACH FOR THE SKY, the story of Douglas Bader, the great legless fighter pilot and air tactician of the last war. In this film KENNETH MORE (*left*, seen shaking hands with CHARLES CARSON, playing Sir Hugh Dowding) gave a great performance as Bader.

Mixed-up foursome—in Rome and Romance—are *(left to right)* DEAN MARTIN, ANNA MARIA ALBERGHETTI, EVA BARTOK and DEWEY MARTIN. The film, *M-G-M's* TEN THOUSAND BEDROOMS, was the first to be made by Martin since he split with partner Lewis.

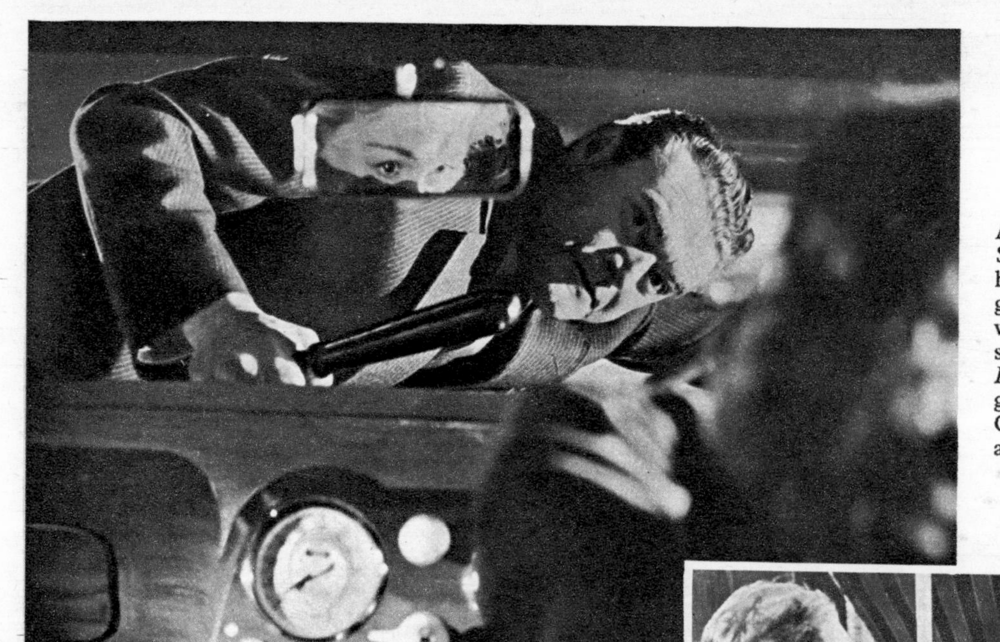

A dangerous moment for C.I.D.' Supt. Halliday (JACK HAWKINS) a he struggles on the bonnet of th getaway car, trying to smash th windscreen while the driver tries t shake him off. It's a scene fron *Ealing's* THE LONG ARM, whicl gave you a good idea of the rea C.I.D. by following the detective as they gradually and painstakingl solved a murder.

Though not as successful as it should have been with the general moviegoing public, or with the critics for that matter, *20th Century-Fox's* THE MAN IN THE GREY FLANNEL SUIT was without doubt one of the best American films of the year. The story of an American executive, his family, his ambitions and his conscience, it was long, intelligent, and gave GREGORY PECK, as the suit-wearer, an opportunity for another fine performance. With him in this scene, boss FREDRIC MARCH and (*left*) HENRY DANIELL.

One of Alfred Hitchcock's greates earlier successes was THE MAN WHO KNEW TOO MUCH and last year he re-made it fo *Paramount*, with Technicolor and VistaVision. JAMES STEWART was the doctor on holiday in Morocco who becomes involved with a gang of crooks. Here he is just in time to hear the last murmured words of stabbed DANIEL GELIN.

*Paramount's* THE BIRDS AND THE BEES (actually a re-make with music of the old Preston Sturges comedy "The Lady Eve") introduced to the screen a new comedian in George Gobel, seen here under the spell of Mitzi Gaynor, who played the lovely daughter of expert card-sharper David Niven.

The starry quartet in *Paramount's* re-make of the successful Cole Porter stage and screen musical ANYTHING GOES are Donald O'Connor, Mitzi Gaynor, Jeanmaire and Bing Crosby.

Bob Hope and Katharine Hepburn made a strange but on the whole successful co-starring team in Betty Box's *Remus* comedy THE IRON PETTICOAT. Miss Hepburn played the Russian aviatrix who in a fit of pique flies her jet through the Iron Curtain and gets Hope as a guide to Democracy—and Love. On the *left*: Alan Gifford.

Guitar strumming JEFF RICHARDS plucks a pretty string against a background of beautiful women, his co-stars in *M-G-M's* re-make of "The Women"—THE OPPOSITE SEX. *Left to right :* JOAN COLLINS, DOLORES GRAY, ANN SHERIDAN, ANN MILLER, JOAN BLONDELL and AGNES MOOREHEAD.

Hell-for-leather, bloody-and-thundery adventure was the basis of the *United Artists* film BANDIDO, in which Robert Mitchum played an adventurer out for an easy buck at the time of the 1916 Mexican revolution. With him, rebel leader Gilbert Roland.

Robert Mitchum was again surrounded by mystery and excitement in another *United Artists'* production, FOREIGN INTRIGUE, in which he was cast as a man investigating the strange life of his deceased boss.

Liam Redmond confirms his suspicions that the man he is drinking with, Van Johnson, is blind and coolly makes plans to rub him out. A scene from the excellent *20th Century-Fox* thriller, set in a somewhat strange London, 23 PACES TO BAKER STREET.

STEWART GRANGER as the British officer who finds the charms of the Anglo-Indian beauty (AVA GARDNER) too great to resist—a scene from *M-G-M's* BHOWANI JUNCTION

OLIVIA DE HAVILLAND played the title role in the *United Artists* film THE AMBASSADOR'S DAUGHTER. Annoyed at the insinuations that the American troops are misbehaving themselves in Paris, she picks one of them (JOHN FORSYTHE) as a guinea-pig to prove that they are not! And of course, it's not long before she's in love with her study . . .

Arthur Grimble and his wife (DENHOLM ELLIOTT and SUSAN STEPHEN) look affectionately at each other in their first great moment of triumph, having brought peace to two warring islands of the Pacific. A scene from John Lawrie's extremely charming PACIFIC DESTINY, based on the book of reminiscences, "A Pattern of Islands," by Sir Arthur Grimble. Also in the scene, MOIRA MACDONALD (*left*) and MICHAEL HORDERN (*right*).

One of the more pleasant, uncomplicated films of the year was *20th Century-Fox's* made-in-Australia SMILEY, a captivating film about a little boy whose ambition to get himself a real "bike" leads indirectly to the uncovering of a dope ring. COLIN PETERSEN as the boy was delightful in every way.

A Western with a difference—a very great difference—was *British Lion's* RAMSBOTTOM RIDES AGAIN, in which ARTHUR ASKEY played the little man out in the woollier wastes of Canada trying against incredible odds to live up to the reputation of his grandfather, Wild Bill Ramsbottom! In this scene Arthur plays a crooked game of poker with the villain—SIDNEY JAMES.

Romantic leads, JANETTE SCOTT and JOHN FRASER, helped considerably to add charm to the *Associated British* film THE GOOD COMPANIONS, a re-make of the J. B. Priestley story, with songs and musical numbers added.

Full of real Irish blarney—and a lot of charm—was George Brown's *J. Arthur Rank* film JACQUELINE. Set in Belfast, it was the story of a shipyard worker who, unfitted for his job, dreams of life on the farm, and drinks to dream the better! Here JOHN GREGSON, as the man, tells his wife (KATHLEEN RYAN) of his problems.

We've seen some clerics do odd things on the screen, but oddest to date was that seen in *Paramount's* THE LEATHER SAINT, in which a young padre (JOHN DEREK) takes up professional boxing in order to raise cash for his pet charity. Also in this scene, RICHARD SHANNON and PAUL DOUGLAS.

THE EDDY DUCHIN STORY (*Columbia*) was one in an ever-lengthening line of films based on the biographical stories of famous American jazz musicians. In this case the story was sad, for Duchin, who had magic fingers, suffered many misfortunes during his short life. Here he is, played by TYRONE POWER, with KIM NOVAK, as his wife.

Hilda, realising that her mother-in-law-to-be's heart attacks are all part of a plan to smash her romance, tells her that she can expect no sympathy from her. A dramatic scene from *20th Century-Fox's* (The Many Loves of) HILDA CRANE, with JEAN SIMMONS as Hilda and EVELYN VARDEN as the mother-in-law-to-be.

*Universal-International* star JULIE ADAMS who, of Scots-English descent, is claimed to have two of the " most beautiful legs in Hollywood ". Among her more recent films was FOUR GIRLS IN TOWN.

JEFF CHANDLER and GEORGE NADER, officers of the Attack Transport ship *Belinda*, watch apprehensively as another wave of Japanese suicide bombers roars into the attack. A scene from *Universal-International's* AWAY ALL BOATS.

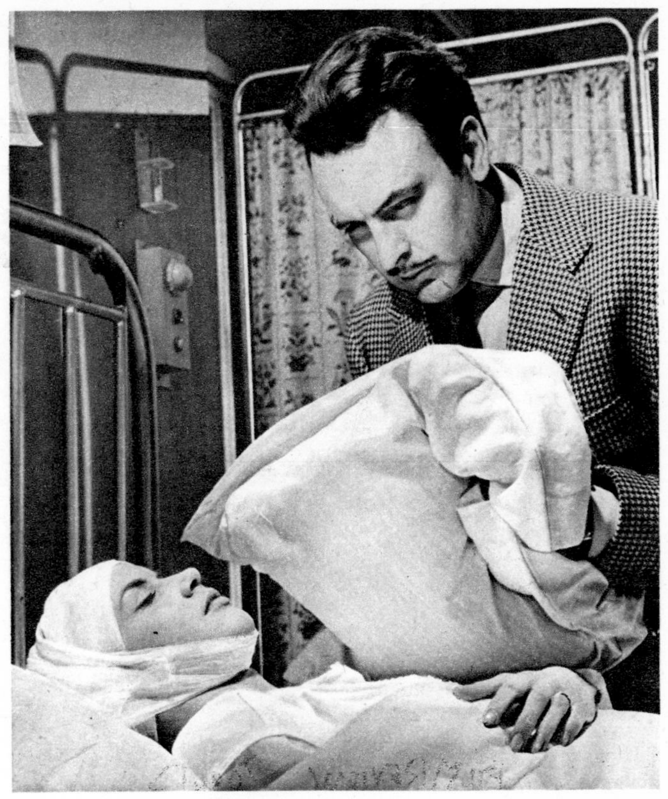

The criminal stands poised above his victim: killer DONALD SINDEN prepares to smother hospital patient MURIEL PAVLOW, the only witness to his crime, in this scene from the Sydney Box production for the *J. Arthur Rank Organisation*, EYEWITNESS.

A sheriff suffering from attacks of blindness (ROBERT RYAN) asks for the support of his fellow-townsmen in combating the death-dealing villain who threatens them in *20th Century-Fox's* handsome and thrilling outdoor epic, THE PROUD ONES.

PAT CROWLEY is introduced by her bridegroom, AUDIE MURPHY, to CHARLES DRAKE in this scene from *Universal-International's* Western, WALK THE PROUD LAND.

In the cramped quarters of their punt in a rainstor two (JIMMY EDWARDS and DAVID TOMLINSON) of th THREE MEN IN A BOAT find the third's (LAURENC HARVEY) playing on his banjo hardly improves th occasion. A scene from the *British Lion* film based o the famous Jerome K. Jerome comedy.

NORMAN WISDOM learns something of the tricks of the stage magician during the cabaret scenes in his third comedy for the *Rank Organisation*, UP IN THE WORLD. The magician is EDWIN STYLES.

KATHLEEN HARRISON takes it hardly that her husband JACK WARNER has had a big win in the pools, while neighbours THORA HIRD and CHARLES VICTOR do their best to comfort her. A scene from *Eros's* HOME AND AWAY.

In *Launder* and *Gilliatt's* comedy THE GREEN MAN ALASTAIR SIM played an international assassin who gets rusty during the war and hilariously fails in his come-back attempt to " remove " a boring British politician. With him in this scene is GEORGE COLE, who was also amusingly involved.

In *Eros's* A TOUCH OF THE SUN, FRANK HOWERD played a hall-porter who suddenly come into a legacy of £10,000 and decides to buy the hote at which he works.

George Minter's IT'S A WONDERFUL WORLD was a jolly comedy about a young composer (GEORGE COLE) who finds a "new sound"—actually old music recorded and then played backwards. TERENCE MORGAN (*left*) played the other half of the song-writing team and the film also introduced to British films France's MYLENE NICOLE (*inset*).

Newlywed GLYNIS JOHNS, ready to symphathise with her hubbie ROSSANO BRAZZI for having lost his remaining few pounds at the gambling tables, finds to her astonishment that he has won a fortune. From *British Lion's* LOSER TAKE ALL, filmed against a Monte Carlo background.

Another very successful—certainly from the box-office point of view—adaptation of a stage farce was *Remus's* SAILOR BEWARE, which was built round the old mother-in-law joke. Here ESMA CANNON's tea-leaves foretell tragedy and THORA HIRD and JOY WEBSTER are suitably shocked.

*Remus's* DRY ROT was a more or less straightforward adaptation of the long-running stage farce of the same title, about three down-and-out bookmakers (SYDNEY JAMES, BRIAN RIX and RONALD SHINER) who plan a big turf coup.

One of the really " big " films of the year—it ran for three-and-a-quarter hours—was *Warner's* GIANT, a sprawling, well acted and generally impressive adaptation of the Edna Ferber novel about Texas. With many themes and several story lines, it was basically a family saga. It was specially interesting in that it contained the last screen performance of the late JAMES DEAN (he was killed almost immediately the film was finished) ; as a young man ruined by love and success. With him in this scene, another young star who made a deep impression this year (both in this film and later in " Baby Doll "), CARROLL BAKER.

One of the smoothest, most successful musicals of the period was *M-G-M's* HIGH SOCIETY, a remake (with music added) of yesteryear's big screen comedy success "The Philadelphia Story." The starry rota of players topping the cast list included BING CROSBY and FRANK SINATRA (seen here after literally getting a bang out of Bing !), GRACE KELLY, and CELESTE HOLM.

In a year notable for many ambitious and large-scale musicals, none was more consistently entertaining than *R K O Radio's* Todd-AO adaptation of the great Rodgers and Hammerstein stage success OKLAHOMA, with GORDON MCRAE as Curly and delightful newcomer SHIRLEY JONES as Laurey, seen here together in the charming "Surrey" number.

One of the biggest things in John Huston's gargantuan adaptation of the Herman Melville story, MOBY DICK, was the white whale of the title, which cost a fortune to construct and played such an important part in the film. In this scene Captain Ahab (GREGORY PECK) has at last caught up with his enemy (the beast which in their former meeting had taken his leg off at the knee) and now begins the fight to the death.

Though hardly pleasant, Tennessee Williams' BABY DOLL as filmed by *Warners* was certainly powerful, and this story of sex in the deep South presented us with a top ranking new star in ELI WALLACH, who made his screen debut in the picture. With him in this scene, KARL MALDEN (*left*) as the " doll's " husband and CARROLL BAKER, as the " doll " herself.

20*th Century-Fox's* THE GIRL CAN'T HELP IT, a witty, gay little comedy with plenty of rock-'n'-roll trimmings, introduced us to a most amusing new star in JAYNE MANSFIELD, who proved an immediate and outstanding success—in more ways than one ! With her, at breakfast, and naturally somewhat overwhelmed by his situation, co-star TOM EWELL.

In the title role DIRK BOGARDE gave an excellent, thoughtful performance in the *Rank* film THE SPANISH GARDENER, which was based on the A. J. Cronin story about a possessive and repressed father's jealousy of his young and lonely son's friendship for the young and virile Spaniard who tends their garden.

It's all routine to test pilot JACK HAWKINS as with co-pilot JOHN STRATTON he takes up a new air freighter on a series of trials for the benefit of a possible client, EDDIE BYRNE, and the Man from the Ministry (DONALD PLEASENCE—in the rear of the plane). A scene from *Ealing's* exciting aerial thriller for *M-G-M*, MAN IN THE SKY.

British agent, Major "Paddy" Leigh-Fermer (DIRK BOGARDE) and his aide Captain Billy Moss (DAVID OXLEY) help their German General prisoner (MARIUS GORING) up the mountainside in an effort to avoid the searching Nazis. A scene from *Powell and Pressburger's Rank* film ILL MET BY MOONLIGHT, a fantastic cloak-and-dagger wartime exploit in Crete which was actually based on fact.

*20th Century-Fox's* Western, LOVE ME TENDER, introduced to moviegoers America's sensational rock-'n'-roll singer Elvis Presley, as a young man who marries his brother's girl friend while the latter is away fighting in the American Civil War. With Presley here are seen his wife —right—(played by Debra Paget) and mother (Mildred Dunnock).

Stepfather Michael Rennie and mother Ginger Rogers face a major problem when the daughter they haven't seen for years arrives home strongly resenting the fact that the father she adores has sent her on this trip. Young Betty Lou Keim gave a delightful performance as the youngster. From *20th Century-Fox's* TEENAGE REBEL.

Alfred Hitchcock went to fact for the first time for the script of his thriller THE WRONG MAN, which he made for *Warners*. It was the story of a man, actually a night club musician (Henry Fonda), picked up, charged and tried for a hold-up of which he was innocent. Here, at the start of it all, insurance clerk Vera Miles suddenly gets the idea he is the same man who had previously stolen money from her at gunpoint.

Also based on truth was *Universal-International's* BATTLE HYMN, the story of a Colonel Dean Hess, World War Two pilot who became a parson and then, plagued by conscience, went back into the U.S. Air Force during the Korean War and eventually found peace by founding a home for Korean orphans. Rock Hudson, seen here with Anna Kashfi, played the Colonel.

A Western with a—most amusing—difference is the best way to describe the *United Artists* production THE KING AND FOUR QUEENS. It presented the situation of crooked (but oh, so charming) CLARK GABLE on a ranch with a fierce old "Ma" (JO VAN FLEET), four lovely and (male) neglected young women and a hidden pot of gold.

Also unusual as films go was *Paramount's* THE RAINMAKER, the screen adaptation of the Richard Nash stage play about a confidence man (BURT LANCASTER) who claims he can bring rain to the parched prairies (and in fact the rain does eventually come) but more quickly brings happiness and love to romance-seeking KATHARINE HEPBURN.

Also well out of the celluloid rut was Jose Ferrer's self-directed film for *Universal-International*, THE GREAT MAN. This was a quietly effective, bitter story of a commentator's investigation into the murky private life of a recently deceased public hero of radio and TV . . . which reveals another idol with feet of—vilest—clay.

One of the most memorable films of the year was *Fox's* ANASTASIA, a polished, beautifully acted screen adaptation of the stage play, which in turn was based on a true story about a mysterious woman who suddenly popped up in Germany to claim to be the daughter of the last Tsar of the Russians, having survived the revolution massacre which was supposed to have wiped out the whole family. In the title rolé INGRID BERGMAN gave a performance of shining worth, deservedly winning with it this year's " Oscar ". Here she is as she appears at the beginning of the story, being introduced by YUL BRYNNER to other members (AKIM TAMIROFF and SACHA PITOEFF) of the association of refugee Russians in Paris who are planning to launch her as the long lost " Last of the Romanoffs ".

Co-stars JAMES MASON and PATRICIA OWENS in a scene from ISLAND IN THE SUN, the *20th Century-Fox* film produced personally by Darryl Zanuck and largely shot on location in Jamaica.

The atmosphere is charged with feline acid in this scene from the *M-G-M* musical THE OPPOSITE SEX, which was a re-make (with musical numbers added) of "The Women." JUNE ALLYSON doesn't know that her husband is being unfaithful to her, and her 'friends' are mostly itching to tell her. *Left to right*: JOAN BLONDELL, DOLORES GRAY, JUNE ALLYSON, ANN SHERIDAN.

A high school dance turns into a sort of free-for-all struggle in this scene from *Universal-International's* teen-age musical ROCK, PRETTY BABY.

HOWARD KEEL surrounded by a whole harem of beauties and watched jealously by the Grand Vizier's wife DOLORES GRAY in a scene from the *M-G-M* screen adaptation of the stage musical KISMET.

ERNEST BORGNINE, GORDON MACRAE and DAN DAILEY as that famous song writing team of the twenties: De Sylva, Brown and Henderson. A scene from the *20th Century-Fox* musical THE BEST THINGS IN LIFE ARE FREE. And with the boys, feminine co-star SHEREE NORTH.

Red-headed, always charming, RHONDA FLEMING is seldom left alone for long ; she is one of the most consistently employed actresses in Hollywood. This year she came to Britain to make a film. This particular portrait comes from one of her more recent movies, *R K O Radio's* TENNESSEE'S PARTNER.

*From Spain came the best film we've yet seen from that country, the moving* Marcelino, *the story of a little boy adopted by some monks and the miracle that comes to him and his guardians. The boy was played by PABLITO CALVO.*

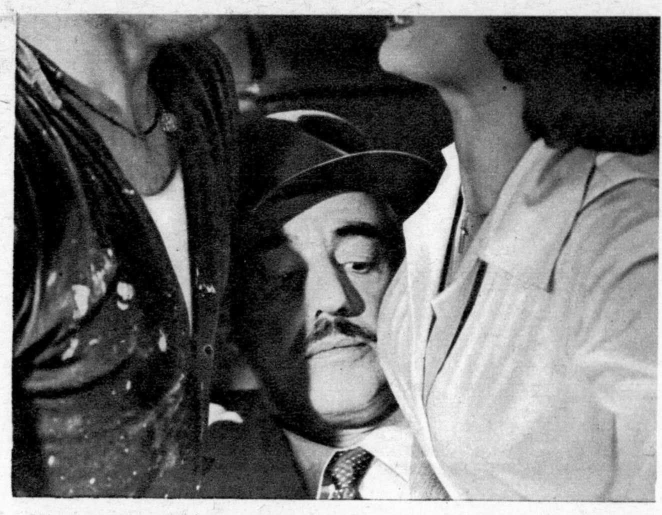

*Vittorio de Sica gets a new angle on a heated argument between a girl acquaintance and her boy-friend in the first of several episodes in the Italian portmanteau picture* Villa Borghese.

of all was Fellini's *La Strada—The Road*, a wonderfully atmospheric film about strolling players in which Guiletta Massima, looking oddly like a tow-headed golliwog, gave such a moving performance. Another of the year's more outstanding Italian movies was *I Vitelloni—Spivs*, also by Fellini, which also had more real atmosphere and feeling than appears in most movies. From Russia came the exciting ballet film *Romeo and Juliet* and from Rene Clair came *Summer Manoeuvres*, in colour and wide-screen; witty, beautifully made and well up to Clair's own high standards even if it is not by any means his best work.

One of the outstanding points of interest with both the French and the Italian movies was the large number which were co-productions, using mixed casts, being made with money from both countries and appealing to both peoples—an astute move necessary in the battle to make the films of these countries pay their way—something which has always been a constant struggle.

I think we shall find that this is only the beginning of what is likely to become an increasingly popular idea, and I also feel that collaboration will extend so that as the world gets smaller the films will become ever more international—something which a few nostalgic purists like myself cannot whole-heartedly welcome.

Of the future? Well, I suppose that we shall see an ever greater proportion of foreign language movies being made in colour and for the new wide screens and I have a feeling that among them we shall get some startling new ways of using these assets . . . as assets I always feel they can so easily—yes, and artistically—be!

*NICOLE COURCEL and PHILIPPE LEMAIRE in* Les Clandestines, *a story of crime seen against a background of Paris's "Call Girl" racket.*

*MARTA TOREN as the girl so cruelly treated in* Maddalena, *a story of a street girl persuaded as a bitter joke to play the Virgin Mary in a Holy Procession and suffers a martyr's death as a result.*

*Temptress* Nana, *played by MARTINE CAROL, in the film of that title based on the famous Emile Zola novel about a femme fatale who inevitably brings trouble to her admirers. Admirer in this scene is NOEL ROQUEVERT.*

*Right)* : Successful sequels are rare : successful sequels o sequels are far rarer : this gave DOCTOR AT LARGE, he third of Betty Box's *Rank* " Doctor " comedies (all ›ased on stories by Richard Gordon), considerable listinction, for it was very funny in its broad way and it leserved its considerable success. In this scene doctors MICHAEL MEDWIN and DIRK BOGARDE talk to pretty nurse SHIRLEY EATON.

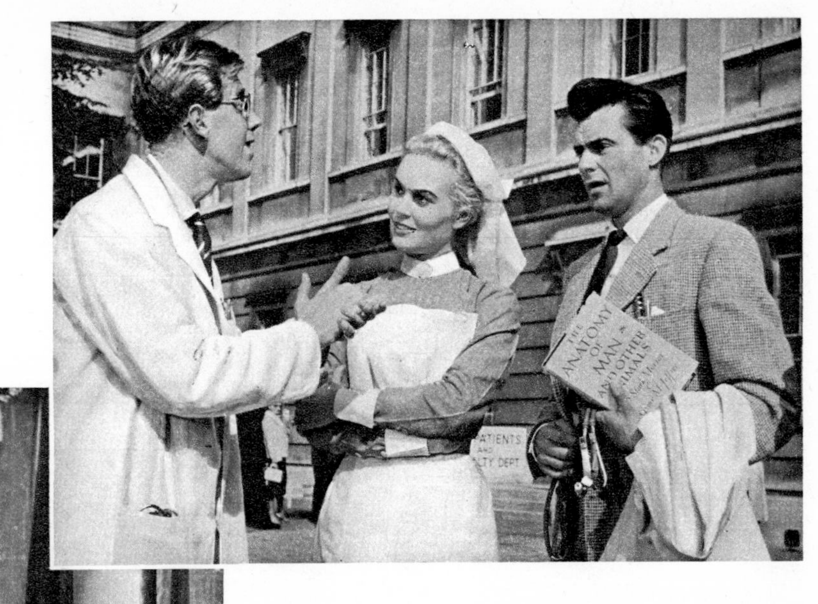


Another Betty Box film was the rather novel comedy THE PASSIONATE STRANGER, which had the original idea of telling a story within a story and separating the sections more completely by telling one—the dream—in colour, and the other—the real-life one—in monotone. CARLO JUSTINI played the Italian chauffeur who gets the wrong—amorous—ideas when he finds that his novelist mistress MARGARET LEIGHTON has put him into her novel as her lover.

*(Right)* : Launder and Gilliatt's production THE SMALLEST SHOW ON EARTH was a minor, essentially British comedy which obtained quite a lot of fun out of the central situation of a young couple, VIRGINIA McKENNA and BILL TRAVERS, being left a " flea-pit " cinema in a small Northern industrial town. Here the legatees meet a part of the legacy they hadn't bargained for, the eccentric old trio of staff : played by BERNARD MILES, PETER SELLERS and MARGARET RUTHERFORD.

*(Left)* : Well up at the top of the year's most highly hilarious British comedies came the Boulting Brothers' BROTHERS IN LAW. This gently, and with wit, " took the mickey "—so to speak—out of the British legal profession. Among those who helped it to success were leading players ERIC BARKER (an excellent screen debut), MILES MALLESON and IAN CARMICHAEL, the last playing the legal pupil whose struggles and misadventures gave the film its main theme. All these players are *(left to right)* in this scene.

*Columbia's Warwick* SEVEN WAVES AWAY posed a problem and left it finally in the laps of the audience. Did skipper TYRONE POWER do right in determining after a disaster at sea to sacrifice a few of the less fit survivors in order to save the remainder? Here ship's nurse MAI ZETTERLING and Power fight the cruel sea at the beginning of the story.

(*Left*): JENNIFER JONES as the invalid Elizabeth Barrett, JOHN GIELGUD as the grim, Victorian papa and VIRGINIA McKENNA as one of his unfortunate daughters in *M-G-M's* polished re-make of the famous story about THE BARRETTS OF WIMPOLE STREET, more especially the romance between poetess Miss Barrett and the poet Robert Browning—the latter role being nicely played by BILL TRAVERS.

(*Below*): Though never highly credible, *M-G-M's* thriller JULIE had its exciting moments. DORIS DAY, now having turned completely away, it seems, from song and dance roles and playing completely "straight", was the girl married to mentally unbalanced LOUIS JOURDAN, and the film largely concerned her efforts to escape his murderous intentions after she has discovered that he had killed her former husband in order to get her for himself.

(*Above*): Once more the problems of the American teenager were examined on the screen in *R K O Radio's* THE YOUNG STRANGER. JAMES MACARTHUR (son of the star HELEN HAYES) played the 17-year-old who is sued for assault on a cinema manager. His parents are played by KIM HUNTER and JAMES DALY. It was easily the best film of this kind of thing yet to be screened.

(*Right*) : Among the several young players who made promising screen debuts during the period under review was JOHN CASSAVETES, who was impressive in *M-G-M's* A MAN IS TEN FEET TALL, which was an excellent, tough movie about the friendship of a young white—an Army deserter (CASSAVETES, seen here in a dangerous position in the New York railyards where the action of the story takes place)—and a young Negro (SIDNEY POITIER) who saves him from himself, so to speak.

(*Left*) : From *Walt Disney* came another vastly entertaining Davy Crockett film, DAVY CROCKETT AND THE RIVER PIRATES. A two-part adventure, it gave our hero plenty of scope in defeating a pack of villains. Here Davy himself (played of course by FESS PARKER) is seen with ever-present pal Georgie (BUDDY EBSEN).

ight) : *Fox's* SEA WIFE skirted quite a lot of the real roblems inherent in its story of four people adrift in the acific Ocean on a raft with little hope of survival. Quartet onsisted of nun (JOAN COLLINS), virile young R.A.F. officer RICHARD BURTON)—both seen here in this scene—and equally irile young negro (CY GRANT) and a colour-conscious blimp (BASIL SYDNEY).

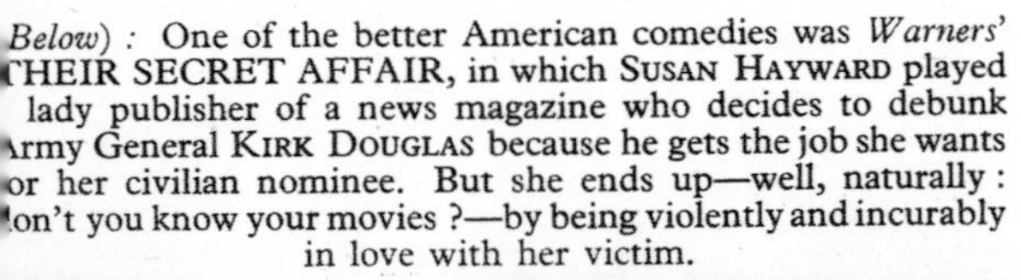

Below) : One of the better American comedies was *Warners'* THEIR SECRET AFFAIR, in which SUSAN HAYWARD played lady publisher of a news magazine who decides to debunk rmy General KIRK DOUGLAS because he gets the job she wants or her civilian nominee. But she ends up—well, naturally : on't you know your movies ?—by being violently and incurably in love with her victim.

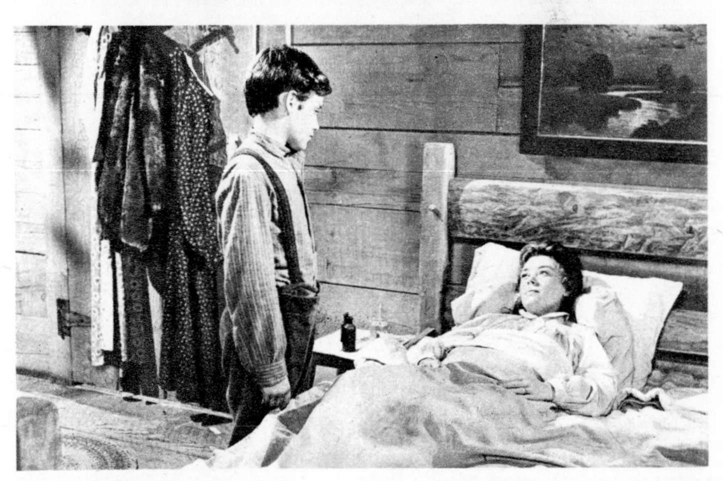

(*Above*) : *R.K.O. Radio's* THE DAY THEY GAVE BABIES AWAY was another of the considerable number of this year's movies which had stories based on fact. This one was a warm, tender tale about a Scots emigrant couple who settle in early Wisconsin and raise a family of six. Here are mother (GLYNIS JOHNS) and son.

(*Left*) : One of the most beautiful backgrounds ever used on the screen was that of the lovingly and lingeringly photographed islands of Greece in *Fox's* BOY ON A DOLPHIN, the story of a treasure discovered at the bottom of the sea and the efforts of various groups of people to raise it. As the sponge diver who first sees the golden boy, SOPHIA LOREN (seen here, with JORGE MISTRAL) in her first English speaking film to be shown in this country, acted everyone else—including co-star ALAN LADD—right off the screen.

(*Right*) : Not for a long time, in fact some thought since before the war, had we seen such a polished, sophisticated and so thoroughly amusing a comedy as *M-G-M*'s DESIGNING WOMAN. It was the story of the sudden romance of sports columnist GREGORY PECK and fashion designer LAUREN BACALL, their sincere but (it sometimes appears) hopeless efforts to make their marriage stick in spite of all the many and often highly hilarious obstacles put in its way by their friends, their enemies and their different ways of life.

(*Left*) : Serious, thoughtful and highly moral, *United Artists*' 12 ANGRY MEN presented the problem of one really honest man (HENRY FONDA, inset) on a jury trying a young lad for stabbing his father. He finds that his eleven fellows (some of them seen here including LEE J. COBB, with knife in hand) are anxious for one reason or another to say " Guilty " and get it over with.

(*Left*) : Kirk Douglas's performance in *M-G-M's* off-beat, unusual picture LUST FOR LIFE—the story in wonderfully correct colour of the tormented painter, Vincent Van Gogh—was one of tremendous integrity. This particular scene from the film (which was premiered at the Curzon in London) comes near the end, when the despairing, mentally sick artist, surrounded by one of the vivid, sun drenched scenes he painted so feverishly and so brilliantly, drops his brush, takes up a revolver and, with a single shot in the head, ends his agony of living.

(*Right*) : Johanna (new young British star Betta St. John) looks at herself in the mirror on her wedding morning, while her parents (Flora Robson and Alexander Knox) proudly watch in the background. Bridesmaid at her side is played by Susan Beaumont. The excellent performances of several most promising youngsters was one of the many good points about the simple, charming *J. Arthur Rank* production HIGH TIDE AT NOON, filmed partly in Nova Scotia.

(*Left*) : In this scene from the *Harlequin* film TIME WITHOUT PITY Ann Todd makes an impassioned plea for the stay of the execution of a young man in whom she has been very interested. Watching her are the lad's father (Michael Redgrave, seated), her husband (Leo McKern, in the background, right), and defence counsel (Peter Cushing, extreme left). Listening sympathetically is an Under Secretary (Ernest Clark).

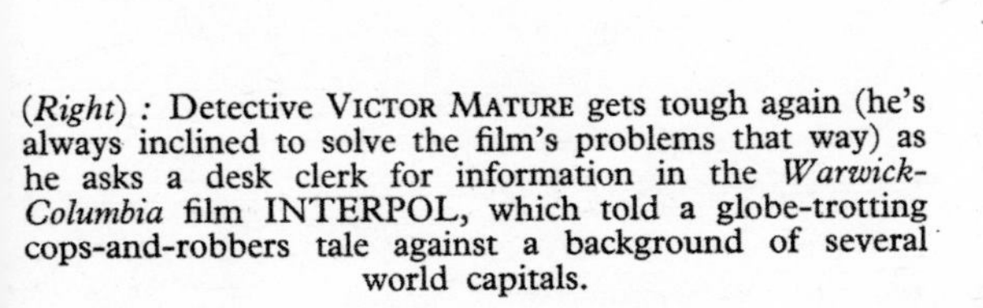

(*Right*) : Detective Victor Mature gets tough again (he's always inclined to solve the film's problems that way) as he asks a desk clerk for information in the *Warwick-Columbia* film INTERPOL, which told a globe-trotting cops-and-robbers tale against a background of several world capitals.

(*Left*) : JEFFREY HUNTER and ROBERT WAGNER as THE JAMES BROTHERS, in *20th Century-Fox's* large-scale Western based on the true story of these notorious outlaws of the old West. In this scene Frank (that's Hunter) pleads with brother Jesse (that's Wagner) to give up his plan to rob the bank at Northfield—a plan which, incidentally, is eventually carried through disastrously.

(*Below*) : A line-up of some of the principal players in the very entertaining *Associated British* musical based on the J. B. Priestley story THE GOOD COMPANIONS. (*Left to right*) : PADDY STONE, JOYCE GRENFELL, JANETTE SCOTT and (*extreme right*) JOHN FRASER.

(*Above*) : The gipsy girl Esmeralda (GINA LOLLOBRIGIDA) takes pity on the tortured dwarf Quasimodo (ANTHONY QUINN) and gives him a drink. A scene from the Franco-English remake of the Victor Hugo story, THE HUNCHBACK OF NOTRE DAME, (released by *Rank*.)

(*Right*) : GINGER ROGERS relaxes on psychiatrist DAVID NIVEN'S couch, with DAN DAILEY an interested spectator. A scene from *20th Century-Fox's* amusing comedy OH, MEN! OH, WOMEN! which got its humour from the current American rage for this kind of self-confession.

Former " Esquire " Calendar Girl Barbara Nichols, a curvey, chromium-blonde who was seen in several films this year including *R.K.O. Radio's* BEYOND A SHADOW OF A DOUBT. Hailed as " Manhattan's answer to Marilyn Monroe " Miss Nichols came to the screen via TV and stage.

Romance : *Columbia's* YOU CAN'T RUN AWAY FROM IT was a remake, with music, of the former Capra classic " It Happened One Night " with JACK LEMMON and JUNE ALLYSON playing the roles formerly taken by Claudette Colbert and Clark Gable.

Romance : In *Fox's* BUS STOP MARILYN MONROE was finally re-vealed as a comedienne of con-siderable merit. Delightfully she played the little cabaret singer (!) wooed and eventually won by rough cowboy DON MURRAY (screen debut) who found that you can't *quite* get away with treating gals like you would steers.

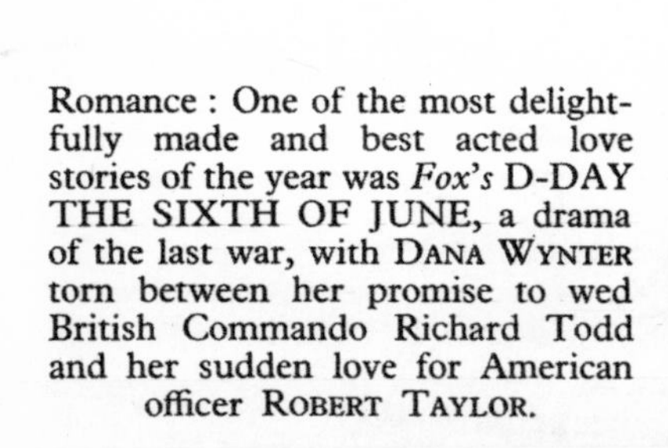

Romance : One of the most delight-fully made and best acted love stories of the year was *Fox's* D-DAY THE SIXTH OF JUNE, a drama of the last war, with DANA WYNTER torn between her promise to wed British Commando Richard Todd and her sudden love for American officer ROBERT TAYLOR.

*Columbia* star VICTORIA SHAW, whose recent films for *Columbia* have included THE EDDY DUCHIN STORY.

Some of the best scenes in Powell and Pressburger's *Rank* film THE BATTLE OF THE RIVER PLATE were those shared by PETER FINCH, as Captain Langsdorf of the German pocket battleship " Graf Spee," and the British merchant ship captain, Dove (BERNARD LEE) who is held as a prisoner on board. This scene is where the German captain explains that after his defeat by the British cruisers he has had to seek shelter in Uruguayan waters. Inset: ANTHONY QUAYLE and IAN HUNTER—as two of the British cruiser captains who defeated the " Spee "—on the bridge of the " Ajax ".

Giving the best performance he has achieved for a long while, JOHN MILLS, as Able Seaman Baker, helped to make Antony Darnborough's THE BABY AND THE BATTLESHIP one the the best British comedy films of the year. And as the baby who causes all the trouble—and the fun—10-months-old MARTYN GARRETT (*inset*) stole practically every scene in which he appeared.

Vivacious brunette COLLEEN MILLER was just about to become a professional dancer when seen and signed by *Universal-International*, for whom she has made—among other films—THE NIGHT RUNNER and (with Jeff Chandler and Orson Welles) PAY THE DEVIL.

One of the most intriguing and unusual musicals of the year was the three-part ballet film made in Britain for *M-G-M* by Gene Kelly, INVITATION TO THE DANCE. It had the novelty of containing no dialogue at all, the whole thing being done by dance and mime. In these two scenes Kelly is seen below as the broken-hearted clown in " The Circus " (the first episode) and then, right with Tamara Toumanova in " Ring Around the Rosy " (the second episode).

The big sensation of *20th Century Fox's* excellent adaptation of the great musical success, THE KING AND I, was a new star, bald-headed Yul Brynner. He played the King in this new version of the former non-musical film "Anna and the King of Siam ", and at once became a great favourite with filmgoers. And as Anna, the British governess, Deborah Kerr also gave a delightful performance.

In Samuel Goldwyn's successful *M-G-M* film of the great stage musical hit of two continents, GUYS AND DOLLS, Jean Simmons, as the little Salvation Army lass who gives her heart to a gambler (played by Marlon Brando), gave a captivating song-and-dance performance. The story was, of course, based on the famous Damon Runyon characters.

A starry quartet from the *Associated British-Marcel Hellman* musical LET'S BE HAPPY. *Left to right :* ZENA MARSHALL, TONY MARTIN, VERA-ELLEN and, in kilt, ROBERT FLEMYNG.

FRANKIE LAINE, the popular singing star, in *Columbia's* HE LAUGHED LAST, which mixed gangsters with fun and music.

A terrifying moment for ESTHER WILLIAMS in *Universal-International's* thriller THE UNGUARDED MOMENT. Miss Williams in her first really dramatic role played a teacher assaulted by a precocious pupil.

JOHN WAYNE as the grimly revengeful Ethan Edwards, sworn to track down the Redskin killers of his brother and wife, and abductors of their children, in John Ford's grand *Warner Bros.* Western THE SEARCHERS.

JACK HAWKINS, as the Pharaoh in Howard Hawks' ancient historical epic for *Warner Brothers*, LAND OF THE PHARAOHS.

Musical Master JOHN MILLS blows his trumpet in this scene from the *Associated British* IT'S GREAT TO BE YOUNG, a musical along rather unusual lines.

GLENN FORD, as THE FASTEST GUN ALIVE—a young man of amazing proficiency with a pistol who has never yet had to depend upon the speed of his "draw" to save his life—takes the first drink that leads directly into his at last having reluctantly to fight it out to the death—against bad man Broderick Crawford. A scene from *M-G-M's* thoughtful, above-average Western. The barman, by the way, is RHYS WILLIAMS.

*RKO-Radio's* superior Western, TENSION AT TABLE ROCK, was firmly in the great "Shane" tradition and concerned a man (RICHARD EGAN) unjustly accused of having shot his best friend in the back. In this scene EGAN is seen with the sheriff's wife (DOROTHY MALONE) and small companion (BILLY CHAPIN).

In *20th Century-Fox's* excellent Western THE LAST WAGON, RICHARD WIDMARK (seen here tied to the wheel of a wagon) played a fugitive wanted by the law for murder who turns over a new leaf and guides a wagon-train of youngsters through Apache country to safety. Also in this scene, FELICIA FARR and RAY STRICKLYN.

It was, as it has proved, an excellent idea on the part of the *Rank* group to lure lovely VIRGINIA MCKENNA from the stage to the screen, for she scored some big successes in the new medium, including SIMBA, THE CRUEL SEA, A TOWN LIKE ALICE and THE BARRETTS OF WIMPOLE STREET.

Large-scale in every way, *M-G-M's* BHOWANI JUNCTION was a sort of love story with many angles, seen against a background of India at the time of the troubles that occurred during the British withdrawal. In this scene: AVA GARDNER, BILL TRAVERS, STEWART GRANGER and LIONEL JEFFRIES.

*M-G-M's* I'LL CRY TOMORROW was based on the best selling autobiography by Lillian Roth, telling the story of a girl whose early unhappiness drove her to the bottle, from which she was only weaned after much agony and humiliation. SUSAN HAYWARD played Lillian and she's seen here with one of her husbands, DON TAYLOR, who himself is a heavy drinker and encourages her in her toping.

*Warners'* THE BAD SEED was an impressive screen adaptation of what appeared to be, basically, a not very credible Maxwell Anderson play about a small girl who inherits a lack of any moral sense and cheerfully kills people if it suits her purpose. Here the girl (played extremely effectively by PATTY McCORMACK—also inset) talks to one of her intended victims, hired help HENRY JONES.

*Associated British* star RICHARD TODD who has done some fine work on the screen this year both for his own and for other companies, including D-DAY THE SIXTH OF JUNE and THE YANGTSE INCIDENT.

'he end of the story. Girl-friend YVONNE DE CARLO nds the " scoundrel " dead in a scene from *RKO-Radio's* DEATH OF A SCOUNDREL, the " success " tory of a very ruthless tycoon. GEORGE SANDERS was excellent in the title role.

JACK PALANCE as the revengeful sergeant in the *United Artists* production, ATTACK, which presented a rather unpleasant picture of graft and corruption among the officers of the U.S. Army during the last war. The film was also noteworthy for some very vivid and terrifyingly realistic scenes of the actual fighting.

Certainly one of the most controversial movies of the year was JAMES MASON'S own production, for *Fox*, BIGGER THAN LIFE, which told the story of a man who is brought to ruin and madness by an addiction to the drug cortisone. In this scene, MASON as the man, CHRISTOPHER OLSEN as his son, and BARBARA RUSH as his wife.

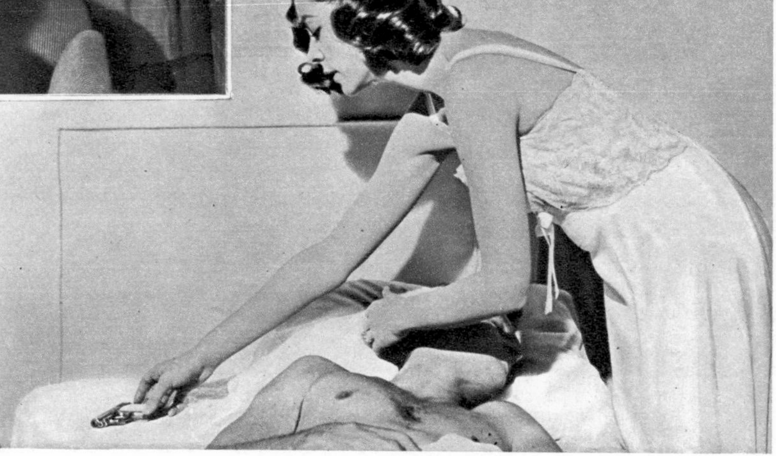

Newlywed LAUREN BACALL makes the disturbing liscovery that her groom (ROBERT STACK) sleeps vith a revolver beneath his pillow, in this scene rom *Universal-International's* drama of an oil-rich family, WRITTEN ON THE WIND.

Singer DORIS DAY, who is singing less and acting more on the screen these days. Her straight role in Hitchcock's THE MAN WHO KNEW TOO MUCH was followed by an even more dramatic role in MISS JULIE for *M-G-M*.

JOAN FONTAINE and DANA ANDREWS were co-stars of *RKO-Radio's* BEYOND A REASONABLE DOUBT, a Fritz Lang drama about a newspaperman who fakes the evidence of a killing and then finds he has woven a net around himself.

Though in his long career SPENCER TRACY has achieved many fine performances, he has seldom done anything better than his portrait of the old guide in *Paramount's* THE MOUNTAIN. The retired climber is persuaded against his better judgement by his young brother to climb the mountain again in order to rob the victims of a plane crash high up in the everlasting snows.

A young actor called PAUL NEWMAN gave an impressive performance in *M-G-M's* SOMEBODY UP THERE LIKES ME, taking the leading role in the autobiographical story of former world middleweight champion Rocky Graziano. In this scene Rocky in prison is being restrained by his fellow prisoners from attacking the warders.

William Wyler's *M-G-M* film FRIENDLY PERSUASION was a long, leisurely and completely charming Quaker family piece set at the period of the American Civil War and showing the effect it had on the individual conscience. A delightful cast included GARY COOPER and DOROTHY McGUIRE, with ANTHONY PERKINS, RICHARD EYER and PHYLLIS LOVE as their children.

Big Chief BOB HOPE says How ! And fellow little chiefs KELLY HOPE and JERRY MATHEWS say How ! too in this scene from *Paramount's* THAT CERTAIN FEELING.

Lovely *20th Century-Fox* contract star RITA MORENO, whose more recent roles have included that of the slave girl in THE KING AND I.

# FILMS GENERALLY RELEASED * DURING THE YEAR *

## * JULY 1st, 1956 TO JUNE 29th, 1957

**A short note as to the nature of each film released generally in this country through the twelve months under review, together with the complete cast, director and producer's name (in some cases the name mentioned may be that of the associate producer), the company which made and distributed the picture and the date when it was generally released. Where in this connection the word "floating" is used it means that the film had no general release on any definite date but has been shown here and there at different times as booked by the cinemas.**

**To conserve space abbreviations of the names of various distributing and producing companies have been made as follows: A.A.—Allied Artists; Anglo—Anglo-Amalgamated; Assoc.—Associated British-Pathe; Ex.—Exclusive; Fox—20th Century-Fox; Ind.—Independent Film Distributors; Lion—British Lion; M-G-M—Metro-Goldwyn-Mayer; Rank—J. Arthur Rank Organisation; R.K.O.—R.K.O. Radio; U.A.—United Artists; U.I.—Universal-International; W.B.—Warner Brothers.**

**The final letters at the end of each paragraph represent the method of production and the colour system used. The key to these letters being as follows: C.—CinemaScope; Col.—Colour where the system is not known; D.—De-Luxe Colour; E.—Eastman Color; G.—Gavaercolour; M.—Metroscope; P.—Pathecolor; S.—Superscope; T.—Technicolor; Tr.—Trucolor; V.—VistaVision; W.—WarnerColor.**

A

**Accused of Murder.** Excellent crime melo from a W. R. Burnett story about a policeman whose faith in a woman accused of murder is finally justified. Cast: *David Brian, Vera Ralston, Sidney Blackmer, Virginia Grey, Warren Stevens, Lee van Cleef, Barry Kelley, Richard Karlan, Frank Puglia, Elisha Cook, Ian MacDonald, Greta Thyssen, Claire Carleton, Hank Worden.* Dir. and Pro.: Joe Kane. (Republic-British Lion.) Rel.: Jan. 14.

**The African Lion.** Walt Disney True Life feature about the King and Queen of Beasts, with family, at home, hunting, and at play. (Disney.) Rel.: April 8.

**Alias John Preston.** Modest British effort about a village finding that the new philanthropist it expected is really a deserter, a racketeer and even a murderer! Cast: *Betta St. John, Alexander Knox, Christopher Lee, Peter Grant, Sandra Dorne, Patrick Holt, John Longden, Bill Fraser, John Stuart, Guido Lorraine, Betty Ann Davies, Gabrielle Gay, Dinah Ann Rogers.* Dir.: David MacDonald. Pro.: Sid Stone. (Lion.) Rel.: July 23.

**The Ambassador's Daughter.** Conducting her own private investigation into the reputed bad behaviour of the American troops abroad, Ambassador *Adolphe Menjou's* daughter *Olivia de Havilland* in Paris falls in love with her first guinea pig, *John Forsythe*. All quite amusing. Rest of cast: *Myrna Loy, Tommy Noonan, Francis Lederer, Edward Arnold, Minor Watson.* Dir. & Pro.: Norman Krasna. (U.A.) Rel.: Sept. 3. (C. & T.)

**Anastasia.** Polished, beautifully produced screen adaptation of the play telling the romanticised story of the girl from a mental home who could be the last Romanoff, surviving daughter of the Tsar. An exquisite (Oscar-winning) performance in the title role by *Ingrid Bergman* lights up the whole movie. Rest of cast: *Yul Brynner, Helen Hayes, Akim Tamiroff, Martita Hunt, Felix Aylmer, Sacha Pitoeff, Ivan Desny, Natalie Schafer, Gregoire Gromoff, Karel Stepanek, Ina de la Haye, Katherine Kath, Hy Hazell, Olga Valery, Tamara Shayne, Peter Sallis, Polycarpe Pavloff.* Dir.: Anatole Litvak. Pro.: Buddy Adler. (Fox.) Rel.: April 15. (T. & C.)

**And Suddenly You Run.** The moral lesson here is, 'don't give way to panic,' and it's pointed by a terrifying story about a detective's fiancee who after accidentally killing a man with her car keeps silence and through this becomes involved in blackmail and murders! Cast: *Scott Brady, Joan Vohs, Frank Faylen, John Dehner, Virginia Gregg, Ric Roman, John Gallaudet, Kem Dibbs, Percy Helton, Francis De Sales, John Maxwell.* Dir.: Franklin Adreon. Pro.: Rudy Ralston. (Republic.) Rel.: Sept. 17.

**Keith Andes, Adele Mara and Robert Ryan in BACK FROM ETERNITY—R.K.O. Radio.**

**Animal World.** A documentary attempt to explain in a simplified form the history of the development of the animal world. Dir. & Pro.: Irwin Allen. (Windsor-W.B.) Rel.: Dec. 17.

**Anything Goes.** Lively, loud and successful remake of earlier Cole Porter stage and screen musical, now with a starry quartet of *Bing Crosby, Donald O'Connor, Jeanmaire* and *Mitzi Gaynor*, with Technicolor and VistaVision too. Rest of cast: *Phil Harris, Kurt Kasznar, Walter Sande.* Dir.: Robert Lewis. Pro.: Robert Emmett Dolan. (Paramount.) Rel.: Aug. 20. (V. & T.)

**Appointment with a Shadow.** *Tony Curtis*, finding he can't catch the killer of his friend (a priest) while a cop, leaves the force to do some private investigation. 'Frisco Italian fishing community background. Rest of cast: *Marisa Pavan, Gilbert Roland, David Leonard, Jay C. Flippen, Ted de Corsia, Argentina Brunetti, Richard Monda, Herbert Vigran.* Dir.: Joseph Pevney. Pro.: Robert Arthur. (V.I.) Rel.: April 15.

**Assignment Redhead.** A plan to find and distribute a twelve million dollar fortune in counterfeit notes defeated by the combined forces of the British and American secret service. Cast: *Richard Denning, Carole Mathews, Ronald Adam, Danny Green, Brian Worth, Jan Holden, Hugh Moxey, Peter Swanwick, Alex Gallier, Bill Nagy, Elwyn Brook-Jones, Robert O'Neil, Robert Crewsdon, Robert Bruce, Paul Hardtmuth, Ronald Leigh Hunt, Edward Forsyth, James Cairns, Theodore Wilhelm.* Dir.: Maclean Rogers. Pro.: W. C. Chalmars. (Butchers). Rel.: Mar. 4.

**Attack.** Brilliantly made, bloody, cynical and horrifying American war story, set at the time of the Battle of the Bulge. How a cowardly, incompetent officer sacrificed his men and was allowed to do so because his superior officer knew that he could be politically useful in the post-war period. Cast: *Jack Palance, Eddie Albert, Lee Marvin, Robert Strauss, Richard Jaeckel, Buddy Ebsen, Strother Martin, Jon Shepodd, Jimmy Goodwin, Steven Geray, Peter Van Eyck, Louis Mercier.* Dir. & Pro.: Robert Aldrich. (Aldrich-U.A.) Rel.: Nov. 5.

**Autumn Leaves.** The usual kind of *Joan Crawford* film: she plays—extremely ably—a brave, lonely stenographer who marries a psychoneurotic boy, suffers and saves him from jail and madness. Rest of cast: *Cliff Robertson, Vera Miles, Lorne Greene, Ruth Donnelly, Shepperd Strudwick, Selmer Jackson, Maxine Cooper, Marjorie Bennett, Frank Gerstle, Leonard Mudie, Maurice Manson, Bob Hopkins.* Dir.: Robert Aldrich. Pro.: William Goetz. (Columbia.) Rel.: Dec. 10.

**Away All Boats.** The story of "Belinda", U.S. Attack Transport ship; of the training of the crew, the battles in the Pacific and the climactic, desperate battle against the Jap suicide planes. Cast: *Jeff Chandler, George Nader, Julie Adams, Lex Barker, Keith Andes, Richard Boone, William Reynolds, Charles McGraw, Jock Mahoney, John McIntire, Frank Faylen, Grant Williams, Floyd Simmons, Don Keefer, Sam Gilman.* Dir.: Joseph Pevney. Pro.: Howard Christie. (U.I.) Rel.: Aug. 6. (V. & T.)

B

**The Baby and the Battleship.** Uproariously funny British satirical comedy about a baby smuggled aboard a battleship and hidden there—if only just—during an exercise. Sterling performances notably by *John Mills* and *Richard Attenborough*. Rest of cast: *Bryan Forbes, Harold Siddons, Clifford Mollison, Lionel Jeffries, Gordon Jackson, Michael Howard, Michael Hordern, Ernest Clark, Thorley Walters, Patrick Cargill, John Forbes-Robertson, Roy Purcell, Kenneth Griffith, Duncan Lamont, Harry Locke, Cyril Raymond, Andre Morell, John Le Mesurier, Ferdy Mayne, Lisa Gastoni, Martin Miller, Jacenta Dicks, Carlo Giustini, Vince Barbi, Vittorio Vittori, Martyn Garrett, D. A. Clarke-Smith, Michael Dear, Barry Foster, Vincent Ball, Robert Ayres, Mark Sheldon, Sam Kydd.* Dir.: Jay Lewis. Pro.: Antony Darnborough. (Lewis-Lion.) Rel.: Oct. 1.

**Baby Doll.** Typical Tennessee Williams story about Sex in the Deep South, telling of a mentally arrested nineteen-year-old married to a man much her senior who has agreed not to consummate the marriage until her twentieth birthday, and of this man's burning down of his rival's cotton gin and the revenge this brings about. Sordid, static, powerful and well-made. Cast: *Carroll Baker, Eli Wallach* (both brilliant screen debuts), *Karl Malden, Mildred Dunnock, Lonny Chapman.* Dir. and Pro.: Elia Kazan. (Warner.) Rel.: February 24.

**Back from Eternity.** Exciting story of a plane-load of crash-landed passengers fighting the surrounding head-hunters and each other in the South American jungle. Cast: *Robert Ryan, Anita Ekberg, Rod Steiger, Phyllis Kirk, Keith Andes, Gene Barry, Fred Clark, Beulah Bondi, Cameron Prud'homme, Jesse White, Adele Mara, Jon Provost.* Dir. & Pro.: John Farrow. (R.K.O.) Rel.: Oct. 1.

**The Bad Seed.** Good Mervyn LeRoy film based on Maxwell Anderson's not-so-good play about an angel-faced little girl who has inherited a penchant for murdering people. Dubious premise, but gripping entertainment. Cast: *Nancy Kelly, Patty McCormack, Henry Jones, Eileen Heckart, Evelyn Varden, William Hopper, Paul Fix, Jesse White, Gage Clarke, Joan Croyden, Frank Cady.* Dir. & Pro.: Mervyn LeRoy. (W.B.) Rel.: Oct. 22.

**Bale Out at 43,000.** *John Payne* finding personal courage: an old story against a new background of experimentation with methods of crew ejection from sound barrier-breaking airplanes. Rest of cast: *Karen Steele, Paul Kelly, Richard Eyer, Constance Ford, Eddie Firestone, George Gay, Steve Ritch, Adam Kennedy, Richard Crane.* Dir.: Francis D. Lyon. Pro.: Wm. C. Thomas and Wm. B. Pine. (Pine-Thomas-U.A.) Rel.: April 22.

**Eric Portman, Mandy Miller and Phyllis Calvert in CHILD IN THE HOUSE—Golden Era.**

**Bandido.** *Robert Mitchum*, as adventurer out for a quick buck in the 1916 Mexican Revolution, mixed up with big-time arms-runner *Zachary Scott*, lovely *Ursula Theiss* and rebel leader *Gilbert Roland*. A roaring, bloody and thundery adventure tale. Rest of cast: *Rudolfo Acosta, Henry Brandon, Douglas Fowley, Jose I. Torvay, Victor Junco, Alfonso Sanchez Tello, Arturo Manrique, Jose A. Espinosa, Margarito Luna, Miguel Inclan, Jose Munoz, Manuel Sanchez Navarro, Antonio Sandoval, Alberto Pedret.* Dir.: Richard Fleischer. Pro.: Robt. L. Jacks. (U.A.) Rel.: Sept. 24. (C. & D.)

**The Barretts of Wimpole Street.** Polished, well acted re-make of the early 30's film based on the play (by Rudolf Besier) which in turn was based on the story of the sad romance between poet Robert Browning and invalid Elizabeth Barrett, who is ruled over by her despotic Victorian father. Cast: *Jennifer Jones, John Gielgud, Bill Travers, Virginia McKenna, Susan Stephen, Vernon Gray, Jean Anderson, Maxine Audley, Leslie Phillips, Laurence Naismith, Moultrie Kelsall, Michael Brill, Kenneth Fortescue, Nicholas Hawtrey, Richard Thorp, Keith Baxter, Brian Smith.* Dir.: Sidney Franklin. Pro.: Sam Zimbalist. (M.G.M.) Rel.: April 1. (C. & M.)

**Battle Hymn.** The true story of Colonel Dean Hess, World War II pilot who became a parson and then, conscience plagued by the memory of the German children he bombed, took to the cockpit again during the Korean War, when he finally found peace by adopting hundreds of little orphans and bringing them to safety. A professional mixture of war, religion and melodrama. Cast: *Rock Hudson* (as Hess), *Anna Kashfi, Dan Duryea, Don DeFore, Martha Hyer, Jock Mahoney, Alan Hale, James Edwards, Carl Benton Reid, Richard Loo, Philip Ahn, Bartlett Robinson, Simon Scott, Teru Shimada, Carleton Young, Jung'Kyoo Pyo.* Dir.: Douglas Sirk. Pro.: Ross Hunter. (U.I.). Rel.: February 25. (C. & T.).

**The Battle of the River Plate.** Long, wonderfully photographed, meticulously correct (from the Naval point of view) reconstruction of the famous British victory in the last war, and its rather shameful (from the German viewpoint) anti-climax, when having escaped the three British cruisers "Ajax", "Exeter" and "Achilles" by going into the neutral harbour of Montevideo the German pocket-battleship "Graf Spee" was scuttled. Cast: *John Gregson, Anthony Quayle, Peter Finch, Ian Hunter, Jack Gwillim, Bernard Lee, Lionel Murton, Anthony Bushell, Peter Illing, Michael Goodliffe, Patrick MacNee, John Chandos, Douglas Wilmer, William Squire, Roger Delgado, Andrew Cruickshank, Christopher Lee, Edward Atienza, April Olrich.* Dir. & Pro.: Michael Powell and Emeric Pressburger. (Rank). Rel.: Dec. 31. (T. & V.)

**Sheldon Lawrence, Karin Booth and Wayne Morris in the CROOKED SKY—Eros.**

**Behind the Headlines.** British murder melo, with boy and girl reporters catching the killer and each other at the same time. Cast: *Alfie Bass, Marianne Brauns, Paul Carpenter, Gaylord Cavallaro, Marian Collins, Sandra Colville, Adrienne Corri, Hazel Court, Harry Fowler, Tom Gill, Olive Gregg, Magda Miller, Trevor Reid, Arthur Rigby, Collin Rix.* Dir.: Chas. Saunders. Pro.: Guido Coen. (Kenilworth-Rank). Rel.: Aug. 6.

**Behind the High Wall.** Grim, forceful prison melodrama about a Warden who lets temptation get the better of him and has to pay the full price for his slip-up. Cast: *Tom Tully, Sylvia Sidney, Betty Lynn, John Gavin, John Larch, Barney Phillips, Ed Kemmer, Don Beddoe, Nicky Blair, John Beradino.* Dir.: Abner Biberman. Pro.: Stanley Rubin. (U.I.). Rel.: January 28.

**Bermuda Affair.** Story of two ex-Korean pilots, partners in an air-line, and their unfortunate choice of wives. Cast: *Gary Merrill, Kim Hunter, Ron Randell, Zena Marshall, Don Gibson, Robert Arden, Elspeth Hoffman, James McLaughlin, Wilbert Smith, Alfred Wagstaff, William Rewalt.* Dir.: Edward Sutherland. Pro.: Coolidge Adams. (Columbia.) Rel.: Nov. 19.

**The Best Things in Life Are Free.** Gay, musically enjoyable, entertaining musical based on the career and some of the private life of the song-writing team of De Sylva, Brown & Henderson, who wrote some of the biggest hit tunes of the 'twenties. Cast: *Gordon MacRae, Dan Dailey, Ernest Borgnine, Sheree North, Tommy Noonan, Murvyn Vye, Phyllis Avery, Larry Keating, Tony Galento, Norman Brooks, Jacques d'Amboise, Roxanne Arlen, Byron Palmer, Linda Brace, Patty Lou Hudson, Julie Van Zandt, Larry Kerr, Charles Victor, Eugene Borden, Harold Miller, Emily Belser, Paul Glass, Bill Foster.* Dir.: Michael Curtiz. Pro.: Henry Ephron. (Fox). Rel.: January 7. (C. & E.).

**Between Heaven and Hell.** Excellently made war film with a thin story but plenty of incident and a lot of excitement: about a young sergeant who comes under a neurotic officer. Cast: *Robert Wagner, Terry Moore, Broderick Crawford, Buddy Ebsen, Robert Keith, Brad Dexter, Mark Damon. Ken Clark, Harvey Lembeck, Skip Homeier, L. Q. Jones, Tod Andrews, Biff Elliot, Bart Burns, Frank Gerstle, Carl Switzer, Gregg Martell, Frank Gorshin Darlene Fields, Ilene Brown, Scotty Morrow, Pixie Parkhurst, Brad Morrow, Scat Man Crothers, Sam Edwards.* Dir.: Richard Fleischer. Pro.: David Weisbart. (Fox). Rel.: February 4. (E. & C.).

**Beyond a Reasonable Doubt.** Newspaper man *Dana Andrews*, trying to prove his point that the innocent sometimes get hanged, deliberately cooks up false evidence to prove himself a killer with the idea of bringing forward an alibi at the right moment. But things go wrong when his alibi crumples and there seems nothing between him and the noose. Rest of cast: *Joan Fontaine, Sidney Blackmer, Philip Bourneuf, Shepperd Strudwick, Arthur Franz, Edward Binns, Robin Raymond, Barbara Nichols, William Leicester, Dan Seymour, Rusty Lane, Joyce Taylor, Carleton Young, Trudy Wroe, Joe Kirk, Charles Evans, Wendell Niles.* Dir.: Fritz Lang. Pro.: Bert Friedlob. (R.K.O.) Rel.: Nov. 11.

**Beyond Mombassa.** Story of five people who, for different reasons, plunged into the African jungle. Cast: *Cornel Wilde, Donna Reed, Leo Genn, Ron Randell, Christopher Lee, Dan Jackson, Eddie Calvert, Bartholomew Sketch, Clive Morton, Macdonald Parke, Virginia Bedard, Julian Sherrier, Ed Johnson Purcell.* Dir.: Geo. Marshall. Pro.: Adrian Worker. (Columbia.) Rel.: Oct. 29. (T.)

**Bhowani Junction.** Long, large-scale film mixing a number of themes and several stories, all set against a background of the riots and uproars that broke out during the British withdrawal from India. *Stewart Granger* as competent British colonel loving half-caste *Ava Gardner*. Rest of cast: *Bill*

**Simone Simon and George Baker in THE EXTRA DAY—British Lion.**

*Travers, Abraham Sofaer, Francis Matthews, Marne Maitland, Peter Illing, Edward Chapman, Freda Jackson, Lionel Jeffries, Alan Tilvern.* Dir.: Geo. Cukor. Pro.: Pandro S. Berman. (M-G-M.) Rel.: Oct. 29. (C. & E.)

**The Big Tip-Off.** *Richard Conte* as ambitious newsman who is prepared to do business with the crooks in order to get scoops and ends up by nearly being scooped into jail himself. Rest of cast: *Constance Smith, Bruce Bennett, Cathy Downs, James Millican, Dick Benedict, Sam Flint, Mary Carroll, Murray Alper, Lela Bliss, G. Pat Collins, Frank Hanley, Harry Guardino, Virginia Carroll, Robert Garraher, Cecil Elliott.* Dir.: Frank McDonald. Pro.: Wm. F. Broidy. (A.A.-Assoc.) Rel.: July 30.

**Bigger Than Life.** *James Mason's* own intelligent, unusual, medically controversial and X-certificated production telling the story of a nice fellow, a schoolteacher, who becomes addicted to the drug Cortisone and through this changes into an obsessed maniac. Very strong, often terrifying and well acted (by Mason himself: *Barbara Rush*). Rest of cast: *Walter Matthau, Robert Simon, Christopher Olsen, Roland Winters, Rusty Lane, Rachel Stephens, Kipp Hamilton, Betty Caulfield, Virginia Carroll, Renny McEvoy, Bill Jones, Lee Aaker, Jerry Mather, Portland Mason, Natalie Masters, Richard Collier, Lewis Charles, William Schallert, John Monoghan, Gus Schilling, Alex Frazer, Mary Carver, Eugenia Paul, Gladys Richards, David Bedell, Ann Spencer, Nan Dolan, Mary McAdoo.* Dir.: Nicholas Ray. Pro.: James Mason. (Fox). Rel.: Oct. 29. (C. & D.)

**The Birds and the Bees.** Comedy with music, actually a remake of "Lady Eve", about the vegetarian son (screen newcomer *George Gobel*) of a multi-millionaire hot-dog king who finds romance with card-sharper *David Niven's* lovely daughter *Mitzi Gaynor*. Rest of cast: *Reginald Gardiner, Harry Bellaver, Fred Clark, Margery Maude, Hans Conried, Mary Treen, Peggy Moffatt, Rex Evans.* Dir.: Norman Taurog. Pro.: Paul Jones. (Paramount.) Rel.: July 9. (T. & V.)

**Birth of a Baby.** A remake, after seventeen years, with the same cast (which is a bit startling on occasions) of the medical film giving advice to parents-to-be. Sincere and useful. Cast: *Eleanor King, Richard Gordon, Ruth Matteson, William Post, Jun.* Pro.: Jack K. Skirball. (Eros). Rel.: Floating.

**The Black Whip.** First-rate Western set at the end of the American Civil War, about a gang of thuggish ex-soldiers who terrorise a district before being finally defeated by the bravery of one man. Cast: *Hugh Marlowe, Coleen Gray, Richard Gilden, Angie Dickinson, Strother Martin, Paul Richards, Charles Gray, William R. Hamel, Patrick O'Moore, Dorothy Schyuler, Sheb Wooley, John Pickard, Adele Mara, Harry Landers, Howard Culver, Rush Williams.* Dir.: Chas. M. Warren. Pro.: Robt. Stabler. (Regal-Fox). Rel.: February 25.

**Blackjack Ketchum, Desperado.** Ex-ace gunslinger, *Howard Duff*, trying to forget his lead-filled past, is persuaded to take up his guns again, this time to aid some outlaw-ruled ranchers. Rest of cast: *Victor Jory, Maggie Mahoney, Angela Stevens, David Orrick, William Tannen, Ken Christy, Martin Garralaga, Robert Roark, Don C. Harvey, Pat O'Malley, Jack Littlefield, Sydney Mason, Ralph Sanford, George Edward Mather, Charles Wagenheim, Wes Hudman.* Dir.: Earl Bellamy. Pro.: Sam Katzman. (Columbia.) Rel.: Nov. 5.

**Bobby Ware is Missing.** Story of a little boy who is found to be missing, and the subsequent demand for a $10,000 ransom received by his frantic parents. Cast: *Neville Brand, Arthur Franz, Jean Willes, Walter Reed, Paul Picerni, Kim Charney, Thorpe Whiteman, Peter Leeds.* Dir.: Thomas Carr. Pro.: Vincent M. Fennelly. (A.A.-Assoc.) Rel.: July 30.

**Border Showdown.** Real-life deputy sheriff *Clint Walker* (as Cheyenne) and buddy *L. Q. Jones* (as Smitty) tangle with a bunch of Mexican border bandits. Rest of cast: *Myron Healey, Richard Reeves, Adele Mara, Lisa Montell, Edward Colmans, Eugene, Inglesias, Frank Yaconelli, James Burke, Martin Garralaga, Lane Chandler, Julian Rivero, Salvador Baguez, Guy Teague,* Dir.: Richard L. Bare. Pro.: Harve Foster. (Warner.) Rel.: Aug. 13.

**The Boss.** The rise and fall of a Mid-Western American politician. His ruthless climb to power and his decision to stay at the top even though it means handing over his "machine" to the racketeers and thugs. Cast: *John Payne, William Bishop, Gloria McGhee, Doe Avedon, Roy Roberts, Rhys Williams, Gil Lamb, Robin Morse, Joe Flynn, Bill Phipp, Bob Morgan.* Dir.: Byron Haskin. Pro.: Frank N. Seltzer. (Seltzer-Window-U.A.) Rel.: Dec. 10.

**Boy on a Dolphin.** Slim, almost tenuous little story about the discovery on the Agean sea-bed of a gold statue, and the efforts of several groups of people to raise it for their own ends. Glorious performance by *Sophia Loren*. Lovingly and lingeringly photographed backgrounds of the exquisite isles of Greece. Rest of cast: *Alan Ladd, Clifton Webb, Alexis Minotis, Jorge Mistral, Laurence Naismith, Piero Giagnoni, Gertrude Flynn.* Dir.: Jean Negulesco. Pro.: Samuel G. Engel. (Fox.) Rel.: June 10. (C. & E.)

**Breakaway.** A lot of skullduggery with crooks pursuing a secret formula and hero *Brian Worth* and private eye *Tom Conway* determined in their separate ways to queer their pitch. Rest of cast: *Michael Balfour, Honor Blackman, Bruce Seton, Freddie Mills, Alexander Gauge, John Horsley, Paddy Webster, John Colicos, Larry Taylor, Arthur Lowe, Frederick Schrecker, Marianne Waller, Russell Westwood.* Dir.: Henry Cass. Pro.: R. S. Baker and Monty Berman. (R.K.O.) Rel.: July 16.

**Brink of Hell.** Discredited test-pilot *William Holden* working his way back into the confidence of his superiors the hard way after a Korean War black mark. Best when it's in the air, of course. Rest of cast: *Lloyd Nolan, Virginia Leith, Charles McGraw, Murray Hamilton, Paul Fix, James Garner, L. Q. Jones, Karen Steele, Bartlett Robinson, Malcolm Atterbury, Ralph Moody, Maura Murphy, Carol Kelly.* Dir. and Pro.: Mervyn Le Roy. (Warner). Rel.: January 6.

**The Broken Star.** Western. Crooked Marshal *Howard Duff* run to earth and suitably punished by erstwhile friend *Bill Williams*, who becomes Marshal in his stead and wins the lovely Latin singer *Lita Baron*. Rest of cast: *Douglas Fowley, Henry Calvin, Addison Richards, Joel Ashley, John Pickard, Wm. (Bill) Phillips, Dorothy Adams, Joe Dominguez*. Dir.: Lesley Selander. Pro.: Howard W. Koch. (U.A.) Rel.: Sept. 3.

**Brothers in Law.** Gently satirical comedy about the legal profession and the struggles of a young man "called to the bar" to make ends meet until he begins to get his briefs—and the awful mess he makes of his first few! Grand fun. Cast: *Richard Attenborough, Ian Carmichael, Terry-Thomas, Jill Adams, Miles Malleson, Raymond Huntley, Eric Barker, Olive Sloane, Nicholas Parsons, John Le Mesurier, Irene Handl, Basil Dignam, Henry Longhurst, Edith Sharpe, Kynaston Reeves, Michael Ward, Everly Gregg, Robert Griffiths, Ian Wilson, John Schlesinger, Margaret Lacey, John Boxer, John Warren, George Rose, Leslie Phillips, Norma Shebbeare, Peggy Ann Clifford, Stuart Saunders, Penny Morell, Maurice Colbourne, Wyndham Goldie, Rolf Le Feuvre, Ian Colin, Brian Oulton, Brian Fox, Ronald Cardew, John Van Eyssen, Bob Gregory, John Welsh, Llewellyn Rees, Bob Vosler, Jack McNaughton, Susan Marryott*. Dir.: Roy Boulting. Pro.: John Boulting. (Tudor-British Lion.) Rel.: April 1.

**Bullets from the Past.** A further episode in the Scotland Yard series: this time a new killing solves a shipboard murder case of twenty-seven years back. Cast: *Ballard Berkeley, Robert Sansom, Philippa Hyatt*. Introduced by Edgar Lustgarten. Dir.: Kenneth Hume. Pro.: Alec Snowden. (Anglo-Amalgamated.) Rel.: June 10.

**Bundle of Joy.** Real-life newlyweds—and themselves recently with a baby of their own—*Debbie Reynolds* and *Eddie Fisher* co-star in unsophisticated little comedy with music about a salesgirl, a baby and a sympathetic boss's son. Rest of cast: *Adolphe Menjou, Tommy Noonan, Nita Talbot, Una Merkel, Melville Cooper, Bill Goodwin, Howard McNear, Robert H. Harris, Mary Treen, Edward S. Brophy, Gil Stratton, Scott Douglas*. Dir.: Norman Taurog. Pro.: Edmund Grainger. (R.K.O.). Rel.: February 18. (T. & R.K.O.-Scope).

**The Burning Hills.** Western. Young *Tab Hunter* struggling against great odds to bring lawful retribution to big-boss cattleman *Skip Homeier* and the thugs responsible for killing his farming brother. Rest of cast: *Natalie Wood, Eduard Franz, Earl Holliman, Claude Akins, Ray Teal, Frank Puglia, Hal Baylor, Tyler MacDuff, Rayford Barnes, Tony Terry*. Dir.: Stuart Heisler. Pro.: Richard Whorf. (W.B.) Rel.: Nov. 11. (C. & W.)

**David Morrell, George Baker and Harry Andrews in A HILL IN KOREA—Wessex-British Lion.**

**Bus Stop.** *Marilyn Monroe* proving herself a first-rate, intelligent comedy actress in amusing story about a dizzy and pretty dumb Ozarkian blonde wooed, lost and won by a 21-year-old cowboy (*Don Murray*) who finds girls (of whom he has not previously met one!) can't be treated exactly like steers. Rest of cast: *Arthur O'Connell, Betty Field, Eileen Heckart, Robert Bray, Hope Lange, Hans Conried, Casey Adams, Henry Slate, Terry Kelman, Linda Brace, Greta Thyssen, Helen Mayon, Lucille Knox, Kate MacKenna, George Selk*. Dir.: Joshua Logan. Pro.: Buddy Adler. (Fox) Rel.: Nov. 19. (C. & E.)

**The Buster Keaton Story.** *Donald O'Connor* giving an extremely good performance in the title role of this biographical movie based on the life of the famous comic of the silent screen. Rest of cast: *Ann Blyth, Rhonda Fleming, Peter Lorre, Larry Keating, Richard Anderson, Dave Willock, Claire Carleton, Larry White, Jackie Coogan, Dan Seymour, Mike Ross, Nan Martin, Robert Christopher, Richard Aherne, Tim Ryan, Joe Forte*. Dir.: Sidney Sheldon. Pro.: R. Smith. (Paramount). Rel.: June 17.(V.).

## C

**Cartouche.** Cartouche (*Richard Basehart*) searching through 18th-century France for the killer of a Prince whose murder has been blamed on the former's old uncle. Rest of cast: *Patricia Roc, Massimo Serato, Akim Tamiroff, Isa Barzizza, Nerio Bernardi, Nino Marchetti, Aldo de Franchi, Vando Trees*. Dir.: Steve Sekely. Pro.: John Nasht. (R.K.O.) Rel.: Floating.

**The Case of the River Morgue.** Another in the long-short Scotland Yard series. Edgar Lustgarten discusses the baffling problem of the body stolen from the morgue, and later returned, but dressed in different clothes! Cast: *Jane Welsh, Gordon Needham, Hugh Moxey*. Dir: Montgomery Tully. Pro.: Alec Snowden. (Anglo.) Rel.: Oct. 29.

**Cell 2455, Death Row.** Fast-paced, fierce gangster film based on the true story of Caryl Chessman, who has spent his six years in a condemned cell by writing and telling the story of his life and so studiously reading law that he has held up his execution all that time! Cast: *William Campbell, Robert Campbell, Marian Carr, Kathryn Grant, Harvey Stephens, Vince Edwards, Allen Nourse, Diane De Laire, Bart Bradley, Paul Dubov, Tyler Mac Duff, Buck Kartalian, Eleanor Audley, Thom Carney, Joe Forte, Howard Wright, Glen Gordon, Jimmy Murphy, Jerry Mickelsen, Bruce Sharpe, Wayne Taylor*. Dir.: Fred F. Sears. Pro.: Wallace MacDonald. (Columbia.) Rel.: Dec. 3.

**Cha-Cha-Cha Boom!** Gay little musical with a strong accent on the Latin-American rhythm. Cast: *Perez Prado, Mary Kaye Trio, Helen Grayco, Luis Arcaraz, Manny Lopez, Steve Dunne, Alix Talton, Jose Gonzales Gonzales, Sylvia Lewis, Dante De Paulo, Charles Evans, Howard Wright*. Dir.: Fred F. Sears. Pro.: Sam Katzman. (Columbia). Rel.: February 11.

**Chain of Evidence.** *James Lydon*, ex-prison inmate with loss of memory due to a revenge beating-up by his former victim, is suspected of murder and only honest detective *Bill Elliott* stands between him and the electric chair. Rest of cast: *Claudia Barrett, Don Haggerty, Tina Carver, Ross Elliott, Hugh Sanders, Timothy Carey, Meg Randall, Don Kerr, Harlan Wade*. Dir.: Paul Landres. Pro.: Ben Schwalb. (A.A.-Assoc.). Rel.: May 27.

**Checkpoint.** British melodrama about an attempt to smuggle a murderer across the border, out of Italy, during the course of a big trans-continent road race. Cast: *Anthony Steel, Odile Versois, Stanley Baker, James Robertson Justice, Maurice Denham, Michael Medwin, Paul Muller, Lee Patterson, Anne Heywood, Anthony Oliver, Philip Gilbert, McDonald Hobley, Robert Rietty, Andrea Malandrinos, Dino Galvani, Jill Dixon, Harold Ayer*. Dir.: Ralph Thomas. Pro.: Betty Box. (Rank). Rel.: January 14. (E.).

**Brenda de Banzie, Gerard Oury, Anton Diffring and Michael Craig in HOUSE OF SECRETS—J. Arthur Rank.**

**Child in the House.** How the impact of *Mandy Miller*, charming little daughter of crooked *Stanley Baker*, on the maritally unhappy household of *Eric Portman* and *Phyllis Calvert* brings about mutual tolerance and understanding after the tantrumic climax. Rest of cast: *Dora Bryan, Joan Hickson, Victor Maddern, Percy Herbert, Joan Benham, Martin Miller, Christopher Toyne, Alfie Bass, Molly Urquhart, Bruce Beeby, Peter Burton*. Dir.: C. Baker Endfield. Pro.: Benjamin Franz. (Golden Era-Eros). Rel.: Sept. 24.

**Christine.** German romance-drama (dubbed into English), with comedy leanings. Cast: *Marianne Cook, Claus Holm, Camilla Spira, Kurt Meisel, Charles Regnier, Helen Vita, Richard Romanowsky, Ethel Reschke, Ernst V. Klipstein, Richard Munch, Josef Dahmen, Albert Florath, Margarete Haagen, Carl Voscherau, Friedrich Schutter, Otta Kuhlmann, Peter Frank, Willy Millowitsch, Horst Beck*. Dir. Gustav Veicky. Pro.: Gyula Trebitsch. (Rank). Rel.: January 14.

**Congo Crossing.** A group of people—a few honest, most of them unscrupulous crooks—struggle in a web of love, hate and greed in a small independent West African state. Cast: *Virginia Mayo, George Nader, Peter Lorre, Michael Pate, Rex Ingram, Tonio Selwart, Kathryn Givney*. Dir.: Joseph Pevney. Pro.: Howard Christie. (U.I.). Rel.: July 2. (T.).

**The Counterfeit Plan.** Escaping the guillotine in France, murderer *Zachary Scott* comes to Britain and with the help of engraver *Mervyn Johns* sets up a giant "fiver" forgery plan, which only goes wrong when he amorously attacks Mervyn's daughter, *Peggie Castle*. Rest of cast: *Sydney Tafler, Lee Patterson, Eric Pohlmann, Robert Arden, Chili Bouchier, John Welsh, Aubrey Dexter, David Lodge, Martin Wyldeck, Mark Bellamy, Arthur Lovegrove, Charles Mortimer, Bernard Fox, Basil Dignam*. Dir.: Montgomery Tully. Pro.: Alec C. Snowden. (Anglo.). Rel.: February 4.

**Crashing Las Vegas.** The Bowery Boys venture into the gambling city, to win and lose and have fun. Cast: *Leo Gorcey, Huntz Hall, Mary Castle, Don Haggerty, David Condon, Jimmy Murphy, Nicky Blair, Mort Mills, Doris Kemper, Jack Rice, Terry Frost*. Dir.: Jean Yarbrough. Pro.: Ben Schwalb. (A.A.-Assoc.). Rel.: February 11.

**Creature with the Atom Brain.** A nice problem for detective *Richard Denning* is how to defeat crook *Michael Granger* and scientist *Gregory Gay* who team up to bring the dead to terrible life by installing "atomic" brains in their craniums! Rest of cast: *Angela Stevens, S. John Launder, Linda Bennett, Tristram Coffin, Harry Lauter, Larry Blake, Charles Evans, Pierre Watkin, Lane R. Chandler, Nelson Leigh, Don C. Harvey, Paul Hoffman, Edward Coch, Karl Davis*. Dir.: Edward L. Cahn. (Clover-Columbia). Rel.: August 20.

**Crime of Passion.** Tragic little story of love, sacred and profane, against a background of the American Police Force. Cast: *Barbara Stanwyck, Sterling Hayden, Raymond Burr, Fay Wray, Virginia Grey, Royal Dano, Robert Griffin, Dennis Cross, Jay Adler, Stuart Whitman, Malcolm Atterbury, Robert Quarry, Gail Bonney, Joe Conley*. Dir.: Gerd Oswald. Pro.: Herman Cohen. (U.A.). Rel.: January 21.

**The Crooked Sky.** American detective *Wayne Morris*, sent to get Scotland Yard out of a little difficulty, solves problem of forged pound notes and the several murders bound up with them. Rest of cast: *Karin Booth, Anton Diffring, Bruce Seton, Sheldon Lawrence, Collette Barthrop, Seymour Green, Frank Hawkins, Murray Kash, Wally Peterson, Richard Shaw, Bill Brandon, Guy Kingsley Poynter*. Dir.: Henry Cass. Pro.: Derek Winn and Henry Cass. (Rank.) Rel.: April 22.

**Crowded Paradise.** The struggling romance of Puerto Rican *Mario Alcade* while trying to become a U.S. citizen in spite of jealous rival *Hume Cronyn's* plans for his early demise. Rest of cast: *Nancy Kelly, Frank Silvera, Enid Rudd, Stefan Schnabel*. Dir.: Fred Pressburger. Pro.: Ben Gradus. (Exclusive). Rel.: March 18.

**A Cry in the Night.** Story of a girl kidnapped by a deranged "Peeping Tom" and the way that the police and her fiance search for her. Cast: *Edmond O'Brien, Brian Donlevy, Natalie Wood, Raymond Burr, Richard Anderson, Irene Hervey, Carol Veazie, Mary Lawrence, Anthony Caruso, George J. Lewis, Peter Hanson, Tina Carver, Herb Vigran*. Dir.: Frank Tuttle. (Jaguar-W.B.). Rel.: October 22.

**The Curse of Frankenstein.** Gory, gruesome British-made spine chiller with poor old Baron Victor Frankenstein (*Peter Cushing*) trying to convince everyone that it's all because of the Thing in the attic. In colour, too. Rest of cast: *Christopher Lee, Hazel Court, Robert Urquhart, Valerie Gaunt, Noel Hood, Marjorie Hume, Melvyn Hayes, Sally Walsh, Paul Hardtmuth, Fred Johnson, Claude Kingston, Henry Caine, Michael Mulcaster, Patrick Troughton*. Dir.: Terence Fisher. Pro.: Anthony Hinds. (Hammer-Warner.) Rel.: May 20.

**The Cyclops.** Science-fiction thriller with *Gloria Talbot* searching for her fiance in remote Mexico and finding the unfortunate results of atomic radiation—a world of giant things. Rest of cast: *James Craig, Lon Chaney, Jun., Tom Drake, Dean Parkin, Vincent Padula, Marlene Kloss, Monuel Lopez*. Dir. and Pro.: Bert I. Gordon. (R.K.O.) Rel.: Floating.

## D

**D-Day The Sixth of June.** Beautifully told, finely acted (by *Dana Wynter, Robert Taylor, Richard Todd*) triangle story set against a background of the last war. Most moving, entirely credible and free from a single false note. The best filmed love story of the year! Rest of cast: *Edmond O'Brien, John Williams, Jerry Paris, Robert Gist, Richard Stapley, Ross Elliott, Alex Finlayson, Cyril Delevanti, Marie Brown, Rama Bai, Dabbs Greer, Geoffrey Steele, George Pelling, Conrad Feia, Boyd "Red" Morgan, Richard Aherne, Victoria Ward, Patricia McMahon, John Damler, Thomas B. Henry, Damien O'Flynn, Ben Wright, Queenie Leonard, Howard Price, Reggie Dvorak, Chet Marshall, Parley Baer, Ashley Cowan, June Mitchell, Grant Scott, Mickey Scott, Joe Garcia, Paul Glass*. Dir.: Henry Koster. Pro.: Chas. Brackett. (Fox). Rel.: Oct. 15 (C. & T.).

**Dance With Me Henry.** *Lou Costello*, adopter of strays and owner of " Kiddyland Fun Fair " is involved through one of his lame dogs, *Bud Abbott*, with the gangsters, the cops, and a murder rap! Rest of cast: *Gigi Perreau, Rusty Hamer, Mary Wickes, Ted De Corsia, Ron Hargrave, Sherry Alberoni, Frank Wilcox, Richard Reeves, Paul Sorenson, Robert Shayne.* Dir.: Charles Barton. Pro.: Bob Goldstein. (U.A.). Rel.: December 17.

**Date With Iris.** Travel documentary. Iris is no lady; it means Inspection of Radio Services and a job of work checking, maintaining, and where necessary improving, the thread of radio communication throughout the world. (Assoc.). Rel.: January 28.

**Davy Crockett and the River Pirates.** Broad, slapstick, extremely amusing sequel to Disney's first Crockett film: now Davy races the King of the Mississippi and cleans up the pirates in their lair. Cast: *Fess Parker, Buddy Ebsen, Jeff York, Kenneth Tobey, Irvin Ashkenazy, Paul Newlan, Troy Melton, Dick Crockett, Clem Bevans, Mort Mills, Frank Richards, Hank Worden, Walter Catlett.* Dir.: Norman Foster. Pro.: Bill Walsh. (Walt Disney.) Rel.: April 8. (T. and Widescreen.)

**The Day They Gave Babies Away.** Warm comedy-drama, from life, about an emigrant Scots couple who settle in early Winconsin and there raise a family of six. Cast: *Glynis Johns, Cameron Mitchell, Rex Thompson, Patty McCormack, Ernest Truex, Hope Emerson, Alan Hale, Sylvia Field, Royal Dano, Reta Shaw, Stephen Wootton, Butch Bernard, Yolanda White, Rita Johnson, Ellen Corby, Rosalyn Boulter, Francis DeSales, Jon Provost.* Dir.: Allen Reisner. Pro.: Sam Wiesenthal. (R.K.O.) Rel.: May 6. (T.)

**Death of a Scoundrel.** *George Sanders* at his considerable, sneering best as a ruthless and crooked financier who treads over anyone in order to reach his golden goal—but eventually brings about his own murder. Rest of cast: *Yvonne De Carlo, Zsa Zsa Gabor, Victor Jory, Nancy Gates, Coleen Gray, John Hoyt, Lisa Ferraday, Tom Conway, Celia Lovsky, Werner Klemperer, John Sutton.* Dir. and Pro.: Charles Martin. (R.K.O.). Rel.: Dec. 3.

**Designing Woman.** Polished, sophisticated, witty, consistently amusing and vintage comedy about the marriage of a sports writer—*Gregory Peck*—and a dress designer—*Lauren Bacall*—and their struggle to make their marriage stick—in spite of their odd friends and enemies. Rest of cast: *Dolores Gray, Sam Levene, Tom Helmore, Mickey Shaughnessy, Jesse White, Chuck Connors, Edward Platt, Alvy Moore, Carol Veazie, Jack Cole.* Dir.: Vincente Minnelli. Pro.: Dore Schary. (M-G-M.) Rel.: June 10. (C. & M.)

**The Desperado.** Routine, well-made Western about an outlaw who dares everything in order to save the life of the young man who had at one time saved his. Cast: *Wayne Morris, James Lydon, Beverly Garland, Rayford Barnes, Dabbs Greer, Lee Van Cleef, Nestor Paiva, Roy Barcroft, John Dierkes, Richard Shackleton, Stanford Jolley, Charles Garland, Florence Lake.* Dir.: Thomas Carr. Pro.: Vincent M. Fennelly. (Assoc.) Rel.: April 23.

**Desperados Are in Town.** *Robert Arthur* as a young Bad Man trying to forget his past and start again. Rest of cast: *Kathy Nolan, Rhys Williams, Rhodes Reason, Dave O'Brien, Kelly Thordsen, Mae Clark, Robert Osterloh.* Dir. and Pro.: Kurt Neumann. (Regal-Fox). Rel.: February 4.

**Destination Death.** Another in the Scotland Yard series of long-short (or short-long) movies: the discovery at London Airport of the body of a poisoned man leads Scotland Yard on the track of a vast international currency smuggling plot. Featuring *Edgar Lustgarten*. Cast: *Russell Napier, Paula Byrne, Melissa Stribling, Arthur Gomez.* Dir.: Montgomery Tully. Pro.: Alec Snowden. (Anglo). Rel.: November 19.

**Dig That Uranium.** The Bowery Boys in the latest racket—finding fun around, in and over a uranium mine. Cast: *Leo Gorcey, Huntz Hall, Mary Beth Hughes, Bernard Gorcey, Raymond Hatton, David Condon, Bennie Bartlett, Harry Lauter, Myron Healey, Richard Powers, Paul Fierro, Carl Switzer.* Dir.: Edward Bernds. Pro.: Ben Schwalb. (A.A.-Assoc.). Rel.: July 16.

**Doctor at Large.** Third of the "Doctor" films based on stories by Richard Gordon. British, broad and occasionally bawdy comedy which in laughs, wit and performances measures up wonderfully well to its record-breaking predecessors. Cast: *Dirk Bogarde, Muriel Pavlow, Donald Sinden, James Robertson Justice, Shirley Eaton, Derek Farr, Michael Medwin, Freda Bamford, Abe Barker, Martin Benson, Cyril Chamberlain, John Chandos, Edward Chapman, Peggy Ann Clifford, Campbell Cotts, George Coulouris, Junia Crawford, Judith Furse, Gladys Henson, Anne Heywood, Ernest Jay, Lionel Jeffries, Mervyn Johns, Geoffrey Keen, Dilys Laye, Harry Locke, Terence Longdon, A. E. Matthews, Guy Middleton, Barbara Murray, Nicholas Phipps, Donald Pickering, Frederick Piper, Wensley Pithey, Maureen Pryor, George Relph, Carol Richmond, Beth Rogan, Barbara Roscoe, Athene Seyler, Jean St. Clair, Ronnie Stevens, Ernest Thesiger, Michael Trubshawe, Molly Urquhart.* Dir.: Ralph Thomas. Pro.: Betty Box. (Rank.) Rel.: April 22. (V. & E.)

Errol Flynn, Cornell Borchers and Werner Klemperer in ISTANBUL—Universal International.

Marlene Dietrich, Vittorio de Sica, Arthur O'Connell, Natalie Trundy and Mischa Auer in THE MONTE CARLO STORY—United Artists.

**Don't Knock the Rock.** The famous *Bill Haley and His Comets*, plus singer *Arnie Haines* in a well-made celluloid apology for Rock-and-Roll. Rest of cast: *Alan Freed, The Treniers, Little Richard, Dave Appell and His Applejacks, Francine MacLaine*, etc. Dir.: Fred F. Sears. Pro.: Sam Katzman (Clover-Columbia). Rel.: February 4.

**Drango.** *Jeff Chandler* giving a fine performance in a thoughtful little drama about a Yankee military governor winning over the residents of a war-ravaged Southern town at the end of the Civil War. Rest of cast: *Joanne Dru, Julie London, Ronald Howard, Donald Crisp, John Lupton, Morris Ankrum, Helen Wallace, Walter Sande, Parley Baer, Amzie Strickland, Charles Horvath, Barney Phillips, David Stollery, Mimi Gibson, Paul Lukather, Damion O'Flynn, Edith Evanson, Phil Chambers, David Saber, Chuck Webster, Katherine Warren, Chubby Johnson, Milburn Stone, Anthony Jochim, Maura Murphy.* Dir.: Hall Bartlett and Jules Bricken. Pro.: Hall Bartlett. (U.A.) Rel.: May 27

**Dry Rot.** The film of the long-running, very successful stage farce about the switching of racehorses, set in a country inn infested with wood fungi! Cast: *Ronald Shiner, Brian Rix, Sidney James, John Chapman, Miles Malleson, Lee Patterson, Michael Shepley, Joan Haythorne, Joan Sims, Heather Sears, Christian Duvaleix.* Dir.: Maurice Elvey. (Remus-International-British Lion). Rel.: December 24.

**Duel at Apache Wells.** *Ben Cooper* comes back to his hometown in time to stop the ruthless *Jim Davis* from ruining his father and stealing his girl-friend. Rest of cast: *Anna Maria Alberghetti, Harry Shannon, Francis J. McDonald, Bob Steele, Frank Puglia, Argentina Brunetti, Ian Macdonald, John Dierkes, Ric Roman.* Dir. and Pro.: Joe Kane. (Republic-British Lion.) Rel.: April 1. (Naturama.)

# E

**The Eddy Duchin Story.** The rather sad biographical tale of famous American musician (portrayed by *Tyrone Power* and played—musically—by Carmen Cavallaro) who during his short life suffered many misfortunes while struggling to fame. Rest of cast: *Kim Novak, Victoria Shaw, James Whitmore, Rex Thompson, Mickey Maga, Shepperd Strudwick, Frieda Inescort, Gloria Holden, Larry Keating, John Mylong, Gregory Gay, Warren Hsieh, Jack Albertson, Carlyle Mitchell, Richard Sternberg, Andy Smith, Lois Kimbrell.* Dir.: Geo. Sidney. Pro.: Jerry Wald. (Columbia). Rel.: August 13. (T. & C.).

**Edge of Hell.** Triple-threat *Hugo Haas*' (he wrote, directed and produced) sentimental little tear jerker about an old man and his dog. Rest of cast: *Francesca De Scaffa, Kem Carlton, June Hammerstein, Jeffrey Stone, Syra Marti, Tracy Roberts, John Vosper, Tony Jochim, Julie Mitchum, Pat Goldin, Michael Mark, Tom Wilson, Sid Melton, William Kahn, Peter Bezbaz and Flip the Dog.* Dir. and Pro.: Hugo Haas. (U.I.). Rel.: Sept. 10.

**Ellie.** Early psychiatrist *Jack Kelly* rescuing girl-friend *Joy Page* from her possessive mother. Charming little 40-minute period piece (*circa* 1900). (W.B.) Rel.: March 25.

**Escape in the Sun.** Millionaire *Martin Bodday* hunting his wife (*Vera Fusek*) and her lover (*Alan Tarlton*) with Intent to Kill, in darkest Africa. Hero in the cast: *John Bentley*. Dir.: George Breakston. Pro.: George Breakston and John R. Carter. (Paramount). Rel.: January 21. (E.).

**Everything But the Truth.** Tiny *Tim Hovey*—Boy Mayor candidate—honestly refuses to retract his true statement that his uncle has dropped the real mayor a cool ten thousand dollars as a bribe! Rest of cast: *Maureen O'Hara, John Forsythe, Frank Faylen, Les Tremayne, Philip Bourneuf, Paul Birch, Barry Atwater, Addison Richards, Jeanette Nolan, Hugh Lawrence, Vernon Rich, Roxanne Arlen.* Dir.: Jerry Hopper. Pro.: Howard Christie. (U.I.). Rel.: February 4. (Col.).

**The Extra Day.** Pleasant little British movie telling a package story about a group of film extras; how their recall for one extra day's shooting on a movie affects their lives. Cast: *Richard Basehart, Simone Simon, George Baker, Josephine Griffin, Colin Gordon, Laurence Naismith, Charles Victor, Sidney James, Joan Hickson, David Hannaford, Olga Lindo, Philip Ray, Jill Bennett, John Humphrey, Dennis Lotis, Meier Tzelniker, Beryl Reid, Shani Wallis, Bryan Forbes, Eddie Byrne, Peter Coke, Tommy Clegg, Hugh Dempster, Gerald Harper, Frank Williams, Elizabeth Wright, Bessie Evans.* Dir.: William Fairchild. Pro.: E. M. Smedley Aston. (Fairchild-Lion). Rel.: July 2. (E.).

**Eye Witness.** Terrified hospital patient *Muriel Pavlow*, sole witness of a murder, knows that killer *Donald Sinden* is out to remove the only evidence against him. Rest of cast: *Ada Reeve, Charles Victor, Leslie Dwyer, Belinda Lee, David Knight, Michael Craig, Nigel Stock, Susan Beaumont.* Dir.: Muriel Box. Pro.: Sydney Box. (Rank). Rel.: August 13.

# F

**The Fastest Gun Alive.** Thoughtful, "psychological" Western, with *Glenn Ford* the ace but untried marksman who is finally faced with proving his skill against a coldly determined killer. Rest of cast: *Jeanne Crain, Broderick Crawford, Russ Tamblyn, Allyn Joslyn, Leif Erickson, John Dehner, Noah Beery, J. M. Kerrigan, Rhys Williams, Virginia Gregg, Chubby Johnson, John Doucette, William "Bill" Phillips, Chris Olsen, Paul Birch, Florenz Ames, Joseph Sweeney.* Dir.: Russell Rouse. Pro.: Clarence Greene. (M-G-M.) Rel.: Dec. 10. (M.)

**Fear Strikes Out.** The story of a baseball player who rose to the top to please his dad, failed to stand the pace, and after a breakdown came slowly back to a sane life. Cast: *Anthony Perkins, Karl Malden, Norma Moore, Adam Williams, Perry Wilson, Peter J. Votrian, Bart Burns.* Dir.: Robt. Mulligan. Pro.: A. Pakula. (Paramount.). Rel.: June 17. (V.).

**Find the Lady.** Neat, if slim British crime melo with model *Beverly Brooks* and doctor *Donald Houston* breaking up a gang of bank-robbers. Rest of cast: *Mervyn Johns, Kay Callard, Maurice Kaufman, Edwin Richfield, Moray Watson, Ferdy Mayne, John Drake, Anne Heywood, Edgar Driver, Nigel Green, Enid Lorimer.* Dir.: Charles Saunders. Pro.: John Temple-Smith. (Rank.) Rel.: Oct. 29.

**Finger Man.** *Frank Lovejoy* as a crook who is let off a life-sentence by agreeing to help convict a bigger-time gangster. Violent crime stuff. Rest of cast: *Forrest Tucker, Peggie Castle, Timothy Carey, John Cliff, William Leicester, Glen Gordon, John Close, Hugh Sanders, Evelynne Eaton, Charles Maxwell.* Dir.: Harold Schuster. Pro.: Lindsley Parsons. (A.A.-Assoc.) Rel.: Oct. 21.

**Firemaidens of Outer Space.** British space-fiction. Cast: *Anthony Dexter, Paul Carpenter, Sydney Taffler, Harry Fowler, etc.* Dir.: Cy Roth. (Eros). Rel.: Floating.

**The First Texan.** *Joel McCrea* as Sam Houston, who led the army which won independence for Texas and the title of first President for himself. Rest of cast: *Felicia Farr, Jeff Morrow, Wallace Ford, Abraham Sofaer, Rudolfo Hoyos, David Silva, Carl Benton Reid, William Hopper, Dayton Lummis, Nelson Leigh, Myron Healy, Jode McCrea, Scott Douglas, William Phipps.* Dir.: Byron Haskin. Pro.: Walter Mirisch. (A.A.-Assoc.) Rel.: July 9. (C. & T.)

**The First Travelling Saleslady.** *Ginger Rogers* goes way out West at the turn of the century determined to sell barbed wire to antipathetic

Texans. Rest of cast: *Barry Nelson, Carol Channing, David Brian, James Arness, Clint Eastwood, Robert Simon, Daniel M. White, John Eldredge, Jack Rice, Edward Cassidy, Frank Wilcox, Harry Cheshire, Robert Hinkle, Kate Drain Lawson, Fred Essler.* Dir. & Pro.: Arthur Lubin. (R.K.O.) Rel.: July 16. (T.)

**Five Steps to Danger.** International espionage thriller. Fishing-trip-bound *Sterling Hayden* meets fleeing *Ruth Roman* and together they crack a very Iron-Curtain plot to recover some new nuclear secrets hidden in a steel mirror. Rest of cast: *Werner Klemperer, Richard Gaines, Charles Davis, Jeanne Cooper, Peter Hansen, Karl Lindt, John Mitchum, John Merrick.* Dir. & Pro.: Henry S. Kesler. (U.A.) Rel.: Nov. 5.

**Flight to Hong Kong.** Tough, fast-moving gangster piece which starts with the forcing down of a diamond-carrying airplane and moves through Hong Kong, Tangier, Macao and Honolulu to a climax in San Francisco. Cast: *Rory Calhoun, Barbara Rush, Dolores Donlan, Soo Young, Pat Conway, Warner Klemperer, Mel Welles, Paul Picerni, Aram Katcher, Rhodes Reason.* Dir. & Pro.: J. M. Newman. (U.A.) Rel.: Nov. 26.

**Footsteps in the Night.** Whodunnit with *Bill Elliot* as the detective taking a big chance on gambling that the man accused of murder (*Douglas Dick*) is really innocent, and letting him free while at the same time setting a trap for the real killer. Rest of cast: *Eleanore Tanin, Don Haggerty, James Flavin, Harry Tyler, Robert Shayne, Gregg Palmer.* Dir.: Jean Yarbrough. Pro.: Ben Schwalb. (A.A.-Assoc.). Rel.: March 18.

**Forbidden Planet.** Adventures of expedition sent —in 2,200—to the star Altaire in an effort to find out what happened to expedition sent there 20 years previously! Cast: *Walter Pidgeon, Anne Francis, Leslie Nielsen, Warren Stevens, Jack Kelly, Richard Anderson, Earl Holliman, George Wallace, Bob Dix, Jimmy Thompson, James Drury, Harry Harvey, Jr., Roger McGee, Peter Miller, Morgan Jones, Richard Grant.* Dir.: Fred M. Wilcox. Pro.: Nicholas Nayfack. (M-G-M.) Rel.: July 16. (C. & E.)

**Foreign Intrigue.** *Robert Mitchum* doggedly trailing through Europe—and plenty of surprises—in an effort to discover just what his late employer was up to when he wrapped himself in mystery during the Hitlerian period. Rest of cast: *Genevieve Page, Ingrid Tulean, Frederick O'Brady, Eugene Deckers, Inga Tidblad, John Padovano, Frederick Schrecker, Lauritz Falk, Peter Copley, Ralph Brown, George Hubert, Jim Gerald, Nil Sperber.* Dir. & Pro.: Sheldon Reynolds. (U.A.) Rel.: July 21. (E)

**Fort Yuma.** Rousing Western, with gallant Apache *John Hudson* saving Fort Yuma from the attack of his tribesmen. Rest of cast: *Peter Graves, Joan Vohs, Joan Taylor, Abel Fernandez, James Lilburn, Bill Phillips, Stanley Clements, John Picard, Addison Richards.* Dir.: Lesley Selander. Pro.: H. W. Koch. (U.A.). Rel.: Floating. (T.).

**Fortune is a Woman.** Neat, pretty credible whodunnit, with fire assessor *Jack Hawkins* mixed up with ex-girl friend *Arlene Dahl* and, through her, fraud and murder in mysterious old manor. Rest of cast: *Dennis Price, Violet Farebrother, Ian Hunter, Malcolm Keen, Geoffrey Keen, Patrick Holt, John Robinson, Michael Goodliffe, Martin Lane, Bernard Miles, Christopher Lee, Greta Gynt, John Phillips, Patricia Marmont.* Dir.: Sidney Gilliat. Pro.: Gilliat and Launder. (Columbia.) Rel.: April 15.

**Four Girls in Town.** Several of U.I.'s most promising youngsters are given a chance in this slim little story about a quartet of girls who are after Hollywood film fame and fortune. Cast: *George Nader, Julie Adams, Marianne Cook, Elsa Martinelli, Gia Scala, Sydney Chaplin, Grant Williams, John Gavin, Ainslie Pryor.* Dir.: Jack Sher. Pro.: Aaron Rosenberg. (U.I.). Rel.: February 4. (T. & C.).

**Francis in the Haunted House.** The funny talking mule gets a new master, *Mickey Rooney*, for this spooky murder comedy-thriller. Rest of cast: *Virginia Welles, Paul Cavanagh, David Janssen, Mary Ellen Kay.* Dir.: Charles Lamont. Pro.: Robert Arthur. (U.I.) Rel.: Dec. 3.

**Friendly Persuasion.** Long, captivating film about the impact of the American Civil War on a rural, warmly human Indiana Quaker family. Charm unlimited. Cast: *Gary Cooper, Dorothy McGuire, Marjorie Main, Anthony Perkins, Richard Eyer, Phyllis Love, Robert Middleton, Mark Richman, Walter Catlett, Richard Hale, Joel Fluellen, Theodore Newton, John Smith, Mary Carr, Edna Skinner, Marjorie Durant, Frances Farewell, Samantha.* Dir. & Pro.: William Wyler. (M-G-M.) Rel.: Dec. 31. (M. & D.)

**Funny Face.** Gay little musical with lens expert *Fred Astaire*, deliberately luring "blue-stocking" *Audrey Hepburn* into becoming the Model of the Year and, unconsciously, into the land of love. Some remarkably fine colour photography, of daring, artistic originality. Rest of cast: *Kay Thompson, Michel Auclair, Robert Flemyng, Dovima.* Dir.: Stanley Donen. Pro.: Roger Edens. (Paramount.) Rel.: May 27. (T. & V.)

Aldo Ray in **NIGHTFALL**—Columbia.

Forrest Tucker and Barbara Britton in **NIGHT FREIGHT**—Allied Artists.

**The Fuzzy Pink Nightgown.** *Jane Russell* as a film star who becomes involved with two amateur kidnappers and changes them into amatory crooks. Neat, sometimes astringent comedy, with film backgrounds and a weakening thread of romance. Rest of cast: *Keenan Wynn, Ralph Meeker, Fred Clark, Adolphe Menjou, Una Merkel, Benay Venuta, Robert H. Harris, Milton Frome, John Truax.* Dir.: Norman Taurog. Pro.: Robt. Waterfield. (U.A.) Rel.: June 3.

## G

**Gaby.** Story of ballerina and boy (an American G.I.) in London in 1944—a kind of modernised (and far less successful) adaptation of yesteryear success "Waterloo Bridge". Cast: *Leslie Caron, John Kerr, Sir Cedric Hardwicke, Taina Elg, Margalo Gillmore, Scott Marlowe, Ian Wolfe, Joe di Reda, Joseph Corey, James Best, Lisa Montell, Ruta Lee, Narda Onyx, Gloria Wood.* Dir.: Curtis Bernhardt. Pro.: E. H. Knopf. (M-G-M.) Rel.: July 23. (C. & E.)

**Garden of Eden.** Naive story about the conversion of an old grumph, thanks to his contact with a nudist camp. Banned in some areas, given a U certificate by the L.C.C., refused any certificate at all by the censor, the film has as a background a famous American nudist camp and its nude inhabitants. Cast: *Mickey Knox, Jamie O'Hara, Karen Sue Trent, R. G. Armstrong, Jane Rose, Paula Morris, Stephen Gray, A. W. Johnson, N. E. Packwood, Jane Sterling.* (Excelsior). Rel.: Floating.

**Giant.** Long (3½-hour), sprawling and impressive film based on the Edna Ferber novel about Texas; several stories, diverse themes. Roughly it's a Family Saga with ironical comments on the oil-rich Texans, the racial (Mexican) question and various other side issues. Cast: *Elizabeth Taylor, Rock Hudson, James Dean, Jane Withers, Chill Wills, Mercedes McCambridge, Carroll Baker, Dennis Hopper, Judith Evelyn, Paul Fix, Rodney Taylor, Earl Holliman, Robert Nichols, Alexander Scourby, Sal Mineo, Fran Bennett, Charles Watts, Elsa Cardenas, Carolyn Craig, Monte Hale, Mary Ann Edwards, Sheb Wooley, Victor Millan, Mickey Simpson, Pilar del Rey, Maurice Jara, Noreen Nash, Napoleon Whiting, Ray Whitley, Tina Menard.* Dir.: George Stevens. Pro.: Stevens and Henry Ginsberg. (Warner). Rel.: March 25. (W.).

**The Girl Can't Help It.** Gay, witty and satirical comedy which has something amusing to say about Rock 'n' Roll, shapely blonde dolls (new star *Jayne Mansfield*, a lovely, really funny performance) and other things. First-rate entertainment. Rest of cast: *Tom Ewell, Edmond O'Brien, Julie London, Ray Anthony, Barry Gordon, Henry Jones, John Emery, Juanita Moore, The Platters.* Dir. and Pro.: Frank Tashlin. (Fox). Rel.: March 11 (C. & E.).

**The Girl in Black Stockings.** Whodunit which is novel in background—that of a small Western town —rather than that of story, which relates the way that the local sheriff trips up a triple murderer. Cast: *Lex Barker, Anne Bancroft, Mamie Van Doren, John Dehner, Ron Randell, Marie Windsor, Joan Holland, Diana Vandervlis, Richard Cutting, Larry Chance, Gene O'Donnell, Norman Leavitt, Gerald Frank, Stuart Whitman, David Dwight, Karl MacDonald, Dan Blocker.* Dir.: H. W. Koch. Pro.: Aubrey Schenck. (U.A.) Rel.: May 27.

**Godzilla, King of the Monsters.** It's a 400-foot high behemoth out of the prehistoric past who pops up to terrorise Tokyo Bay and defeat everything in the way of lethal weapons that the Japanese Army and Navy can throw at him! *Raymond Burr* and Japanese cast. Dir.: Terry Morse and Ishiro Honda. Pro.: Tomoyuki Tanaka. (U.A.). Rel.: Floating.

**The Good Companions.** Cheerful, gay British musical based on the Priestley story about a band of struggling players who meet a good deal of adversity before some of them meet West End success. Cast: *Eric Portman, Celia Johnson, Hugh Griffith, Janette Scott, John Fraser, Bobby Howes, Rachel Roberts, John Salew, Mona Washbourne, Paddy Stone, Irving Davies, Shirley Ann Field, Margaret Simons, Kim Parker, Beryl Kaye, Thora Hird, Beatrice Varley, Alec McCowen, Jimmy Caroll, Jeremy Burnham, Anna Turner, Fabia Drake, Brian Oulton, Lloyd Pearson, Ralph Truman, Joyce Grenfell, John Le Messurier, Agnes Bernelle, Lloyd Lamble, Nicholas Bruce, Leslie Carol, Larry Cross, Campbell Cotts, Shane Cordell, Tom Gill, Marianne Stone, Max Butterfield, Marjorie Rhodes, Richard Leech, Barbara Archer, George Rose, Ian Wilson, Melvyn Hayes, Claude Bonser, Olwen Brookes, Anthony Newley, Richard Thorp, George Woodbridge.* Dir.: J. Lee Thompson. Pro.: H. G. Inglis and J. Lee Thompson. (Assoc.) Rel.: April 22. (C. & T.)

**Goodbye My Lady.** Enchanting little film about a boy and a basenji—the dog which laughs and cries but never barks—and the lad's old uncle (*Walter Brennan*) and their free, simple life in the Mississippi swampland country. Rest of cast: *Phil Harris, Brandon de Wilde, Sidney Poitier, William Hopper, Louise Beavers.* Dir: Wm. A. Wellman. (Warner.) Rel.: June 3.

**The Great American Pastime.** Sad-faced comic *Tom Ewell* shoulders this slim little comedy about a lawyer who took over a baseball team and found that it didn't do him much good. Rest of cast: *Anne Francis, Dean Jones, Rudy Lee, Judson Pratt, Raymond Bailey, Wilfred Knapp, Bob Jellison, Todd Ferrell, Raymond Winston, Paul Angle, Ann Morriss, Gene O'Donnell.* Dir.: Herman Hoffman. Pro.: Henry Berman. (M-G-M.) Rel.: April 15.

**The Great Locomotive Chase.** Lively, exciting Walt Disney re-creation of an American Civil War incident, when Union spies (headed by *Fess Parker*) stole a Confederate ammunition train in the State of Georgia. Rest of cast: *Jeffrey Hunter, George Robotham, Stan Jones, Marc Hamilton, John Wiley, Slim Pickens, Morgan Woodward, W. S. Bearden, Harvey Hester, Douglas Bleckley, Jeff York, John Lupton, Eddie Firestone, Kenneth Tobey, Don Megowan, Claude Jarman, Jr., Harry Carey, Jr., Lennie Geer.* Dir.: Francis D. Lyon. Pro.: L. E. Watkin. (Disney). Rel.: November 26. (C. & T.).

**The Great Man.** Unusual, bitter, and quietly effective story of a radio reporter who, set to do an hour's obituary programme about a great and much loved personality, finds in his private life the idol had feet of basest, vilest clay. Cast: *Jose Ferrer, Dean Jagger, Keenan Wynn, Julie London, Joanne Gilbert, Ed Wynn, Jim Backus, Russ Morgan, Robert Foulk.* Dir.: Jose Ferrer. Pro.: Aaron Rosenberg. (U.I.). Rel.: March 25.

**The Green Man.** Extremely amusing comedy-thriller about expert assassin (wonderful *Alastair Sim*) who, out of practice, bungles an assignment—the blowing up of boring politician *Raymond Huntley*—and pays the price of his mistake. Rest of cast: *George Cole, Terry-Thomas, Jill Adams, Avril Angers, John Chandos, Dora Bryan, Vivienne Wood, Colin Gordon, Eileen Moore, Cyril Chamberlain, Doris Yorke, Arthur Brough, Maria Burke.* Dir. Robert Day. (Launder & Gilliat-British Lion). Rel.: Oct. 22.

**Gun Brothers.** Two brothers meet after a lapse of years to find they are now on different sides of the legal fence: one leads the hold-up gang, the other leads the law! Good Western. Cast: *Buster Crabbe, Ann Robinson, Neville Brand, Michael Ansara, Walter Sande, Lita Milan, James Seay, Roy Barcroft, Slim Pickens, Dorothy Ford.* Dir.: Sidney Salkow. (U.A.) Rel.: Dec. 24.

**Gun for a Coward.** Western. The story of two brothers, the younger of which, *Jeffrey Hunter*, is taken to be a coward because he likes to think before he acts. Rest of cast: *Fred MacMurray, Janice Rule, Chill Wills, Dean Stockwell, Josephine Hutchinson, John Larch, Paul Birch.* Dir.: Abner Biberman. Pro.: William Allard. (U.I.). Rel.: January 6. (C. & T.).

**The Gun Runner.** Cuban-helping hero *Alan Ladd* fighting the Spaniards, rival gun-runner *Lloyd Nolan* and his own bitterness for being unjustly cashiered from the American army; and falling in love with *Rossana Podesta.* Rest of cast: *Chill Wills, Paul Fix, L. Q. Jones, Frank de Kova, George J. Lewis, Royal Dano, Don Blackman, Francisco Ruiz, Clegg Hoyt, Ernest Sarracino.* Dir.: Gordon Douglas. Pro.: Martin Rackin. (Warner). Rel.: November 26.

**The Guns of Fort Petticoat.** Somewhat unusual Western, with *Audie Murphy,* suspected renegade, returning to his own country after the end of the Civil War and organising a local women's army to keep back the Redskins. Rest of cast: *Kathryn Grant, Hope Emerson, Jeff Donnell, Jeanette Nolan, Sean McClory, Ernestine Wade, Peggy Maley, Isobel Elsom, Patricia Livingston, Kim Charney, Ray Teal, Nestor Paiva, James Griffith, Charles Horvath, Ainslie Pryor, Madge Meredith.* Dir.: George Marshall. Pro.: Harry Joe Brown. (Columbia.) Rel.: May 13. (T.)

**Gunslinger.** *Anthony Ireland,* as a gunman hired by the local bad men (actually a woman), finds his job is to rub out the marshal's pretty widow with whom he's falling in love. Rest of cast: *Beverly Garland, Allison Hayes, Martin Kingsley, Jonathan Haze, Chris Alcaide, Richard Miller, Bruno Ve Sota, Margaret Campbell, William Schallert, Aaron Saxon, Chris Miller.* Dir. and Pro.: Roger Corman. (Anglo-Amalgamated). Rel.: March 10. (Col. and WideVision).

**Guys and Dolls.** Samuel Goldwyn's very large-scale, large-screen adaptation of the popular stage musical, with *Marlon Brando* the gambler who wins pretty little Salvation Army lass *Jean Simmons*—a wonderful, stand-out performance. Rest of cast: *Frank Sinatra, Vivian Blaine, Robert Keith, Stubby Kaye, B. S. Pully, Johnny Silver, Sheldon Leonard, Dan Dayton, George E. Stone, Regis Toomey, Kathryn Givney, Veda Ann Borg, Mary Alan Hokanson, Joe McTurk, Kay Kuter, Stapleton Kent, Renee Renor.* Dir.: Joseph L. Mankiewicz. Pro.: S. Goldwyn. (M-G-M.). Rel.: December 24. (C. & E.).

## H

**The Halliday Brand.** Bitter, adult Western about a bad, bad cattle baron (*Ward Bond*) who is also the local sheriff and abuses both positions so much that his son (*Joseph Cotten*) sets out ruthlessly to ruin him. Rest of cast: *Viveca Lindfors, Betsy Blair, Bill Williams, Jay C. Flippen, Christopher Dark, Jeanette Nolan.* Dir.: J. H. Lewis. Pro.: Collier Young. (U.A.). Rel.: March 25.

**He Laughed Last.** Popular singing star *Frankie Laine* in a musical which mixes gangsters, murder and melody. Rest of cast: *Lucy Marlow, Anthony Dexter, Alan Reed, Florenz Ames, Paul Dubov, Dick Long, Jesse White, Henry Slate, Peter Brocco.* Dir.: Blake Edwards. Pro.: Jonie Taps. (Columbia). Rel.: September 17. (T.).

**The Hefferan Family.** Warm and friendly little film—one of Fox's "pocket editions"—about a good man (*Paul Douglas*) and his wife (*Alexis Smith*) seen against a cosy small-town background. Dir.: Jules Bucken. (Fox). Rel.: January 6.

**Hidden Guns.** Brave Sheriff *Richard Arlen* and singing son *Faron Young* (debut) stand up to frontier villain *Bruce Bennett* and in the end, with the townspeople behind them, chalk up another win for justice. Rest of cast: *John Carradine, Lloyd Corrigan, Angie Dickinson, Damian O'Flynn, Irving Bacon, Tom Hubbard, Ron Kennedy, Bill Ward, Raymond L. Morgan, Edmund Cobb, Bill Weldon, Guinn "Big Boy" Williams, Gordon Terry, Charles Heard, Bill Coonty, Michael Darris.* Dir. and Pro.: Al Gannaway. (Republic-British Lion). Rel.: January 21.

**The Hide-out.** British crime melo. Insurance company investigator *Dermot Walsh* finding it is his own friend who leads the fur-smuggling gang he is paid to smash. Cast: *Rona Anderson, Ronald Howard, Sam Kydd, Howard Lang, Edwin Richfield, Arnold Diamond, Trevor Reid, Richard Shaw, Tommy Clegg, Jessica Cairns, Frank Hawkins, Jack Taylor, Angela Krefeld.* Dir.: Peter Graham Scott. Pro.: John Temple-Smith (Major-Rank). Rel.: December 31.

**High Society.** Elaborate, shiny re-make (with music) of "The Philadelphia Story": about a Society girl who finds that perfect husbands are very rare indeed! Cast: *Bing Crosby, Grace Kelly, Frank Sinatra, Celeste Holm, John Lund, Louis Calhern, Sidney Blackmer, Louis Armstrong, Margalo Gillmore, Lydia Reed, Gordon Richards, Richard Garrick.* Dir.: Chas. Walters. Pro.: Sol Siegel. (M-G-M). Rel.: Feb. 4. (T. & V.).

Lloyd Nolan and Alan Ladd in THE GUN RUNNER—Warner Bros

**The High Terrace.** Modest, entertaining back-stage British whodunnit with star, playwright and theatre manager among the suspects after an unpopular producer has been found murdered. Cast: *Dale Robertson, Lois Maxwell, Derek Bond, Eric Pohlmann, Mary Laura Wood, Lionel Jeffries, Jameson Clark, Carl Bernard, Garard Green, Olwen Brookes, Benita Lydal, Marianne Stone, Frederick Treves, Jonathan Field, Gretchen Franklin, Alan Robinson, Jack Cunningham.* Dir.: Henry Cass. Pro.: R. S. Baker. (Cipa-R.K.O.). Rel.: Oct. 1.

**High Tide at Noon.** Pleasing, simple, unusual film about love and lobster fishing on an island off the Nova Scotian mainland. A mostly young, very promising cast: *Betta St. John, William Sylvester, Michael Craig, Flora Robson, Alexander Knox, Peter Arne, Patrick McGoohan, Patrick Allen, Jill Dixon, Susan Beaumont, John Hayward, Errol MacKinnon, Stuart Nichol, George Murcell, Anthony Bate, Stella Bonheur, Bernard Bresslaw, Victor Chenet, Franklin Fox, John Stevenson Lang, Gerald Lawson, Arthur Massey, Bill Nagy, Charles Richardson, Evan Roberts, Ryck Rydon, Richard Shaw, Nicholas Stuart, Garry Thorne.* Dir.: Philip Leacock. Pro.: Julian Wintle. (Rank.) Rel.: April 22.

**A Hill in Korea.** Factual, documentary-like film about a group of untried young soldiers suddenly faced with desperate fighting in Korea. Cast: *George Baker, Harry Andrews, Stanley Baker, Michael Medwin, Ronald Lewis, Stephen Boyd, Victor Maddern, Harry Landis, Robert Brown, Barry Lowe, Robert Shaw, Charles Laurence, Percy Herbert, Eric Corrie, David Morrell, Michael Caine.* Dir.: Julian Amyes. Pro.: Anthony Squire. (British Lion). Rel.: October 22.

**Hit and Run.** Another of *Hugo Haas's* one-man efforts; built around the tragic consequences of the marriage of an old man to a young girl. Rest of cast: *Cleo Moore, Vince Edwards, Julie Mitchum, Dolores Reed.* Dir. and Pro.: Hugo Haas. (Haas-United Artists) Rel.: February 11.

**Hold Back the Night.** About the big Korean retreat and the bottle of whisky which became a symbol to a decimated American company of marines. Cast: *John Payne, Mona Freeman, Peter Graves, Chuck Connors, Audrey Dalton, Bob Nichols, John Wilder, Bob Easton, Stanley Cha, Nicky Blair, John Craven, Nelson Leigh.* Dir.: Allan Dwan. Pro.: Hayes Goetz. (Assoc.) Rel.: April 1.

**Hollywood or Bust.** *Dean Martin* and *Jerry Lewis,* joint owners of a new car, set out for fame and fortune in Hollywood. Rest of cast: *Anita Ekberg, Pat Crowley, Maxie Rosenbloom, Willard Waterman, Jack McElroy, Mike Ross, Wendell Niles, Frank Wilcox, Kathryn Card, Richard Karlan, Tracey Roberts, Ben Welden, Ross Westlake, Sandra White, Gretchen Houser, Adele August.* Dir.: Frank Tashlin. Pro.: Hal Wallis. (Paramount.) Rel:. December 24. (V. & T.)

Kieron Moore, Jimmy Hanley and Donald Wolfit in SATELLITE IN THE SKY—Warner.

**Home and Away.** The unfortunate results when one member of a typical British family finds they have won a fortune on the pools! Cast: *Jack Warner, Kathleen Harrison, Lana Morris, Charles Victor, Thora Hird, Valerie White, Harry Fowler, Merrie Carroll, Bernard Fox, Margaret St. Barbe West, Ross Pendleton, Leslie Henson, Sam Kydd.* Dir.: Vernon Sewell. Pro.: George Maynard. (Eros). Rel.: October 15.

**Hot Cars.** Out-of-work *John Bromfield* becomes involved in American stolen car racket and ends up, when he tries to get out of it, by being framed for murder. Rest of cast: *Joi Lansing, Mark Dana, Carol Shannon, Ralph Clanton, Robert Osterloh, Dabbs Greer, Charles Keane, Kurt Katch, George Sawaya, John Merrick, Jean Sinclair, Maurice Marks, Marilee Earle, Vic Cutrier, Paula Hill.* Dir.: Donald McDougall. Pro.: Howard W. Koch. (Bel-Air-U.A.). Rel.: August 20.

**Hot Summer Night.** Tense, convincing and well observed thriller about young reporter's adventures with a gang of killers when he tries to gain an exclusive interview with the Boss. Background is a small Ozarkian town sweltering in midsummer heat. Cast: *Leslie Nielsen, Colleen Miller, Edward Andrews, Jay C. Flippen, James Best, Paul Richards, Robert Wilke, Claude Akins, Marianne Stewart.* Dir.: David Friedkin. Pro.: Morton Fine. (M-G-M.) Rel.: May 13.

**Hour of Decision.** British crime reporter finds, while helping the police solve the problem of the murdered gossip columnist, that his own wife is suspected of the crime, and he alone may be able to save her. Cast: *Jeff Morrow, Hazel Court, Anthony Dawson.* Dir.: Monty Berman. Rel.: May 17.

**House of Secrets.** Well-made, actionful thriller with newcomer *Michael Craig* as a young seaman mistaken for an international crook and because of this launched by the police into some very tough adventures while trying to counter a counterfeiting gang. Rest of cast: *Julia Arnall, Brenda de Banzie, Barbara Bates, David Kossoff, Gerard Oury, Geoffrey Keen, Anton Diffring, Eric Pohlmann, Eugene Deckers, Jacques Brunius, Alan Tilvern, Carl Jaffe, Gordon Tanner, David Lander, Balbina, Violet Gould, John Serrett, Jean Driant, Patrick Westwood, Yves Chanteau.* Dir.: Guy Green. Pro.: Vivian A. Cox. (Rank). Rel.: November 19. (V. & T.).

**Huk.** Philippine war story (1951) about some rebels who try to destroy American installations on the islands. Cast: *George Montgomery, Mona Freeman, John Baer, James Bell, Teddy Benavedes, Ramio Barri, Ben Perez.* Dir.: John Barnwell. Pro.: Collier Young. (U.A.). Rel.: July 9. (E.).

**The Hunchback of Notre Dame.** Free adaptation of the Victor Hugo story about the gipsy girl, the hunchback bell-ringer and the man whose passion led them all to tragedy. Beautifully photographed, but script-ually thin. Cast: *Gina Lollobrigida, Anthony Quinn, Jean Danet, Alain Cuny, Robert Hirsch, Danielle Dumont, Philippe Clay, Maurice Sarfati, Jean Tissier, Valentine Tessier, Jacques Hilling, Jacques Dufilho, Roger Blin, Marianne Oswald, Roland Bailly, Pieral, Camille Guerini, Damia, Robert Lombard, Albert Remy, Hubert Lapparent, Boris Vian, Georges Douking, Paul Bonifas, Madeleine Barbulee, Albert Michel, Daniel Emilfork.* Dir.: Jean Delannoy. Pro.: R. Hakin. (Rank.) Rel.: April 1. (C. & T.)

## I

**I'll Cry Tomorrow.** *Susan Hayward* giving one of her very best performances in a screen adaptation of the real-life story of ex-film star Lillian Roth, who took to the booze and let it drag her through hell before she finally beat it with the help of A.A. Rest of cast: *Richard Conte, Eddie Albert, Jo Van Fleet, Don Taylor, Ray Danton, Margo, Virginia Gregg, Don Barry, David Kasday, Carole Ann Campbell, Peter Leeds, Tol Avery.* Dir.: Daniel Mann. Pro.: Lawrence Weingarten. (M-G-M). Rel.: October 8. (M.).

**Ill Met By Moonlight.** An incredible (but apparently true) story of the war, based on the book of the same title. The way that a couple of British officers, with the help of some Cretan partisans, kidnap a German General in the island and whisk him off to Cairo. An exciting, well told tale shown against breathtakingly beautiful backgrounds. Cast: *Dirk Bogarde, Marius Goring, David Oxley, Cyril Cusack, Laurence Payne, Wolfe Morris, Michael Gough, Rowland Bartrop, Brian Worth, Paul Stassino, Adeeb Assaly, John Cairney, George Egeniou, Demitri Andreas, Theo Moreas, Takis Frangofinos.* Dir. and Pro.: Powell and Pressburger. (Archer-Rank.) Rel.: March 4. (V.)

**The Incredible Shrinking Man.** About the odd case of a man stricken with a strange complaint which gradually reduces him to nothing! Fascinating fantasy. Cast: *Grant Williams, Randy Stuart, April Kent, Paul Langton, Raymond Bailey, William Schallert, Frank Scannell, Helene Marshall, Diana Darrin, Bill Marshall.* Dir.: Jack Arnold. Pro.: Albert Zugsmith. (U.I.) Rel.: June 24.

**Indestructible Man.** Revived murderer becomes almost indestructible monster—real horror stuff! Cast: *Lon Chaney, Marian Carr, Casey Adams, Ross Elliott.* Dir. and Pro.: Jack Polloxfen. (A.A.-Assoc.). Rel.: October 8.

**Interpol.** International drug smuggling melo, with *Victor Mature* as the brawny but awfully unsubtle cop after cool villain *Trevor Howard* and lovely but rather dumb aide *Anita Ekberg*. Rest of cast: *Bonar Colleano, Andre Morell, Martin Benson, Dorothy Alison, Peter Illing, Eric Pohlmann, Sidney Tafler, Alec Mango, Lionel Murton, Danny Green, Yana, Sidney James, Marne Maitland, Harold Kasket, Van Boolen, Brian Nissen, Peter Elliott, Charles Lloyd Pack, Al Mulock, Alfred Burke, Maurice Browning, Cyril Shaps, Paul Strassino, Gaylord Cavallaro.* Dir.: John Gilling. Pro.: Phil Samuel. (Warwick-Columbia.) Rel.: May 6. (C.)

**Introduction to Erica.** Sentimental, simple but rather charming little story of German immigrant *Maria Palmer* who finds romance with crusty doctor *Victor Jory* when chicken-pox brings her to the little Kansas town of Kings Row. Rest of cast: *Jack Kelly, John Anderson, Nadine Ashdown, Isa Ashdown, Tony Hughes, Nesdon Booth.* Dir.: Paul Stewart. Pro.: Roy Huggins. (Warner). Rel.: September 24.

**Invasion of the Body Snatchers.** Walter Wanger chiller-thriller about plant spores from outer space taking possession of both bodies and personalities of the inhabitants of our earth. Cast: *Kevin McCarthy, Dana Wynter, Larry Gates, King Donovan, Carolyn Jones, Jean Willes, Ralph Dumke, Virginia Christine, Tom Fadden, Kenneth Patterson, Whit Bissell.* Dir.: Don Siegel. Pro.: Walter Wanger. (A.A.-Assoc.). Rel.: October 8.

**Invitation to the Dance.** Wonderful Gene Kelly-directed three-part picture telling three diverse stories in dance and mime, without one word of dialogue. **A**: The Clown, danced movingly by *Gene Kelly* and telling the old sad story. **B**: Ring Around Rosy, a kind of cautionary tale along modern "La Ronde" lines about a gift bracelet which makes the rounds. **C**: The Magic Lamp, an Arabian Nights fairy story brilliantly mixing real and cartoon figures against a drawn-in background. In sum total a novel, intelligent and technically outstanding picture with wonderful dancing, fine colour and a great deal of real art. Casts: **A**: *Igor Youskevitch, Claire Sombert, Gene Kelly.* **B**: *Gene Kelly, Igor Youskevitch, Tommy Rall, David Paltenghi, Claude Bessy, Tamara Toumanova, Diana Adams, Belita, Daphne Dale, Irving Davies.* **C**: *Carol Haney, David Kasday, Gene Kelly.* Dir.: Gene Kelly. Pro.: Arthur Freed. (Cartoon sequences by Fred Quimby). (M-G-M). Rel.: Floating. (T. & M.).

**The Iron Petticoat.** Often very funny British comedy, modelled vaguely along "Ninotchka" lines. *Katharine Hepburn* as Russian air ace who in a fit of feminine pique flies her jet across the iron curtain and becomes involved with American escort *Bob Hope*. Rest of cast: *James Robertson Justice, Robert Helpmann, David Kossoff, Alan Gifford, Paul Carpenter, Noelle Middleton, Nicholas Phipps, Sidney James, Alexander Gauge, Doris Goddard, Tutte Lemkow, Sandra Dorne, Richard Wattis, Maria Antippas, Martin Boddey.* Dir.: Ralph Thomas. Pro.: Betty Box. (Romulus-Remus-Ind.-Lion). Rel.: September 17. (T. & V.).

**Istanbul.** *Errol Flynn* struggling against about half the crooked citizens of that city to hang on to some hidden diamonds they all appear to want. Rest of cast: *Cornell Borchers, John Bentley, Torin Thatcher, Leif Erickson, Peggy Knudsen, Martin Benson, Werner Klemperer, Nat "King" Cole.* Dir.: Joseph Pevney. Pro.: Albert Cohen. (U.I.). Rel.: December 3. (T.).

**It's A Wonderful World.** Cheery, entertainment-packed British comedy with music, highlighted by *George Cole's* performance as an astute song-writer who discovers that he can sell old tunes recorded backwards as the music of tomorrow, and *James Hayter's* delicious comedy work as an actual music publisher. Rest of cast: *Terence Morgan, Kathleen Harrison, Ted Heath and His Music, Mylene Nicole, Harold Lang, Richard Wattis, Reginald Beckwith, Dennis Lotis, Maurice Kaufman, Charles Clay, Derek Blomfield, Jock McKay, Douglas Blackwell, Keith Sawbridge, Angela Braemar, Stan Thomason, Charles Brodie, Brian Sunners, Hal Osmond, Sam Kydd, George Moon, Leslie Weston, Patricia Ryan, Avril Sadler, Jeanette Pearce, Howard Williams, Maya Koumani, Shirley Ann Field, Colin Croft, Roger Snowdon, Douglas Bradley-Smith, Bernard Rebel, Walter Crisham, Francesco Russo, Lellah Sabarathy.* Dir.: Val Guest. Pro.: Denis O'Dell. (Geo. Minter-Renown). Rel.: October 8. (T. & SpectaScope).

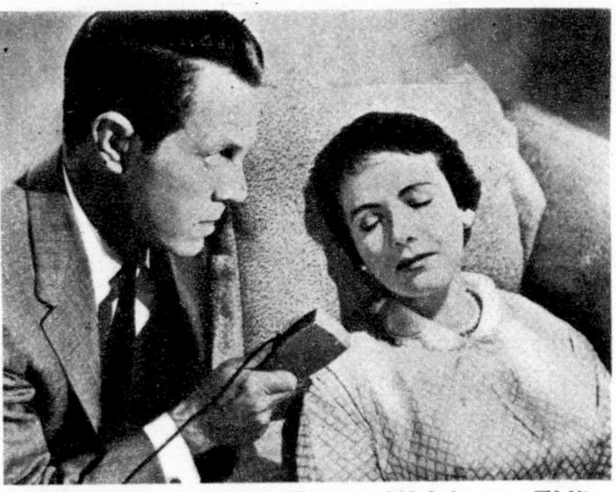

**Louis Hayward and Teresa Wright in THE SEARCH FOR BRIDEY MURPHY—Paramount.**

**It's Great To Be Young.** Lively musical about a school orchestra (organised by youthful, eccentric housemaster *John Mills*) and the battle they have before they win over new headmaster *Cecil Parker*. Rest of cast: *John Salew, Elizabeth Kentish, Mona Washbourne, Mary Merrall, Derek Blomfield, Jeremy Spenser, Dorothy Bromiley, Brian Smith, Wilfred Downing, Robert Dickens, Dawson France, Carole Shelley, Marjorie Rhodes, Eddie Byrne, Russell Waters, Richard O'Sullivan, Norman Pierce, Eleanor Summerfield, Bryan Forbes.* Dir.: Cyril Frankel. Pro.: Victor Skutezky. (Marble Arch-Assoc.) Rel.: August 6.

**I've Lived Before.** *Jock Mahoney* convincing fiancee *Leigh Snowden* and Dr. *John McIntyre* that he has in fact lived before. Also *Ann Harding*. Dir.: Richard Bartlett. Pro.: Howard Christie. (U.I.) Rel.: November 19.

## J

**Jacqueline.** Winning little comedy-drama—with Belfast backgrounds—about a drunken shipyard worker who yearns to go back to the farm. Delightfully played by *John Gregson, Kathleen Ryan* and little *Jacqueline*. Rest of cast: *Noel Purcell, Cyril Cusack, Liam Redmond, Maureen Swanson, Tony Wright.* Dir.: Roy Baker. Pro.: George Brown. (Rank). Rel.: July 23.

**The James Brothers.** Super-Western about the notorious outlaw brothers who made history—of a violent kind—in the Old West just after the end of the Civil War. Cast: *Robert Wagner, Jeffrey Hunter, Hope Lange, Agnes Moorehead, Alan Hale, Alan Baxter, John Carradine, Rachel Stephens, Barney Phillips, Biff Elliot, Barry Atwater, Chubby Johnson, Frank Gorshin, John Doucette, Robert Adler, Clancy Cooper, Sumner Williams, Tom Greenway, Mike Steen, Aaron Saxon, Marian Seldes, Anthony Ray, Clegg Hoyt, Tom Pittman, Louis Zito, Carl Thayler, Mark Hickman, Adam Marshall, Frank Overton, Joseph Di Reda, J. Frederick Albeck, Kellogg Junge, Jr.* Dir.: Nicholas Ray. Pro.: Herbert B. Swope, Jun. (Fox.) Rel.: May 20. (C. & E.)

**Jedda.** Australian romantic melo about the problem of a native girl brought up by whites and then tempted by the underlying wildness of her nature when she grows up. Cast: *Ngaria Kinoth, Robert Tudwali.* Dir.: Charles Chavvel. (Independent-Australian). Rel.: August 13. (G.).

**Joe Butterfly.** Fun and frolics among the Army newspaper men in post-war Japan. Cast: *Audie Murphy, George Nader, Keenan Wynn, Keiko Shima, Fred Clark, John Agar, Charles McGraw, Shinpei Shimazaki, Reiko Higa, Tatsuo Saito, Chizu Shimazaki, Herbert Anderson, Eddie Firestone, Frank Chase, Harold Goodwin, William Willingham, Burgess Meredith.* Dir.: Jesse Hibbs. Pro.: Aaron Rosenberg. (U.I.). Rel.: June 10. (C. and T.).

**Marjorie Rambeau, Dana Wynter and Richard Egan in SECRET INTERLUDE—20th Century-Fox.**

**Julie.** Poor *Doris Day*, married to a man who killed her first husband in order to get her and who is determined to kill her when he finds out that she knows it! So Julie runs. . . Rest of cast: *Louis Jourdan, Barry Sullivan, Frank Lovejoy, John Gallaudet, Harlan Warde, Jack Kruschen, Hank Patterson, Aline Towne, Ann Robinson, Ed Hinton, Jack Kelly, Barney Phillips, Carleton Young, Pamela Duncan, Mae Marsh, Edward Marsh.* Dir.: Andrew L. Stone. Pro.: Martin Melcher. (M-G-M.) Rel.: April 15.

## K

**Kelly and Me.** The story of a man—vaudevillian *Van Johnson*—a dog—wonder Alsatian *Kelly*—and a girl—film producer's daughter *Piper Laurie*—and the way that the first teams up with the second, develops a swollen head, is duly deflated before teaming up with the third (and second, again) for a happy ending. Rest of cast: *Martha Hyer, Onslow Stevens, Herb Anderson, Frank Wilcox, Gregory Gay, Maurice Manson.* Dir.: R. Z. Leonard. Pro.: Robert Arthur. (U.I.) Rel.: January 6. (T. & C.)

**The Killing.** Laconic tense and effective little crime melo about plot, to steal two million dollars from a race-track—and the way the whole thing comes unstuck. Cast: *Sterling Hayden, Coleen Gray, Vince Edwards, Jay C. Flippen, Marie Windsor, Ted DeCorsia, Elisha Cook, Joe Sawyer, Tim Carey, Jay Adler, Joseph Turkell, Maurice Oboukhoff.* Dir.: Stanley Kubrick. Pro.: James B. Harris. (U.A.). Rel.: July 21.

**The King and Four Queens.** Amusing Western. Crooked but so charming adventurer *Clark Gable* on a run-down ranch near Touchstone with a grim old "Ma," four lovely young women, (one of whom can match him in guile) and a large pot of buried gold. Rest of cast: *Eleanor Parker, Jo Van Fleet, Jean Willes, Barbara Nichols, Sara Shane, Roy Roberts, Arthur Shields, Jay C. Flippen.* Dir.: Raoul Walsh. Pro.: David Hempstead. (U.A.) Rel.: February 11. (C. & D.)

**The King and I.** Very wide, high and handsome screen adaptation of the great Rodgers and Hammerstein stage musical success, with *Yul Brynner* a most impressive King of Siam and *Deborah Kerr* at her very best as the British governess who comes to admire and even love him in the end. Rest of cast: *Rita Moreno, Martin Benson, Terry Saunders, Rex Thompson, Carlos Rivas, Patrick Adiarte, Alan Mowbray, Geoffrey Toone, Yuriko, Marion Jim, Robert Banas, Dusty Worrall, Gemze de Lappe, Thomas Bonilla, Dennis Bonilla, Michiko Iseri, Charles Irwin, Leonard Strong.* Dir.: Walter Lang. Pro.: Charles Brackett. (Fox) Rel.: October 8. (C. & E.).

**Kismet.** Lavish screen adaptation of the stage show—set in old Baghdad and using Borodin's themes for the music. Cast: *Howard Keel, Ann Blyth, Dolores Gray, Vic Damone, Monty Woolley, Sebastian Cabot, Jay C. Flippen, Mike Mazurki, Jack Elam, Ted de Corsia, Patricia Dunn, Reiko Sato, Wonci Lui, Julie Robinson.* Dir.: Vincente Minnelli. Pro.: Arthur Freed. (M-G-M.) Rel.: March 18. (C. & E.)

## L

**Land of the Pharaohs.** Ancient Egypaint history. *Jack Hawkins* as the Pharaoh building a pyramid; *Joan Collins* as the ruthless neighbourhood Princess who covets his treasure; thousands of toiling extras being whipped into work in a way the T.U. would certainly not like! Rest of cast: *James Robertson Justice, Sidney Chaplin, James Hayter, Dewey Martin, Alexis Minotes, Luisa Boni, Kerima, Piero Gragnoni.* Dir. and Pro.: Howard Hawks. (Warner.) Rel.: August 13. (C. & W.).

**The Last Man to Hang?** How a man, accused of the murder of his wife, is found not guilty and then discovers that the lady is not dead at all! Cast: *Tom Conway, Elizabeth Sellars, Eunice Gayson, Freda Jackson, Hugh Latimer, Raymond Huntley, Margaretta Scott, Victor Maddern, Anthony Newley, Tony Quinn, Leslie Western, Jack Lambert, Hal Osmond, Anna Turner, Harold Goodwin, Bill Shine, David Horne, Russell Napier, Olive Sloane, Michael McKeag, Joan Newall, John Stuart, Thomas Heathcote, Joan Hickson, Shelagh Fraser, Dan Cunningham, Charles Lloyd Pack, John Warren, Walter Hudd.* Dir.: Terence Fisher. Pro.: John Gossage. (A.C.T.-Columbia.) Rel.: Sept. 17.

**Last of the Badmen.** Somewhat unusual Western with *George Montgomery* as the undercover detective playing a hazardous game in trying to smash a gang who do business killing bandits (after building them up) for the reward money. Rest of cast: *James Best, Douglas Kennedy, Keith Larsen, Robert Foulk, William Bouchey, John Doucette, Meg Randall, Tom Greenway, Addison Richards, Michael Ansara, John Damler, Harlan Warde.* Dir.: Paul Landres. Pro.: Vincent M. Fennelly. (A.A.-Assoc.) Rel.: June 24. (C. and D.).

**The Last Wagon.** Hard, tough, very well made Indian-fighting Western. A fugitive wanted for murder (*Richard Widmark*) risks life to guide orphaned youngsters through war-ridden Apache country. Breathtaking scenic backgrounds of Northern Arizona. Rest of cast: *Felicia Farr, Susan Kohner, Tommy Rettig, Stephanie Griffin, Ray Stricklyn, Nick Adams, Carl Benton Reid, Douglas Kennedy, George Mathews, James Drury, Ken Clark, Timothy Carey, George Ross, Juney Ellis, Abel Fernandez.* Dir.: Delmer Daves. Pro.: William B. Hawks. (Fox). Rel.: November 26. (C. & E.).

**The Leather Saint.** The Minister takes to fisticuffs in order to raise money for his favourite charity, an iron lung for local polio victims. Cast: *Paul Douglas, John Derek, Jody Lawrence, Cesar Romero, Ernest Truex, Richard Shannon, Ricky Vera, Robert Cornthwaite, Edith Evanson, Lou Nova, Baynes Barron, Mary Benoit, Thomas B. Henry, Bill Baldwin.* Dir.: Alvin Ganzer. Pro.: N. Ratchin. (Paramount). Rel.: July 9. (V.).

**Lisbon.** *Ray Milland*, working for master crook *Claude Rains*, is set the task of smuggling some quarter of a million dollars through the Iron Curtain. Instead, he smuggles lovely *Maureen O'Hara.* Lovely backgrounds of the title city. Rest of cast: *Yvonne Furneaux, Francis Lederer, Percy Marmont, Jay Novello, Edward Chapman, Harold Jamieson, Humberto Madeira.* Dir. and Pro.: Ray Milland. (Rep.-British Lion.) Rel.: January 14. (T. & Naturama.)

**The Littlest Outlaw.** Charming Disney film, made in Mexico in colour, about wonderful friendship of boy and horse. Cast: *Pedro Armendariz, Joseph Calleia, Rodolfo Acosta, Andres Velasquez, Laila Maley, Gilberto Gonzales, Jose Torvay, "Ferrusquilla", Enriqueta Zazueta, Senor Lee, Carlos Ortigoza.* (Disney). Rel.: July 9. (T.).

**The Lonely House.** One of the Scotland Yard series. This time the Yard is faced with a body in a barrel of tar and only one clue, a set of false teeth! Cast: *Russell Napier, Dorothy Bramhall, Bettina Dickson.* Introduced by Edgar Lustgarten. Dir.: Montgomery Tully. Pro.: Alec Snowden. (Anglo-Amalgamated.) Rel.: February 4.

**The Long Arm.** First-rate Ealing film which reveals something of the real workings of the C.I.D. by presenting a routine robbery and then showing how by hard work, much tedious detail and a lot of puzzling, the case is solved. Cast: *Jack Hawkins, John Stratton, Dorothy Alison, Michael Brooke, Sam Kydd, Glyn Houston, Richard Leech, Newton Blick, Geoffrey Keen, Sydney Tafler, Peter Burton, George Rose, Arthur Rigby, Ralph Truman, Ian Bannen, Maureen Davis, John Warwick, Joss Ambler, Barry Keagan, Alec McOwen, Harry Locke, Nicholas Parsons, Warwick Aston, Ursula Howells, David Davies, Julie Milton, Meredith Edwards, Harold Goodwin, John Welsh, Gillian Webb, Maureen Delany, Jameson Clark, William Mervyn.* Dir.: Charles Frend. Pro.: Tom Norsham. (Ealing-Rank.). Rel.: September 10.

**Loser Takes All.** Mild, thin little comedy based on a story by Graham Greene, about two young people in Monte Carlo. He finds a system which can't lose, but nearly loses her before he learns his lesson. Cast: *Rossano Brazzi, Glynis Johns, Robert Morley, Tony Britton, Felix Aylmer, Albert Lieven, A. E. Matthews, Joyce Carey, Geoffrey Keen, Peter Illing, Walter Hudd, Charles Lloyd Pack, Guido Lorraine, Joan Benham, Carl Bernard.* Dir.: Ken Annakin. Pro.: John Stafford. (British Lion.) Rel.: January 14. (C. & E.)

**Love Me Tender.** Fairly leisurely Western set at the tail-end of the Civil War. *Richard Egan* as one of three brothers who rob a Federal train and are eventually forced to give back their loot. Introducing *Elvis Presley*, rock-'n-roll singer, as Egan's younger brother who has married Egan's former girl friend, *Debra Paget.* Rest of cast: *Robert Middleton, William Campbell, Neville Brand, Mildred Dunnock, Bruce Bennett, James Drury, Russ Conway, Ken Clark, Barry Coe, L. Q. Jones, Paul Burns, Jerry Sheldon.* Dir.: Robert D. Webb. Pro.: David Weisbart. (Fox.) Rel.: January 14.

**Victor Mature in THE SHARKFIGHTERS—United Artists.**

**Lovers and Lollipops.** Romance of attractive widow is menaced by small daughter. Cast: *Lori March, Gerald O'Loughlin, Cathy Dunn, William Ward.* Dir. and Pro.: Morris Engel and Ruth Orkin. (Rank.) Rel.: April 29.

# M

**Magnificent Roughnecks.** *Jack Carson* and *Mickey Rooney* as two husky oil men sweltering, swearing and fighting other oil-well men in the South American jungle. Rest of cast: *Nancy Gates, Jeff Donnell, Myron Healey, Willis Bouchey, Eric Feldary, Alan Wells, Frank Gerstle.* Dir.: Sherman A. Rose. Pro.: Herman Cohen. (A.A.-Assoc.). Rel.: August 5.

**Man Afraid.** *George Nader* as a cleric who accidentally kills a prowler assaulting his wife and is thereafter marked down by the dead man's father, who seeks to get even through the minister's young son. Rest of cast: *Phyllis Thaxter, Tim Hovey, Eduard Franz, Harold J. Stone, Judson Pratt, Reta Shaw, Butch Bernard, Mabel Albertson, Martin Milner.* Dir.: Harry Keller. Pro.: Gordon Kay. (U.I.) Rel.: May 13.

**The Man from Del Rio.** *Anthony Quinn* as a revenge-seeking, ruthless gunman turning over to law and order in order to win lovely *Katy Jurado.* Rest of cast: *Peter Whitney, Douglas Fowley, John Larch, Whit Bissell, Douglas Spencer, Guinn "Big Boy" Williams, Marc Hamilton, Adrienne Marden, Barry Atwater, Carl Thayler.* Dir.: Harry Horner. Pro.: Robert L. Jacks. (U.A.). Rel.: December 17.

**Man from the Black Hills.** Western. *Jimmy Ellison* fighting the impostor who has installed himself with a blind man and hopes to collect the latter's gold mine. Rest of cast: *Johnny Mack Brown, Rand Brooks, Lane Bradford, Stanford Jolley, Stanley Andrews, Denver Pyle, Roy Bennett, Robert Bray, Florence Lake, Stanley Price, Joel Allen, Bud Osborne.* Dir.: Thomas Carr. Pro.: Vincent M. Fennelly. (A.A.-Assoc.). Rel.: September 3.

**The Man in the Grey Flannel Suit.** The story of a young American business executive, his worries, his wife and his vivid memories of the war; in its way a detailed picture of a way of life. Intelligent, long, but always absorbing account of a man, his family and his conscience. Cast: *Gregory Peck, Jennifer Jones, Fredric March, Marisa Pavan, Lee J. Cobb, Ann Harding, Keenan Wynn, Gene Lockhart, Gigi Perreau, Portland Mason, Arthur O'Connell, Henry Daniell, Connie Gilchrist, Joseph Sweeney, Sandy Descher, Mickey Maga.* Dir.: Nunnally Johnson. Pro.: Darryl F. Zanuck. (Fox). Rel.: September 3. (C. & T.).

**The Man in the Sky.** Middle-aged test pilot *Jack Hawkins*, finds himself aloft in a fire-wrecked plane and knows there's not much chance of him getting it down safely. Beautifully tense, exciting thriller; modestly, but very well made. Rest of cast: *Elizabeth Sellars, Jeremy Bodkin, Gerald Lohan, Walter Fitzgerald, John Stratton, Eddie Byrne, Victor Maddern, Lionel Jeffries, Donald Pleasence, Catherine Lacey, Megs Jenkins, Ernest Clark, Raymond Francis, Russell Waters, Howard Marion Crawford.* Dir.: Charles Crichton. Pro.: Seth Holt. (Ealing-M-G-M.) Rel.: February 18.

**The Man is Armed.** Rough-and-tumble crime melo about lorry driver driven off his trolley when he is "framed" for smuggling. Cast: *Dane Clark, William Talman, May Wynn, Robert Horton, Barton MacLane, Fred Wayne, Richard Benedict, Richard Reeves, Harry Lewis, Bob Jordan, Larry J. Blake, Darlene Fields, John Mitchum.* Dir.: Franklin Adreon. Pro.: Edward J. White. (Republic). Rel.: September 10.

**A Man is Ten Feet Tall.** Tough, realist film about a U.S. Army deserter who gets a job in the New York railyards and is there "sorted out" psychologically by a young negro who befriends and helps him. Cast: *John Cassavetes, Sidney Poitier, Jack Warden, Kathleen Maguire, Ruby Dee, Robert Simon, Ruth White, William A. Lee, Val Avery, John Kellogg, David Clarke, Estelle Hemsley, Charles Jordan, Ralph Bell.* Dir.: Martin Ritt. Pro.: David Susskind. (M-G-M.) Rel.: April 1.

**The Man Who Knew Too Much.** Alfred Hitchcock's re-make of one of his more famous earlier thrillers, now with colour, VistaVision, some remarkable photography, London and Morocco backgrounds and a fine cast. Cast: *James Stewart, Doris Day, Bernard Miles, Brenda de Banzie, Chris Olsen, Ralph Truman, Daniel Gelin, Mogens Wieth, Alan Mowbray, Reggie Nalder, Hillary Brooke, Richard Wattis, Noel Willman, Alix Talton, Carolyn Jones, Yves Brainville, Betty Baskcomb.* Dir. and Pro.: Alfred Hitchcock. (Paramount). Rel.: July 30. (V. & T.).

**(The Many Loves of) Hilda Crane.** *Jean Simmons* giving a wonderfully subtle and extremely sensitive performance as a girl whose restless seeking of "freedom" leads her to a constant dependence on men, including several husbands. Rest of cast: *Guy Madison, Jean Pierre Aumont, Judith Evelyn, Evelyn Varden, Peggy Knudsen, Gregg Palmer, Richard Garrick, Jim Hayward, Sandee Marriot, Don Shelton, Helen Mayon, Blossom Rock, Jay Jostyn.* Dir.: Philip Dunne. Pro.: Herbert B. Swope, Jr. (Fox). Rel.: August 27. (C. & T.).

**The Melbourne Olympiad.** The film of the 1956 Olympic Games. Dir.: Ian K. Barnes. Narration by Eamonn Andrews, Robert Beatty, Nancy Spain. (Renown.) Rel.: Jan. 6.

**Miami Expose.** Modest and conventional little crime melo, mostly notable for containing one of the last screen performances by the late *Edward Arnold.* Rest of cast: *Lee J. Cobb, Patricia Medina, Michael Granger.* Dir.: Fred Sears. Pro.: Sam Katzman. (Columbia). Rel.: October 29.

**Mister Cory.** *Tony Curtis* as a fugitive from the Chicago slums gambling his way to the top of the tree and into the hearts of both *Kathryn Grant* and *Martha Hyer.* Rest of cast: *Charles Bickford, William Reynolds, Henry Daniell, Russ Morgan, Willis Bouchey, Louise Lorimer, Joan Banks, Harry Landers, Glen Kramer, Dick Crockett.* Dir.: Blake Edwards. Pro.: Robert Arthur. (U.I.) Rel.: Mar. 25. (C. & E.)

**Moby Dick.** John Huston's fortune-costing, epic-proportioned adaptation of the strange Melville classic about the half-crazy Captain Ahab and his relentless, tragic-ending hunt for the great white whale. Wonderful colour Cast: *Gregory Peck, Richard Basehart, Leo Genn, James Robertson Justice, Harry Andrews, Bernard Miles, Mervyn Johns, Noel Purcell, Edric Connor, Joseph Tomelty, Francis de Wolff, Philip Stainton, Royal Dano, Seamus Kelly, Friedrich Ledebur, Ted Howard, Tamba Alleney, Tom Clegg, Orson Welles.* Dir. and Pro.: John Huston. (Moulin-Warner.) Rel.: January 27. (T.)

**Mohawk.** Western along fairly routine lines, with strife between U.S. Cavalry and Redskins along the frontier, *circa* 1800. Cast: *Scott Brady, Rita Gam, Neville Brand, Lori Nelson, Allison Hayes, John Hoyt, Vera Vague, Rhys Williams, Ted de Corsia, Mae Clarke, John Hudson, Tommy Cook, Michael Granger, James Lilburn, Chabon Jadi.* Dir.: Kurt Neumann. Pro.: Edward L. Alperson. (Fox). Rel.: July 2. (E.).

**The Monte Carlo Story.** Gossamer-light little story about gamblers *Vittorio de Sica* and *Marlene Dietrich* deciding to play the rest of their cards together. Background is glamorous Monte Carlo. Rest of cast: *Arthur O'Connell, Natalie Trundy, Jane Rose, Clelia Matania, Alberto Rabagliati, Mischa Auer, Renato Rascel, Carlo Rizzo, Truman Smith, Mimo Billi, Marco Tulli, Guido Martufi, Jean Combal.* Dir.: Samuel Taylor. Pro.: Marcello Girosi. (Titanus-U.A.) Rel.: April 22. (T. and Technirama.)

**The Mountain.** Terribly tense, dizzily exciting story of an old guide (*Spencer Tracy*) forced by his horrible brother into making one last mountain climb in order to rob the victims of an airplane crash. And what happened when they eventually got there. Wonderful photography. Rest of cast: *Robert Wagner, Claire Trevor, Anna Kashfi, Barbara Darrow, William Demarest, Richard Arlen, E. G. Marshall, Richard Garrick, Harry Townes.* Dir. and Pro.: Edward Dmytryk. (Paramount). Rel.: November 12.

**Mountain Fortress.** Western. How Cheyenne (*Clint Walker*) persuades a gang of desperadoes to join him in fighting their way out of a Redskin trap. Rest of cast: *L. Q. Jones, Bob Wilke, Ann Robinson, Peter Coe, Jeff Silver, John Garner, Phil Rich, John Doucette, George Wallace, Rush Williams, Tom Hennesy.* Dir.: Richard Bare. Pro.: Harve Foster. (Warner). Rel.: September 3.

**Paul Douglas and Judy Holliday in THE SOLID GOLD CADILLAC—Columbia.**

**Murder Reported.** Neat little crime melo. Newspaperman *Paul Carpenter* tracking down a killer with the aid of his boss's daughter, *Melissa Stribling*. Rest of cast: *John Laurie, Maurice Durant, Peter Swanwick, Yvonne Warren, Ewen Solon, Patrick Holt, Anne Blake, Georgia Brown, Hal Osmond, Reginald Hearne*. Dir.: Chas. Saunders. Pro.: Guidd Coen. (Fortress-Columbia.) Rel.: May 6.

**My Teenage Daughter.** *Anna Neagle* as the bewildered business mother of problem child *Sylvia Sims*; a topical theme at the heart of a domestic drama. Rest of cast: *Norman Wooland, Wilfrid Hyde White, Kenneth Haigh, Julia Lockwood, Helen Haye, Josephine Fitzgerald, Wanda Ventham, Murray Mayne, Michael Shepley, Avice Landone, Michael Meacham, Ballard Berkeley, Edie Martin, Myrette Morven, Grizelda Hervey, Betty Cooper, Launce Maraschal, Lesley Osmond, Diana King, Daphne Cave, Laidman Brown*. Dir. and Pro.: Herbert Wilcox. (Wilcox-Lion.) Rel.: August 27.

**My Wife's Family.** Broad British comedy based on successful play of same title about the uproar that follows Ma-in-law's discovery of what she thinks is a plot to deceive her poor little married daughter. Cast: *Ronald Shiner, Ted Ray, Diane Hart, Fabia Drake, Greta Gynt, Robertson Hare, Zena Marshall, Jessica Cairns, Benny Lee, James Mageean, Virginia Clay, Martin Wyldeck, Patrick Westwood, Robert Dickens, Charles Wright, Peggy Ann Clifford, Laurie Main, Frank Hawkins, Ian Whittaker, Audrey Nicholson, Ian Wilson, Charles Doran, Frank Royde*. Dir.: Gilbert Gunn. Pro.: Hamilton Inglis. (Forth-Assoc.) Rel.: February 11. (E.)

**N**

**The Naked Hills.** *David Wayne* as an ambitious chap trying to get rich in the 19th-century Californian gold rush, but dogged by ill luck, crooked prospectors and hard-hearted businessmen. Rest of cast: *Keenan Wynn, James Barton, Marcia Henderson, Jim Backus, Denver Pyle, Myrna Dell, Lewis Russell, Frank Fenton, Fuzzy Knight, Jim Hayward, Chris Olsen, Steven Terrell*. Dir. and Pro.: Joseph Shaftel. (A.A.-Assoc.). Rel.: October 8. (P.).

**The Narrowing Circle.** A story about an innocent man framed for a triple murder, his efforts to escape the noose and put it round the neck of the real killer. Cast: *Paul Carpenter, Hazel Court, Russell Napier, Trevor Reid, Ferdy Mayne, Alan Robinson, June Ashley, Basil Dignam, Paula Byrne, Mary Jones, Ronald Stevens, Hugh Latimer*. Dir.: Charles Saunders. Pro.: Frank Bevis. (Fortress-Eros). Rel.: September 24.

**Night in Havana.** *Errol Flynn* as card-dealer in Cuban club involved in a plot to smuggle counterfeit cash. Rest of cast: *Rossana Rory, Gia Scala, Pedro Armandariz, Sandro Giglio, Jacques Aubuchon, Carlos Rivas, Charles Todd, Guillerme Alvarez Guedes, Carlos Mas, Rogelio Hernandez, Velia Martinez, Aurora Pita*. Dir.: Richard Wilson. Pro.: Lewis F. Blumberg. (U.A.) Rel.: May 20.

**Nightfall.** Laconic, confusing (deliberately), violent and pretty well-made American crime thriller with commercial artist *Aldo Ray* and new friend *Anne Bancroft* being doubly on the run: from the police who suspect him of murder and from the crooks who suspect he may have taken their loot. Rest of cast: *Brian Keith, Jocelyn Brando, James Gregory, Frank Albertson, Rudy Bond*. Dir.: Jacques Tourneur. Pro.: Ted Richmond. (Columbia) Rel.: Sept. 19.

**Night Freight.** Brothers *Forrest Tucker* and *Keith Larsen*, railroad owners, sink their differences and join forces to defeat the crooks, who are planning to smash their line and replace it with lorries. Rest of cast: *Barbara Britton, Thomas Gomez, Michael Ross, Myrna Dell, Lewis Martin, G. Pat Collins, Sam Flint, Ralph Sanford, George Sanders, Joe Kirk, Jim Alexander, Charles Fredericks, Guy Rennie, Michael Dale*. Dir.: Jean Yarborough. Pro.: Ace Herman. (A.A.-Assoc.) Rel.: July 16.

**No Road Back.** Efficient crime melo about a diamond robbery—planned by a blind and deaf woman fence—which goes wrong and leads to several murders. Cast: *Skip Homeier, Paul Carpenter, Patricia Dainton, Norman Wooland, Margaret Rawlings, Eleanor Summerfield, Alfie Bass, Sean Connery, Robert Bruce, Philip Ray, Thomas Gallagher*. Dir.: Montgomery Tully. Pro.: Steve Pallos. (Gibraltar-R.K.O.) Rel.: February 18.

**O**

**Odongo.** Another tough, brusque Big White Hunter (*Macdonald Carey* this time) caught, tamed and completely defeated by the woman wished upon him—flame-headed, perfectly cool vet *Rhonda Fleming*. Rest of cast: *Juma, Eleanor Summerfield, Francis de Wolff, Earl Cameron, Dan Jackson, Michael Carridia, Errol John, Leonard Sachs, Paul Hardtmuth, Bartholomew Sketch, Lionel Ngakane*. Dir.: John Gilling. Pro.: Max Varmel. (Warwick-Columbia) Rel.: July 9. (T. & C.)

**Oh, Men! Oh, Women!** Quite delicious, sophisticated comedy, a satire on the current American craze for the psychiatrist's couch, with *David Niven* as the "head-shrinker" who has to prove his theories the harder, more personal way. Rest of cast: *Dan Dailey, Ginger Rogers, Barbara Rush, Tony Randall, Natalie Schafer, Rachel Stephens, John Wengraf, Cheryl Clarke, Charles Davis*. Dir. and Pro.: Nunnally Johnson. (Fox.) Rel.: May 20. (C. & D.)

**Oklahoma.** Long, lavish and vastly entertaining adaptation of the Rodgers and Hammerstein stage success which revolutionised the musical theatre. Cowboy *Gordon MacRae* masculinely wooing wonderful *Shirley Jones* and defeating horrid villain *Rod Steiger*. Great numbers, lovely performances, nice backgrounds. Rest of cast: *Gloria Grahame, Gene Nelson, Charlotte Greenwood, Eddie Albert, James Whitmore, Barbara Lawrence, Jay C. Flippen, Roy Barcroft, James Mitchell, Bambi Lynn*. Dir.: Fred Zinnemann. Pro.: Arthur Hornblow, Jun. (Magna-R.K.O.) Rel.: March 10. (T. & C.)

**Oklahoma Woman.** *Peggie Castle* as a whip-wielding, gun-toting outlaw queen who can't persuade honest *Richard Denning* to ride with her to a senatorship and great but crooked power. Rest of cast: *Cathy Downs, Tudor Owen, Martin Kingsley, Touch Connors*. Dir.: & Pro.: Roger Corman. (Anglo-Amalgamated.) Rel.: Oct. 1.

Alan Ladd in STAMPEDED—Warner.

**The Oklahoman.** Western. *Joel McCrea* in trouble in 1870 Oklahoma because, he a doctor, is friendly with an Indian and takes his part against the local cattle baron. Rest of cast: *Barbara Hale, Brad Dexter, Gloria Talbot, Verna Fenton, Douglas Dick, Michael Pate, Anthony Caruso, Esther Dale*. Dir.: F. D. Lyon. Pro.: Walter Mirisch. (A.A.-Assoc.). Rel.: June 3. (C. and D.).

**Operation Murder.** *Tom Conway* persuaded by fellow doctor *Patrick Holt* to plan the perfect murder—and how a small boy spoils it all. Rest of cast: *Sandra Dorne, John Stone, Virginia Keiley, Rosamund John, Frank Hawkins, Robert Ayres, Gilbert Winfield, Timothy Fitzgerald, Alastair Hunter, Tony Quinn*. Dir.: Ernest Morris. Pro.: Edward J. and Harry Lee Danziger. (Assoc.) Rel.: January 6.

**The Opposite Sex.** A re-make of the sizzling film (which in turn was based on the Claire Boothe play) "The Women" which, in telling the story of an innocent caught up and cruelly wounded in the New York feminine jungle, takes some hefty, deft swipes at the Gentle Sex. Cast: *June Allyson, Joan Collins, Dolores Gray, Ann Sheridan, Ann Miller, Leslie Nielsen, Jeff Richards, Agnes Moorehead, Charlotte Greenwood, Joan Blondell, Sam Levene, Bill Goodwin, Alice Pearce, Barbara Jo Allen, Sandy Descher, Carolyn Jones, Jerry Antes, Alan Marshal, Jonathan Hole*. Dir.: David Miller. Pro.: Joe Pasternak. (M-G-M.) Rel.: March 4. (C. & M.)

**Our Miss Brooks.** *Eve Arden* takes to Hollywood and the larger screen the character she originally created on T.V.—and the result is a pretty mild, conventional comedy. Rest of cast: *Gale Gordon, Don Porter, Robert Rockwell, Jane Morgan, Richard Crenna, Nick Adams, Leonard Smith, Gloria MacMillan, Joe Kearns, William Newell, Philip Van Zandt*. Dir.: Al Lewis. Pro.: David Weisbart. (W.B.) Rel.: Nov. 26.

**Outside the Law.** How ex-convict smashes international crime ring and at same time finds romance. Cast: *Ray Danton, Leigh Snowden, Grant Williams, Onslow Stevens, Judson Pratt, Jack Kruschen, Floyd Simmons, Raymond Bailey, Mel Welles, Arthur Hanson, Vernon Rich*. Dir.: Jack Arnold. Pro.: A. J. Cohen. (U.I.) Rel.: July 23.

**Over Exposed.** The sad story of a nighterie hostess whose driving ambition takes her into the news-photographer business and then lets it drive her on into such deep and crooked waters that her lover only just saves her in the nick of time. Cast: *Cleo Moore, Richard Crenna, Isobel Elsom, Raymond Greenleaf, Shirley Thomas, James O'Rear, Donald Randolph, Dayton Lummis, Jeanne Cooper, Jack Albertson, William McLean, Edna M. Holland, Edwin Parker*. Dir.: Lewis Seiler. Pro.: Lewis J. Rachmil. (Columbia) Rel.: Oct. 1.

**P**

**Pacific Destiny.** Enchanting adaptation of Sir Arthur Grimble's book, "A Pattern of Islands"—about his early memories as a young member of H.M. Colonial Service in Samoa, made on the spot in fine colour. Cast: *Denholm Elliot, Susan Stephen, Felix Felton, Peter Bathurst, Clifford Buckton, Michael Hordern, Gordon Jackson, Inia Te Wiata, Henrietta Godinet, Ollie Crichton, Hans Kruse, Moira Macdonald, Rosie Leavasa*. Dir.: Wolf Rilla. Pro.: Jas. Lawrie. (Lion) Rel.: July 16. (C. & E.)

**Pardners.** *Martin* and *Lewis* go Way Out West. Rest of cast: *Lori Nelson, Jeff Morrow, Jackie Loughery, John Baragrey, Agnes Moorehead, Lon Chaney Jr., Milton Frome, Richard Ahearn, Lee Van Cleef, Stuart Randall, Scott Douglas, Jack Elam, Bob Steel, Mickey Finn*. Dir.: Norman Taurog. Pro.: Paul Jones. (Paramount) Rel.: Sept. 10 (V. & T.)

**Paris Follies of 1956.** Slender story tying together an actual performance of title show at the American (Los Angeles) "Moulin Rouge" nite spot! Cast *Forrest Tucker, Margaret Whiting, Dick Wesson, Martha Hyer, Barbara Whiting, Lloyd Corrigan, Wally Cassell, Fluff Charlton, James Ferris, William Henry, The Sportsmen, Frank Parker*. Dir.: Leslie Goodwin. Pro.: Bernard Tabakin. (A.A.-Assoc.) Rel.: Sept. 9. (D.)

Leo Genn and Robert Brown in THE STEEL BAYONET—United Artists.

**The Passionate Stranger.** Neat British comedy about the Italian chauffeur of a British couple who, reading his mistress's new novel, of which he is the inspiration, gets some amorous ideas—to the lady's intense embarrassment. The "novel" is shown in Technicolor, the rest in monotone—a nice touch. Cast: *Ralph Richardson, Margaret Leighton, Patricia Dainton, Carlo Justini, Ada Reeve, Andree Melly, Frederick Piper, Michael Shepley, Thorley Walters, George Woodbridge, Allan Cuthbertson, John Arnatt, Barbara Archer, Marjorie Rhodes, Megs Jenkins, Michael Trubshawe, Alexander Gauge, Barbara Graley, C. Witty, Fred Tooze*. Dir.: Muriel Box. Pro.: Peter Rogers. (British Lion.) Rel.: March 4. (T.)

**Passport to Treason.** Private eye *Rod Cameron*, ably assisted by cheery *Lois Maxwell*, escapes death by the skin of his teeth and reveals villain *Clifford Evans*' Peace League as a kind of neo-Fascist ring. Rest of cast: *Ballard Berkeley, Douglas Wilmer, Andrew Faulds, John Colicos, Derek Sydney, Barbara Burke, Marianne Stone, Peter Illing, Trevor Reid, Neil Wilson*. Dir.: Robt. S. Baker. Pro.: Baker and Monty Berman. (Mid-Century-Eros.) Rel.: Sept. 24.

**Pay the Devil.** The struggle between dictator-rancher *Orson Welles* and dedicated obstinate sheriff *Jeff Chandler* in Texas, ending with another step forward by law and order. Rest of cast: *Colleen Miller, John Larch, Joe Schneider, Leo Gordon, Martin Garraglia, Ben Alexander*. Dir.: Jack Arnold. Pro.: Albert Zugsmith. (U.I.). Rel.: June 10. (C.).

**Person Unknown.** Another Scotland Yard adventure: how the discovery of a body in quarry leads the detectives on an international quest and an unexpected end to the trail. Cast: *Russell Napier, Marianne Stone, etc*. Featuring: *Edgar Lustgarten*. Dir.: Montgomery Tully. Pro.: Alec Snowden. (Anglo.) Rel.: Dec. 31.

**Please Murder Me.** Story of passion. *Angela Lansbury* as the faithless wife and mistress, *Dick Foran* as her unfortunate husband and *Raymond Burr* as the instrument of revenge. Rest of cast: *John Dehner, Lamont Johnson, Robert Griffin, Denver Pyle, Alex Sharpe, Lee Miller, Madge Blake, Russ Thorson*. Dir.: Peter Godfrey. Pro.: Donald Hyde. (W.B.) Rel.: Nov. 12.

**The Power and the Prize.** *Robert Taylor*, representative of American Big (and pretty crooked) Business, learns honesty from British business executive *Sir Cedric Hardwicke* and love from German *Elizabeth Muller*. Rest of cast: *Burl Ives, Charles Coburn, Mary Astor, Nicola Michaels,*

*Cameron Prud'homme, Richard Erdman, Ben Wright, Jack Raine, Tom Browne Henry, Richard Deacon.* Dir.: Henry Koster. Pro.: Nicholas Nayfack. (M-G-M.) Rel.: January 28. (C.)

**The Proud and the Profane.** Conventional wartime romance: Red Cross worker *Deborah Kerr* and half-breed Marine Colonel *William Holden* going the way of all flesh in the Guadalcanal area. Rest of cast: *Thelma Ritter, Dewey Martin, William Redfield, Ross Bagdasarian, Theodore Newton, Ward Wood, Adam Williams, Marion Ross, Genevieve Aumont.* Dir.: George Seaton. Pro.: William Perlberg. (Paramount.) Rel.: Oct. 8. (V).

**The Proud Ones.** Flat Rock Sheriff *Robert Ryan*, having previously climbed down for the sake of peace in Keystone, now grimly takes his stand against crooked and death-dealing villain *Robert Middleton*. Handsome and thrilling Western. Rest of cast: *Virginia Mayo, Jeffrey Hunter, Walter Brennan, Arthur O'Connell, Ken Clark, Rodolfo Acosta, George Mathews, Fay Roope, Edward Platt, Whit Bissell, Paul Burns, Richard Deacon, Frank Gerstle, Charles Tannen, Lois Ray, Jack Low, Ken Terrell, Harrison Lewis, Don Brodie, William Fawcett, Ed Mundy, Jackie Coogan, Juanita Close.* Dir.: Robert D. Webb. Pro.: Robert L. Jacks. (Fox.) Rel.: July 30. (C. & E.)

## Q

**Quatermass Two.** Professor *Brian* (Quatermass) *Donlevy* struggling against the evil, permeating influence of the things from another world. Rest of cast: *John Longden, Sidney James, Bryan Forbes, William Franklyn, Vera Day, Charles Lloyd Pack, Tom Chatto, John Van Eyssen, Percy Herbert, Michael Ripper, John Rae, Marianne Stone, Ronald Wilson, Jane Aird, Betty Impey, Lloyd Lamble, John Stuart, Gilbert Davies, Joyce Adams, Edwin Richfield, Howard Williams, Philip Baird and Robert Raikes, John Fabin, George Merritt, Arthur Blake, Michael Balfour, Jan Holden.* Dir.: Val Guest. Pro.: Anthony Hinds. (Hammer-U.A.). Rel.: June 10.

**The Quiet Gun.** Villain, Hero and Indian Girl triangle troubles in the Old West, with sheriff *Forrest Tucker* defeating villain *Lee Van Cleef* and mob violence. Rest of cast: *Mara Corday, Jim Davis, Kathleen Crowley, Tom Brown, Lewis Martin, Hank Worden, Gerald Milton, Everett Glass, Edith Evanson.* Dir.: William Claxton. Pro.: Earle Lyon. (Regal-Fox.) Rel.: May 6. (Regalscope.)

## R

**The Rainmaker.** Excellent screen adaptation of the charming American play by Richard Nash about confidence man *Burt Lancaster* who says he can bring rain to the parched prairies, but does in fact bring love to *Katharine Hepburn*. Rest of cast: *Wendell Corey, Lloyd Bridges, Earl Holliman, Cameron Prud'homme, Yvonne Lime, Wallace Ford.* Dir.: Joseph Anthony. Pro.: Hal Wallis. (Paramount.) Rel.: March 18. (T. & V.)

**Ramsbottom Rides Again.** British emigrant *Arthur Askey* made sheriff of the lawless Canadian town of Lonesome. Rest of cast: *Glenn Melvyn, Betty Marsden, Shani Wallis, Danny Ross, Anthea Askey, Sidney James, Frankie Vaughan, June Grant, Jerry Desmonde, Sabrina, Donald Stewart, Campbell Singer, Marne Maitland, Beckett Bould, Billy Percy, Gary Wayne, Sam Kydd, Deryck Guyler, Edie Martin, Leonard Williams, Denis Wyndham, Jack Carson.* Dir. and Pro.: John Baxter. (Hylton-Lion.) Rel.: July 30.

**Raw Edge.** *Herbert Rudley* as a British dictator of the Oregon frontier country being forced out of business by hero *Rory Calhoun*. Rest of cast: *Yvonne DeCarlo, Mara Corday, Rex Reason, Neville Brand, Emile Meyer, Robert Wilkie.* Dir.: John Sherwood. Pro.: Albert Zugsmith. (U.I.) Rel.: July 2. (T.)

**Reach For The Sky.** Polished, entertaining and generally finely made adaptation of Paul Brickhill book telling inspiring story of Douglas Bader, legless airman who became one of the great fighter pilots and air-warfare tacticians of the last war. *Kenneth More* outstanding as Bader. Rest of cast: *Muriel Pavlow, Lyndon Brook, Lee Patterson, Alexander Knox, Dorothy Alison, Michael Warre, Sydney Tafler, Howard Marion Crawford, Jack Watling, Nigel Green, Anne Leon, Charles Carson, Ronald Adam, Walter Hudd, Basil Appleby, Philip Stainton, Eddie Byrne, Beverly Brooks, Michael Ripper, Derek Blomfield, Avice Landone, Eric Pohlmann, Michael Gough, Harry Locke, Sam Kydd.* Dir.: Lewis Gilbert. Pro.: Daniel M. Angel. (Angel-Rank). Rel.: August 27.

**Rebel in Town.** Post-American Civil War story of lingering hatreds, of a near-lynching, and of a couple's renewed love for each other. Cast: *John Payne, Ruth Roman, J. Carrol Naish, Ben Cooper, John Smith, James Griffith, Mary Adams, Bobby Clark, Mimi Gibson, Sterling Franck, Joel Ashley, Ben Johnson.* Dir.: Alfred Werker. Pro.: Howard W. Koch. (Bel-Air-U.A.). Rel.: October 15.

**Reprisal.** Unusual, off-key Technicolored Western, with *Guy Madison* as the part-Redskin trying to hide his parentage in a town seething with prejudice against the Indians, and nearly being lynched when his secret comes out. Rest of cast: *Felicia Farr, Kathryn Grant, Michael Pate, Edward Platt, Otto Hulet, Wayne Mallory, Robert Burton, Ralph Moody, Frank de Kova, Addison Richards.* Dir.: George Sherman. Pro.: Louis J. Rachmil. (Rachmil-Columbia.) Rel.: February 18. (T.)

**Leslie Nielsen and Debbie Reynolds in TAMMY—Universal-International.**

**George Tobias, Jeanne Crain, Jeff Chandler, Elaine Stewart and Philip Reed in THE TATTERED DRESS—Universal-International.**

**The Revolt of Mamie Stover.** The story of a very bad girl who in Hawaii during the war made good in a very big way, by selling herself and investing the proceeds in real estate! Cast: *Jane Russell, Richard Egan, Joan Leslie, Agnes Moorehead, Jorja Curtright, Michael Pate, Richard Coogan, Alan Reed, Eddie Firestone, Jean Willes, Leon Lontoc, Kathy Marlowe, Margia Dean, Jack Mather, Boyd "Rod" Morgan, John Halloran.* Dir.: Raoul Walsh. Pro.: Buddy Adler. (Fox). Rel.: Sept. 17. (T. & C.)

**Rock Around the Clock.** Title is explanatory, especially to Rockers and Rollers. Story is about *Johnny Johnston's* efforts to get this new rhythm going. With *The Platters, Tony Martinez* and his band, *Freddie Bell* and his Bellboys, *Bill Haley* and his Comets and other modern dance organisations. Also *Alix Talton, Lisa Gaye, John Archer, Henry Slate, Earl Barton.* Dir.: Fred F. Sears. Pro.: Sam Katzman. (Columbia). Rel.: August 27.

**Rock, Pretty Baby.** All the hep cats or whatever they are, who like this new kind of dance music, will enjoy this "rock 'n roll" film, with *Sal Mineo, John Saxon, Luana Patten, Edward C. Platt, Fay Wray, Rod McKuen, John Wilder, Alan Reed, Jr., Bob Courtney, Douglas Fowley, George Winslow, Johnny Grant, April Kent, Sue George, Susan Volkmann, Caryl Volkmann, Shelley Fabares.* Dir.: Richard Bartlett. Pro.: Edmond Cherie. (U.I.) Rel.: March 25.

**Rock, Rock, Rock.** A sort of vaudeville bill with song, dance and other speciality acts, many with a Rock-'n-Roll flavour. Cast includes *Alan Freed, Frankie Lymon, La Vern Baker*, etc. Dir.: Will Price. Pro.: Max J. Rosenberg and Milton Subotsky. (W.B.) Rel.: April 8.

**Run for the Sun.** Highly melodramatic story about publicity-shy author residing in Mexico, *Richard Widmark*, lovely newshound *Jane Greer* sent to get his story, and their joint adventure when plane-stranded among some nasty ex-war criminals including *Trevor Howard, Peter Van Eyck* and *Carlos Henning*. Dir.: Roy Boulting. Pro.: Harry Tatelman. (Russ-Field-U.A.). Rel.: October 15. (T. & S.)

## S

**Sailor Beware.** Roaring screen farce—based on the hoary old mother-in-law joke—adapted from the stage success, with *Peggy Mount* nearly ruining her daughter's marriage by her ferocious organising. Rest of cast: *Cyril Smith, Shirley Eaton, Ronald Lewis, Thora Hird, Esma Cannon, Gordon Jackson, Joy Webster, Geoffrey Keen, Jack MacGowran, Charles Houston, Peter Collingwood, Anne Blake, Henry McGee, Fred Griffiths, Douglas Blackwell, Edie Martin, Eliot Makeham, Margaret Moore, Barbara Hicks.* Dir.: Gordon Parry. Pro.: Jack Clayton. (Remus-Lion). Rel.: October 15.

**Satellite in the Sky.** A British addition to the science-fiction cycle, this tells of a space ship sent to explode a new titanium-bomb in space! Cast: *Kieron Moore, Lois Maxwell, Donald Wolfit, Bryan Forbes, Jimmy Hanley, Thea Gregory, Barry Keegan, Alan Gifford, Shirley Lawrence, Walter Hudd, Donald Gray, Peter Neil, Rick Rydon, Ronan O'Casey, Robert O'Neil, Charles Richardson, Carl Jaffe, Trevor Reid, Alastair Hunter, John Baker.* Dir.: Paul Dickson. Pro.: Edward J. and Harry Lee Danziger. (W.B.). Rel.: December 17. (W. & C.)

**Sea Wife.** About a young and pretty nun (*Joan Collins*), a young and virile Britisher (*Richard Burton*), an equally young and virile negro (*Cy Grant*) and a blimp type (*Basil Sydney*) on a survivors' raft in the open sea for days on end . . . a position full of possibilities, many of them delicious, not more than superficially explored in the film. Rest of cast: *Ronald Squire, Harold Goodwin, Gibb McLaughlin, Roddy Hughes, Lloyd Lamble, Ronald Adam, Nicholas Hannen, Otokichi Ikeda, Tenji Takagi, Beatrice Varley.* Dir.: Bob McNaught. Pro.: Andre Hakim. (Sumar-Fox.) Rel.: May 6. (C. & T.)

**The Search for Bridie Murphy.** Unusual, serious and somewhat strange film giving a semi-documentary account of a small town amateur hypnotist who experiments with a neighbour's wife and brings to light an occult experience which may have a number of diverse explanations. Cast: *Teresa Wright, Louis Hayward, Nancy Gates, Kenneth Tobey, Richard Anderson, Tom McKee, Janet Riley, Charles Boaz, Lawrence Fletcher, Charles Maxwell, Walter Kingsford, Noel Leslie, William J. Barker, Eilene Janssen, Bradford Jackson, James Kirkwood, Hallene Hill, Denis Freeborn, Ruth Robinson.* Dir.: Noel Langley. Pro.: Pat Duggan. (Paramount.) Rel.: March 18. (V.)

**The Searchers.** Very good John Ford Western made in Monument Valley. *John Wayne* as the grimly revengeful ex-soldier who for years tracks down the Comanches who have killed his brother and brother's wife and taken away their two little girls. Rest of cast: *Jeffrey Hunter, Vera Miles, Ward Bond, Natalie Wood, John Qualen, Olive Carey, Henry Brandon, Ken Curtis, Harry Carey Jr., Antonio Moreno, Hank Worden, Lana Wood, Walter Coy, Dorothy Jordan, Pippa Scott, Pat Wayne, Beulah Archuletta.* Dir. and Pro.: John Ford. (Warner). Rel.: September 23. (T. & V.)

**Secret Interlude.** Somewhat sentimental story of a man who goes back to the Southern States and there catches up with his past, in the person of a lovely young married woman, involved in the mystery of the novelist going blind at Pompey's Head. Cast: *Richard Egan, Dana Wynter, Cameron Mitchell, Sidney Blackmer, Marjorie Rambeau, Dorothy Patrick Davis, Rosemarie Bowe, Jerry Paris, Ruby Goodwin, Pamela Stufflebeam, Evelyn Rudie, Howard Wendell, Dayton Lummis, Bess Flowers, Cheryl Calloway, Charles Herbert, De Forrest Kelly, Florence Mitchell, Robert Johnson, Anna Mabry.* Dir. and Pro.: Philip Dunne. (Fox). Rel.: July 2. (E. & C.)

**The Secret of Treasure Mountain.** Western with an original story about a treasure hunt for gold buried 200 years previously by a Spaniard in the country of the Apache. Cast: *Valerie French, Raymond Burr, William Prince, Lance Fuller, Susan Cummings, Pat Hogan, Reginald Sheffield, Rodolfo Hoyos, Paul McGuire, Tom Hubbard, Boyd Stockman.* Dir.: Seymour Friedman. Pro.: Wallace MacDonald. (Columbia). Rel.: August 6.

**The Secret Place.** Low-toned, effective British crime film with authentic East London slum backgrounds. About the planning of a robbery by a few amateur crooks, their success (a brilliant sequence) and the sorry aftermath, when with a fortune they cannot translate into cash, everything goes wrong. Cast: *Belinda Lee, David McCallum, Anne Blake, Ronald Lewis, Michael Gwynn, George Selway, George A. Cooper, John Welsh, Michael Brooke, Maureen Pryor, Geoffrey Keen, Brendon Hanley, Hugh Manning, Philip Ray, Wendy Craig.* Dir.: Clive Donner. Pro.: John Bryan. (Rank.) Rel.: March 25.

**Serenade.** *Mario Lanza* returns to the screen in fine voice after three years to sing sixteen songs and struggle gamely through a heavily dramatic story of passion. Rest of cast: *Joan Fontaine, Sarita Montiel, Vincent Price, Joseph Calleia, Harry Bellaver, Vince Edwards, Silvio Minciotti, Frank Puglia, Edward Platt, Frank Yaconelli, Mario Siletti, Maria Serrano, Eduardo Noriega, Licia Albanese, Jean Fenn.* Dir.: Anthony Mann. Pro.: Henry Blanke. (W.B.). Rel.: September 3. (W.)

**Seven Men from Now.** Ex-sheriff *Randolph Scott* grimly tracking down and meting out justice to the seven men who killed his wife during a hold-up. Rest of cast: *Gail Russell, Lee Marvin, Walter Reed*

**Sylvia Syms and Anna Neagle in MY TEENAGE DAUGHTER—British Lion.**

*John Larch, Donald Barry, Fred Graham, John Barradino, John Phillips, Chuck Roberson, Steve Mitchell, Pamela Duncan, Stuart Whitman.* Dir.: Budd Boetticher. Pro.: A. V. McLaglen and R. E. Morrison. (W.B.) Rel.: April 8. (W.)

**Seven Waves Away.** A maritime drama which sets an unanswered problem. *Tyrone Power* as the captain of a small boat-load of survivors, the only one left afloat after their ship has been torpedoed, who sets adrift all those not likely to survive, so giving a chance to the few who might. Was he right? Rest of cast: *Mai Zetterling, Lloyd Nolan, Stephen Boyd, Moira Lister, James Hayter, Marie Lohr, Laurence Naismith, Eddie Byrne, Clare Austin, Orlando Martins.* Dir.: Richard Sale. Pro.: J. R. Sloan. (Copa-Columbia.) Rel.: April 8.

**Seventh Cavalry.** Unjustly suspected of cowardice, Captain *Randolph Scott* of the U.S. 7th Cavalry beats a mutiny and the redskins to prove his bravery. Rest of cast: *Barbara Hale, Jay C. Flippen, Jeanette Nolan, Frank Faylen, Leo Gordon, Denver Pyle, Harry Carey Jr., Michael Pate, Donald Curtis, Frank Wilcox, Pat Hogan, Russell Hicks, Peter Ortiz.* Dir.: J. H. Lewis. Pro.: Harry Joe Brown. (Columbia). Rel.: Oct. 14. (T.)

**Shack Out on 101.** Spy thriller set in an eating shack on Highway 101, just by which is one of America's secret electronic laboratories. Waitress *Terry Moore* and the F.B.I. uncover a plot to steal those secrets. Rest of cast: *Frank Lovejoy, Keenan Wynn, Lee Marvin, Whit Bissell, Jess Barker, Donald Murphy, Frank De Kova, Len Lesser.* Dir.: Edward Dein. Pro.: Mort Millman. (Wm. F. Broidy-A.A.-Assoc.) Rel.: August, 26.

**The Shadow on the Window.** Chase melodrama with the police trying to catch up with the heroine before the crooks (who have kidnapped her) decide to kill her—something about which they are divided. Compact; exciting. Cast: *Phil Carey, Betty Garrett, John Barrymore, Jr., Corey Allen, Gerald Sarracini, Jerry Mathers, Sam Gilman, Rusty Lane, Ainslie Pryor, Paul Picerni, William Leslie, Doreean Woodbury, Ellie Kent, Angela Stevens, Mort Mills, Carl Milletaire, Julian Upton, Nesdon Booth, Jack Lomas.* Dir.: Wm. Asher. Pro.: Jonie Taps. (Columbia). Rel.: June 10.

**The Sharkfighters.** *Victor Mature* bravely making himself sharkbait in order to prove successful a 1942 U.S. Navy experiment to save ditched fliers from the wolves of the deep. Smoothly made, in colour, on and off the Cuban coastline. Rest of cast: *Karen Steele, James Olson, Philip Coolidge, Rafael Campos, George Neise, Nathan Yates, Jesus Hernandez, Claude Akins, Charles Collingwood* Dir.: Jerry Hopper. Pro.: Sam Goldwyn, Jun. (U.A.). Rel.: November 26. (C. & T.)

**Showdown at Abilene.** Adult Western about an ex-sheriff who comes back to Abilene after four years of war, is persuaded to take up his old job—though he won't use his guns any more—and the eventful violent showdown that removes the villain, brings back the girl-friend and renews our hero's dexterity with the side-arms. Cast: *Jock Mahoney, Martha Hyer, Lyle Bettger, David Janssen, Grant Williams, Ted de Corsia, Harry Harvey, Dayton Lummis, John Maxwell, Richard Cutting, Robert Anderson, Lane Bradford.* Dir.: Charles Haas. Pro.: Howard Christie. (U.I.-Rank.) Rel.: April 22. (T.)

**Sierra Stranger.** *Howard Duff* struggling against odds and a ruthless gang in a routine Western. Rest of cast: *Gloria McGhee, Dick Foran, John Hoyt, Barton MacLane, George E. Stone, Ed Kemmer, Robert Foulk, Eve McVeagh, Henry "Bomber" Kulky, Byron Foulger.* Dir.: Lee Sholem. Pro.: N. T. Herman. (Columbia.) Rel.: April 8.

**The Silent World.** Wonderful French underseas documentary, the result of many thousands of dives and long months of patience and work. Dir.: Jacques-Yves Cousteau and Louis Malle. (Rank.) Rel.: March 10. (Colour)

**Tony Wright and Donald Sinden in TIGER IN THE SMOKE—J. Arthur Rank.**

**The Silken Affair.** *David Niven* as an accountant whose head is turned (to the large-scale cooking of books) by French charmer *Genevieve Page.* Rest of cast: *Ronald Squire, Beatrice Straight, Wilfrid Hyde White, Howard Marion Crawford, Dorothy Alison, Miles Malleson, Richard Wattis, Joan Sims, Irene Handl, Charles Carson, Harry Locke, Martin Boddey, Colin Morris, Leonard Sharp, John Carroll.* Dir.: Roy Kellino. Pro.: Fred Feldkamp. (R.K.O.) Rel.: May 6.

**Slander.** American melodrama aimed at the sensational smear magazines in that country and the kind of harm they do. Cast: *Van Johnson, Ann Blyth, Steve Cochran, Marjorie Rambeau, Richard Eyer, Harold J. Stone, Philip Coolidge, Lurene Tuttle, Lewis Martin.* Dir.: Roy Rowland. Pro.: Armand Deutsch. (M-G-M.) Rel.: February 18.

**The Slave Woman.** A bit of Babylonian history, with *Rhonda Fleming* the lovely slave who becomes mistress of the king, is desired by the Prime Minister and outlives them both to find, as Queen, romance with her faithful, humble lover *Ricardo Montalban.* Rest of cast: *Roldano Lupi, Carlo Ninchi, Tamara Lees.* Dir.: Carlo Bragaglia. Pro.: Nat Wachsberger. (Pantheon-British Lion). Rel.: December 3. (T.)

**Slightly Scarlet.** Rough, tough gangster piece, with *John Payne* as the gang boss's first lieutenant whose ambition leads him into plenty of trouble—as well as *Rhonda Fleming's* arms. Rest of cast: *Arlene Dahl, Kent Taylor, Ted de Corsia, Lance Fuller, Frank Gerstle, Buddy Baer, George E. Stone, Ellen Corby, Roy Gordon.* Dir.: Allan Dwan. Pro.: B. Bogeaus. (R.K.O.). Rel.: July 2. (T.)

**The Smallest Show on Earth.** Thoroughly entertaining, fairly broad British comedy about a young couple who inherit an old and almost derelict "flea-pit" cinema in a Northern industrial town—together with the odd trio of staff—and their efforts to make a "go" of it. Cast: *Bill Travers, Virginia McKenna, Leslie Phillips, Peter Sellers, Margaret Rutherford, Bernard Miles, Francis de Wolff, June Cunningham, Sidney James.* Dir.: Basil Dearden. Pro.: Michael Relph. (Launder and Gilliatt—Relph-Dearden—British Lion.) Rel.: May 6.

**Smiley.** Charming, made-in-Australia film about a little boy whose ambition to get himself a real bike leads indirectly to the uncovering of a dope ring. *Colin Peterson* delightful as the tow-headed lad. Rest of cast: *Chips Rafferty, John McCallum, Ralph Richardson, Jocelyn Hernfield, Bruce Archer, Margaret Christensen, Reg Lye, Charles Tingwell, Marion Johns, Guy Doleman, William Rees, Gavin Davies, Chow Sing, Bob Simm, Reggie Weigand.* Dir. and Pro.: Anthony Kimmins. (Fox). Rel.: July 23. (C. & D.)

**The Solid Gold Cadillac.** *Judy Holliday* giving delightful comedy performance as the girl who with honest *Paul Douglas's* help defeats on behalf of the small shareholders the wicked machinations of a crooked board of directors. Rest of cast: *Fred Clark, John Williams, Hiram Sherman, Neva Patterson, Ralph Dumke, Ray Collins, Arthur O'Connell, Richard Deacon, Marilyn Hanold, Anne Loos, Audrey Swanson, Larry Hudson, Sandra White, Harry Antrim, George Burns.* Dir.: Richard Quine. Pro.: Fred Kohlmar. (Columbia). Rel.: October 17.

**Somebody Up There Likes Me.** The tough, rough story of U.S. prizefighting champ Rocky Graziano—his path from juvenile delinquent, jailbird, Army deserter, to hero of the small square ring. The world championship fight climax is one of the finest boxing sequences ever screened. Cast: *Paul Newman* (Rocky), *Pier Angeli, Everett Sloane, Eileen Heckart, Sal Mineo, Harold J. Stone, Joseph Buloff, Sammy White, Arch Johnson, Robert Lieb, Theodore Newton, Robert Loggia, Judson Pratt, Matt Crowley, Harry Wismer, Sam Taub, Donna Jo Gribble, Robert Easton, Ray Stricklyn, John Rosser, Frank Campanella, Ralph Vitti.* Dir.: Robert Wise. Pro.: Charles Schnee. (M-G-M). Rel.: November 19. (M.)

**The Spanish Gardener.** Adaptation of the A. J. Cronin story about a frustrated Foreign Office official in Spain who bitterly resents the young and virile Spanish gardener's friendship with his son. Adult, cool and excellent. Cast: *Dirk Bogarde, Jon Whiteley, Michael Hordern, Cyril Cusack, Maureen Swanson, Lyndon Brook, Josephine Griffin, Bernard Lee, Rosalie Crutchley, Ina de la Haye, Geoffrey Keen, Harold Scott, Jack Stewart, Richard Molinas, Susan Lyall Grant, John Adderley, David Lander.* Dir.: Philip Leacock. Pro.: John Bryan. (Rank.) Rel.: January 28. (T. & V.)

**Spring Reunion.** A much-restrained *Betty Hutton* comes back to the screen in a mild little melodrama about a high school class reunion. Rest of cast: *Dana Andrews, Jean Hagen, Laura La Plante, Robert Simon, Gordon Jones, Irene Ryan, Herbert Anderson, Richard Shannon, Kerr Curtis, Vivi Janis, Mimi Doyle, Florence Sundstrom, Richard Benedict.* Dir.: Robert Pirosh. Pro.: Jerry Bresler. (Bryna-U.A.) Rel.: January 21.

**Spy Chasers.** The Bowery Boys join the Cloak and Dagger Brigade! In their 39th film they are involved with exiled royalty. Cast: *Leo Gorcey, Huntz Hall, Bernard Gorcey, Leon Askin, Sig Ruman, Veola Vonn, Lisa Davis, David Condon, Bennie Bartlett, Richard Benedict, Frank Richards, Linda Bennett.* Dir.: Edward Bernds. Pro.: Ben Schwalb. (Assoc.). Rel.: July 30.

**Stagecoach to Fury.** Tense and exciting Western about a group of stagecoach passengers held prisoner by a Mexican bandit and their different reactions to this situation. Cast: *Forrest Tucker, Mari Blanchard, Wallace Ford, Rudolfo Hoyos, Paul Fix, Rico Alaniz, Wright King, Margia Dean, Ian Macdonald.* Dir.: William Claxton. Pro.: Earle Lyon. (Fox.) Rel.: February 11.

**Stampeded.** Western. *Alan Ladd* as the strong man curing weak man *Edmond O'Brien* of his addiction to the bottle and persuading him to build a new town that cattlemen can make a base for business and transport. Rest of cast: *Virginia Mayo, Anthony Caruso, Julie Bishop, John Qualen, Don Castle, David Ladd, Jack Wrather, Jnr., George J. Lewis, James Anderson, Don Kelly, Charles Watts.* Dir.: Gordon Douglas. Pro.: George Bertholon (Warner.) Rel.: June 3.

**The Steel Bayonet.** The brutal, bloody but convincing and expert telling of a story of an incident during the Tunis campaign of 1943: the hopeless last stand of a group of British infantry defending a forward artillery spotting post. Cast: *Leo Genn, Kieron Moore, Michael Medwin, Robert Brown, Michael Ripper, John Paul, Shay Gorman, Tom Bowman, Bernard Horsfall, John Watson, Arthur Lovegrove, Percy Herbert, Paddy Joyce, Jack Stewart, David Crowley, Barry Lowe, Michael Dear, Ian Whittaker, Michael Balfour, Raymond Francis, Anthony Warren, Rolf Carston, Gerard Green, Wolf Frees, Jeremy Longhurst, David Ritch, Abdul Noor, Victor Platt.* Dir. and Pro.: Michael Carreras. (U.A.) Rel.: June 3.

**A Strange Adventure.** Young hot-rod enthusiast *Ben Cooper* finds his interest in *Marla English* leads him into plenty trouble—but a new romance too. Rest of cast: *Joan Evans, Jan Merlin, Nick Adams, Peter Miller, Paul Smith, Emlen Davies, Frank Wilcox.* Dir.: William Witney. Pro.: William J. O'Sullivan. (Republic). Rel.: November 12.

**Street of Sinners.** *George Montgomery* as brave, straight policeman on New York's toughest East Side beat, having to fight teenage rebels, big crime boss and even his own superiors. Hair-raising in its picture of the other side of town; exciting, too. Rest of cast: *Geraldine Brooks, Nehemiah Persoff, Marilee Earle, Stephen Joyce, William Harrigan, Clifford David, Diana Milay, Sandra Rehn, Danny Dennis, Melvin Decker, Joey Fay, Billy James, Ted Irwin, Fred Herrick, Wolf Barzell, Lou Gilbert, Stephen Eliot, Bob Duffy.* Dir. and Pro.: William Berke. (U.A.). Rel.: Floating.

**Sunshine in Soho.** An interesting documentary in colour of that famous London quarter, with commentary by Howard Marion Crawford. Dir. and Pro.: Burt Hyams. (Diploma-Columbia). Rel.: August 13.

**Suspended Alibi.** How a features editor, caught in a web of lies he has woven to hide an *affaire* from his wife, is sentenced to death for a murder of which he is innocent. Cast: *Patrick Holt, Honor Blackman, Valentine Dyall, Andrew Keir, Naomi Chance, Lloyd Lamble, Viola Lyel, Frederick Piper, Bryan Coleman, Wally Patch, Jeanette Hutchinson, Tony Winterbottom, Madoline Thomas, Edgar Wreford, John Baker, Ian Whittaker, Brown Derby, Vincent Lawson, Walter Horsburgh, Richard McNeff.* Dir.: Alfred Shaughnessy. Pro.: Robert Dunbar. (Rank.) Rel.: February 25.

**T**

**Tammy.** *Debbie Reynolds* as the charming little innocent from the Bayou backwoods country who brings happiness and a new hope to a number of people. Rest of cast: *Leslie Nielsen, Walter Brennan, Mala Powers, Sidney Blackmer, Mildred Natwick, Fay Wray, Philip Ober, Craig Hill, Louise Beavers, April Kent.* Dir.: Joseph Pevney. Pro.: Ross Hunter. (U.I.) Rel.: April 15. (C. & T.)

**The Tattered Dress.** Slick, successful New York lawyer, *Jeff Chandler*, is brought back to humility and integrity when he is framed for and nearly convicted of bribery. Rest of cast: *Jeanne Crain, Jack Carson, Gail Russell, Elaine Stewart, George Tobias, Edward Andrews, Philip Reed, Edward C. Platt, Floyd Simmons.* Dir.: Jack Arnold. Pro.: Albert Zugsmith. (U.I.) Rel.: April 29. (C.)

**Teenage Rebel.** Pleasant little film based on the theme of the harm caused to children by divorce, with *Ginger Rogers* (a delightful performance) trying to win the fifteen-year-old daughter she hasn't seen for eight years. Three extremely promising performances by youngsters *Betty Lou Keim, Diane Jergens and Warren Berlinger.* Rest of cast: *Michael Rennie, Mildred Natwick, Rusty Swope, Lili Gentle, Louise Beavers, Irene Hervey, John Stephenson, Susan Luckey, James O'Rear, Gary Gray, Pattee Chapman, Wade Dumas, Richard Collier.* Dir.: Edmund Goulding. Pro.: Charles Brackett. (Fox.) Rel.: February 11. (C. & T.)

**Ten Thousand Bedrooms.** Quite pleasant musical, the first to be made by *Dean Martin* after his split with Jerry Lewis: he's a hotelier on the grand scale who comes to Rome and there runs into a lot of girl trouble. Rest of cast: *Anna Maria Alberghetti, Eva Bartok, Dewey Martin, Walter Slezak, Paul Henreid, Jules Munshin, Marcel Dalio, Evelyn Varden, Lisa Montell, Lisa Gaye, John Archer, Steve Dunne, Dean Jones, Monique Van Vooren.* Dir. and Pro.: Joe Pasternak. (M-G-M.) Rel.: May 13. (C. & M.)

**Tension at Table Rock.** Superior Western in the great "Shane" tradition about a stranger (*Richard Egan*) who arrives in town and is found to be a man with the unjustified reputation of shooting his pal in the back. He stays just long enough to back up timid sheriff *Cameron Mitchell* and restore law and order before jogging on. Rest of cast: *Dorothy Malone, Billy Chapin, Royal Dano, Edward Andrews, John E. Dehner, De Forest Kelley, Joe De Santis, Angie Dickinson.* Dir.: Charles Marquis Warren. (R.K.O.). Rel.: December 3. (T.).

**Texas Rose.** Jack Slade, a Pinkerton Guard, tangles with the Suttons' Wyoming Gang and falls in love with one of its prettiest members, the Rose of the title. Cast: *John Ericson, Mari Blanchard, Neville Brand, Casey Adams, Jon Shepodd, Howard Petrie, John Dennis, Angie Dickinson, Donna Drew, Mike Ross, Lyla Graham, Alan Wells, Raymond Bailey.* Dir.: Harold Schuster. Pro.: Lindsley Parsons. (A.A.-Assoc.). Rel.: September 16.

**That Certain Feeling.** *Bob Hope* comedy—all about the revenge that a shy strip-cartoonist has on his pompous boss, who is to marry the artist's ex-wife. Rest of cast: *Eva Marie Saint, George Sanders, Pearl Bailey, David Lewis, Jerry Mathers, Al Capp.* Dir. and Pro.: Norman Panama and Melvin Frank. (Paramount). Rel.: December 24. (T. & V.).

**That Woman Opposite.** Who killed Sir Maurice Lawes in the quiet French village of La Bandelette? And why? That is the problem facing shrewd Inspector *Guido Lorraine* and his private-eye friend *Dan O'Herlihy.* Rest of cast: *Phyllis Kirk, Wilfrid Hyde White, Petula Clark, Jack Watling, William Franklyn, Margaret Withers, Jacques Cey, Andre Charisse, Robert Raikes, Tita Dane, Balbina, Irene Moore, Concepta Fennell, Campbell Gray, John Serett.* Dir.: Compton Bennett. Pro.: Wm. Gell. (Monarch). Rel.: June 3.

**Their Secret Affair.** Another, sometimes amusing, variation of the routine movie theme about the girl starting by disliking a man and ending up by marrying him. In this case the girl is the queen-pin of a big New York news empire and the man is a two-star U.S. Army General whom she is trying to belittle so he will lose the atomic executive job she wants for somebody else. Cast: *Susan Hayward, Kirk Douglas, Paul Stewart, Jim Backus, John Cromwell, Roland Winters, A. E. Gould-Porter, Michael Fox, Frank Gerstle, Charles Lane.* Dir.: H. C. Potter. Pro.: Martin Rackin. (W.B.) Rel.: April 29.

**Jon Whiteley in THE WEAPON—Eros.**

**There's Always a Thursday.** A somewhat bitter little comedy about a man who is accused of having an affair, and who thus at last finds success in the world which has denied it to him for so long as a good, sober citizen. Cast: *Marjorie Rhodes, Charles Victor, Jill Ireland, Richard Thorp, Bruce Seton, Lance George, Patrick Holt, Deirdre Mayne, Frances Day, Howard Green, Lloyd Lamble, Peter Fontain, Geoff Goodhart, Reginald Hearne, Glen Alyn, Ewen Solon, Martin Boddy, Alexander Field, Robert Raglan, Yvonne Savage, Margaret Rowe, Yvette Davis, Alex MacIntosh, E. Malin.* Dir.- Chas. Saunders. Pro.: Guidd Coen. (Rank.) Rel.: April 1.

**These Wilder Years.** Ruthless tycoon *James Cagney* tries to find the son he sired but refused to acknowledge twenty years back, and finds his way barred by equally determined, dedicated welfare worker *Barbara Stanwyck.* Rest of cast: *Walter Pidgeon, Betty Lou Keim, Don Dubbins, Edward Andrews, Basil Ruysdael. Grandon Rhodes, Will Wright, Lewis Martin, Dorothy Adams, Dean Jones, Herb Vigran,* Dir.: Roy Rowland. Pro.: Jules Schermer. (M-G-M). Rel.: December 10. (M.)

**Three Brave Men.** American political drama which seeks in an odd kind of way to justify the modern witch-hunts which go on there from time to time. Cast: *Ray Milland, Ernest Borgnine, Frank Lovejoy, Nina Foch, Dean Jagger, Virginia Christine, Edward Andrews, Frank Faylen, Diane Jergens, Warren Berlinger, Andrew Duggan, Joseph Wiseman, James Westerfield, Richard Anderson, Olive Blakeney, Robert Burton, Jason Wingreen, Ray Montgomery, Sandy Descher, Patty Ann Gerrity, Jonathan Hole, Barbara Gould, Fern Barry, Joseph McGuinn, Samuel Colt.* Dir.: Philip Dunne. Pro.: H. B. Swope, Jr. (Fox.) Rel.: February 25. (C.)

**Three for Jamie Dawn.** Naughty playgirl kills her lover and shyster lawyer tries to bribe a jury to acquit her. Cast: *Laraine Day, Ricardo Montalban, Richard Carlson, June Havoc, Maria Palmer, Eduard Franz, Regis Toomey, Scotty Beckett, Herb Vigran, Marilyn Simms, Dorothy Adams.* Dir.: Thomas Carr. Pro.: Hayes Goetz? (Assoc.) Rel.: May 6.

**Three Men in a Boat.** A pretty free adaptation of the Jerome K. Jerome story about three friends —*Jimmy Edwards, David Tomlinson* and *Laurence Harvey*—who find that a quiet holiday on the River Thames can be quite exciting—in a broad and funny way. Rest of cast: *Noelle Middleton, Shirley Eaton, Jill Ireland, Lisa Gastoni, Campbell Cotts, Joan Haythorne, Robertson Hare, Adrienne Corri, Martha Hunt.* Dir.: Ken Annakin. (British Lion.) Rel.: January 21. (C. & E.)

**Three Violent People.** Confederate captain *Charlton Heston,* returning to uneasy private life in Texas after the war, has to fight his brother, his new wife and the carpet-baggers. Rest of cast: *Anne Baxter, Gilbert Roland, Tom Tryon, Forrest Tucker, Bruce Bennett, Elaine Stritch, Barton MacLane, Peter Hansen, John Harmon, Ross Bagdasarian, Bobby Blake, Jameel Farah, Leo Castillo, Don Devlin, Raymond Greenleaf, Roy Engel, Argentina Brunetti.* Dir.: Rudolph Mate. Pro.: Hugh Brown. (Paramount). Rel.: January 21. (T. & V.)

**Thunder Over Arizona.** Western with *Skip Homeier,* hired by bad man *George Macready* to do his dirty work, switching over to the forces of law and order and wiping out the whole gang. Rest of cast: *Kristine Miller, Wallace Ford.* Dir. and Pro.: Joe Kane. (Republic-British Lion.) Rel.: March 4. (T. & Naturama.)

**Thunderstorm.** Uninhibited melodrama about a girl who comes from the sea and brings the passions of a group of Spanish villagers to boiling point before returning whence she came. Cast: *Linda Christian, Carlos Thompson, Charles Korvin, Garry Thorne, Tito Junco, Felix de Pomes.* Dir.: John Guillermin. Pro.: Binnie Barnes. (Hemisphere-Lion). Rel.: July 2.

**Tiger in the Smoke.** Pretty consistently thrilling (if incredible) thriller which starts in the London fog and keeps you fogged almost until the climax in the Brittany sunshine. About a murderer, his war-time buddies and a buried treasure. Cast: *Donald Sinden, Muriel Pavlow, Tony Wright, Bernard Miles, Alec Clunes, Laurence Naismith, Christopher Rhodes, Charles Victor, Thomas Heathcote, Sam Kydd, Kenneth Griffith, Gerald Harper, Wensley Pithy, Stanley Rose, Stratford Johns, Brian Wilde, Hilda Barry, Beatrice Varley.* Dir.: Roy Baker. Pro.: Leslie Parkyn. (Rank). Rel.: December 17.

**Time Without Pity.** Sincere, uneven but interesting British drama about a hopeless alcoholic who comes from a Canadian sanitorium with just 24 hours to spare before his son is hanged for murder, and his desperate efforts to save his boy. Cast: *Michael Redgrave, Ann Todd, Leo McKern, Peter Cushing, Alec McCowen, Renee Houston, Paul Daneman, Lois Maxwell, Richard Wordsworth, George Devine, Joan Plowright, Ernest Clarke, Peter Copley, Hugh Moxey, Julian Somers, John Chandos, Dickie Henderson, Jnr.* Dir.: Joseph Losey. Pro.: John Arnold and Anthony Simmons. (Eros.) Rel.: May 13.

**The Tommy Steele Story.** The success story—and a true one—of Bermondsey boy Tommy, who rose to the top of the bill from playing his guitar in a London coffee bar. Rest of cast: *Patrick Westwood, Hilda Fenemore, Charles Lamb, Peter Lewiston, John Boxer, Mark Daly, Lisa Daniely, Bryan Coleman, Cyril Chamberlain and Steele's own Band as well as other groups.* Dir.: Gerard Bryant. Pro.: Hernert Smith. (Anglo-Amalgamated). Rel.: June 24.

**A Touch of the Sun.** *Frankie Howerd* finds the real South of France very different to his dream country, but luckily disillusionment leads to his making his fortune and winning pretty *Ruby Murray.* Rest of cast: *Dorothy Bromiley, Dennis Price, Gordon Harker, Reginald Beckwith, Alfie Bass, Willoughby Goddard, Richard Wattis, Edna Morris, Ian Whittaker, Brian Sunners, Lee Young, George Margo, Miriam Karlin, Ann Goerge, Jed Brown, Lucy Griffith, Eshma Cannon, Evelyn Roberts, John Vere.* Dir.: Gordon Parry. Pro.: Raymond Stross. (Eros). Rel.: November 12.

**Town on Trial.** Outstanding British whodunnit with *John Mills* rather roughly but very efficiently sorting out the suspects in a small town when a young girl is violated and strangled. Rest of the cast: *Charles Coburn, Barbara Bates, Derek Farr, Alex McCowen, Elizabeth Seal, Geoffrey Keen, Margaretta Scott, Fay Compton, Meredith Edwards, Harry Locke, Maureen Connell, Magda Miller, David Quitak, Dandy Nichols, Raymond Huntley.* Dir.: John Guillermin. Pro.: Maxwell Setton. (Setton-Columbia.) Rel.: February 18.

**Trapeze.** Carol Reed's imaginative and intelligent treatment of the old, old story about a circus act whose miracles on the high trapeze are interfered with by a glamorous, man-eating girl who decides to join them! Wonderful atmosphere caught in the Paris circus; superb and exciting camera-work; first-class performances by *Burt Lancaster, Gina Lollobrigida* and *Tony Curtis.* Rest of cast: *Katy Jurado, Thomas Gomez, Johnny Puleo, Minor Watson, Gerald Landry, J. P. Kerrien, Sidney James, Gabrielle Fontan, Pierre Tabard, Gamil Ratab, Edward Hagopian, Michel Thomas.* Dir.: Carol Reed. Pro.: James Hill. (U.A.) Rel.: August 20. (C. & D.)

**True as a Turtle.** Pleasant British comedy about a group of people bound for the coast of France on a rather old craft called "The Turtle." Cast: *John Gregson, June Thorburn, Cecil Parker, Keith Mitchell, Elvi Hale, Avis Landone, Jacques Brunius, Gabrielle Brune, Charles Clay, Betty Stockfield, Michael Briant, Pauline Drewett, John Harvey.* Dir.: Wendy Toye. Pro.: Peter de Sarigny. (Rank.) Rel.: March 18. (E.)

**12 Angry Men.** Unusual, absorbing and intelligent motion picture about the way that eleven men on an American jury trying a young man accused of murder are brought to a sense of their immense responsibility by the integrity and doubt of their twelfth man. Cast: *Henry Fonda, Lee J. Cobb, Ed Begley, E. G. Marshall, Jack Warden, Martin Balsam, John Fiedler, Jack Klugman, Edward Binns, Joseph Sweeney, George Voskovec, Robert Webber, Rudy Bond, James A. Kelly, Bill Nelson, John Savoca.* Dir.: Sidney Lumet. Pro.: Henry Fonda and Reginald Rose. (U.A.) Rel.: May 20.

**23 Paces to Baker Street.** Blind playwright *Van Johnson* stumbles on a kidnap plot and after having the devil's own job in convincing the police of the fact, himself becomes involved so deeply that the kidnapper determines to remove him. Rest of cast: *Vera Miles, Cecil Parker, Patricia Laffan, Maurice Denham, Estelle Winwood, Liam Redmond, Isobel Elsom, Martin Benson, Natalie Norwick, Terence de Marney, Queenie Leonard, Charles Keane, Lucie*

**Bette Davis, Barry Fitzgerald and Ernest Borgnine in WEDDING BREAKFAST—Metro-Goldwyn-Mayer.**

*Lancaster, A. Cameron Grant, Ashley Cowan, Les Sketchly, Ben Wright, Reginald Sheffield, Janice Kane, Robert Raglan, Howard Lang, Margaret McGrath, Walter Horsborough, Fred Griffith, Charles Stanley, Robin Alalouf, Yorke Sherwood.* Dir.: Henry Hathaway. Pro.: Henry Ephron. (Fox). Rel.: September 24. (C. & E.)

U **The Unguarded Moment.** *Esther Williams* as a teacher involved in a rather unpleasant murder. Rest of cast: *George Nader, Edward Andrews, John Saxon, Les Tremayne, Jack Albertson, John Wilder, Dani Crayne.* Dir.: Harry Keller. Pro.: Gordon Kay. (U.I.). Rel.: September 3.

**The Unholy Wife.** In the first of her Hollywood films to be shown here, *Diana Dors* plays British no-good girl (married to Californian vinery owner *Rod Steiger*) who plans to murder her husband but kills the wrong man and pays, ironically, for the wrong crime. Rest of cast: *Tom Tryon, Beulah Bondi, Marie Windsor, Arthur Franz, Louis Van Rooten, Joe DeSantis, Argentina Brunetti, Tol Avery, James Burke, Steve Pendleton, Gary Hunley, Douglas Spencer.* Dir. and Pro.: John Farrow. (R.K.O.). Rel.: June 24. (T.).

**Unidentified Flying Objects.** A film telling in "March of Time" manner the story of the American Flying Saucers, examining all evidence and finally suggesting that there may well be more things in heaven and earth. . . .! Dir.: Winston Jones. Pro.: Clarence Greene. (U.A.) Rel.: Floating.

**Up in the World.** *Norman Wisdom* as a window cleaner who accidentally saves a rich young milord from a kidnapping plot and finds romance with pretty housemaid *Maureen Swanson.* Rest of cast: *Jerry Desmonde, Ambrosine Phillpotts, Colin Gordon, Michael Caridia, Michael Ward, Jill Dixon, Cyril Chamberlain, William Lucas, Eddie Leslie, Hy Hazell.* Dir.: John Paddy Carstairs. Pro.: Hugh Stewart. (Rank). Rel.: December 30.

**Utah Blaine.** Hard ridin', shootin' and fisticuffin' Western, with *Rory Calhoun* as Utah, so known because he and his guns brought law and order to that state.. Rest of cast: *Susan Cummings, Angela Stevens, Max Baer, Paul Langton, Ray Teal, George Keymas, Gene Roth, Norman Fredric, Ken Christy, Dennis Moore, Steve Darrell, Terry Frost, Jack Ingram.* Dir.: Fred F. Sears. Pro.: Sam Katzman. (Columbia.) Rel.: April 15.

V **Valerie.** Three stories about a single incident, the killing of *Anita Ekberg's* parents by husband *Sterling Hayden*...as padre *Anthony Steel* tells it and as Hayden and wounded wife Anita tell it. Rest of cast: *Peter Walker, John Wengraf, Iphigenie Castiglioni, Jerry Barclay, Robert Adler, Tom McKee, Gage Clarke, Sydney Smith, Norman Leavitt, Juney Ellis, Malcolm Atterbury, Stanley Adams, Brian O'Hara.* Dir.: Gerd Oswald. Pro.: Hal R. Makelim. (U.A.) Rel.: June 10.

**The Village.** Moving film based on the work of the Pestalozzi Children's Village in Switzerland. About an orphan D.P. girl and her affection for a Polish boy; coupled with the love story of an English teacher (*John Justin*) and his Polish colleague (*Eva Dahlbeck*). Rest of cast: *Sigfrit Steiner, Mary Hinton, M. Woyetcki, Guido Lorraine, Maurice Regamey, Rolando Catalano, Krystina Bragiel, Voytek Dolinsky, Trevor Hill.* Dir.: Leopold Lindtberg. Pro.: Lazer Wechsler and Kenneth L. Maidment. (Assoc.). Rel.: August 20.

**Viva Las Vegas!** Routine little musical set in the gambling city of the title, with cheerful gambler *Dan Dailey* and lovely dancer *Cyd Charisse* finding that they make sweet music (the chink of won money) together! Rest of cast: *Agnes Moorehead, Lili Darvas, Jim Backus, Oscar Karlweis, Liliane Montevecchi, Cara Williams, George Kerris, Betty Lynn, The Slate Brothers, Pete Rugolo, John Brascia, John Harding, Benny Rubin, Jack Daly, Henny Backus,* Guest Stars: *Jerry Colonna, Paul Henreid, Lena Horne, Frankie Laine, Mitsuko Sawamura.* Dir.: Roy Rowland. Pro.: Joe Pasternak. (M-G-M). Rel.: September 17. (C. & E.)

W **Walk the Proud Land.** Western. The story, based on fact, about the way that Indian Agent J. P. Clum in 1874 fought, eventually successfully, for a new and less militaristic approach to the Apache problem and how that approach paid off. Cast: *Audie Murphy, Anne Bancroft, Pat Crowley, Charles Drake, Tommy Rall, Jay Silverheels, Robert Warwick, Victor Millan, Eugene Mazzola, Anthony Caruso, Morris Ankrum, Addison Richards, Ainslie Pryor.* Dir.: Jesse Hibbs. Pro.: Aaron Rosenberg. (U.I.). Rel.: September 3. (C. & T.)

**Way to the Gold.** Rather strange mixture of comedy, crime and romance in a story about an ex-convict searching for the ill-gotten gold buried by his cell-mate. Cast: *Jeffrey Hunter, Sheree North, Barry Sullivan, Walter Brennan, Neville Brand, Jacques Aubuchon, Ruth Donnelly, Tom Pittman, Philip Ahn, Geraido Mandia, Ted Edwards, Alan Jeffrey.* Dir.: R. D. Webb. Pro.: David Weisbart. (Fox). Rel.: June 24.

**The Weapon.** The story of a young boy who finds a gun, discharges it in a struggle with his friends and thinking he is a killer runs off, pursued by Scotland Yard, the U.S. Army, his mother and a real killer. Cast: *Steve Cochran, Lizbeth Scott, George Cole, Herbert Marshall, Nicole Maurey, Jon Whiteley, Stanley Maxted, Laurence Naismith, John Horsley, Denis Shaw, Fred Johnson, Basil Dignam, Arthur Lovegrove, Felix Felton, Joan Schofield, Myrtle Reed, Roland Brand, Ryck Ryden, Vivian Matalon, Peter Augustine, George Bradford, Peter Godsell, Fraser Hines, Joe Aston and Rene, Richard Goolden.* Dir.: Val Guest. Pro.: Frank Bevis. (Eros). Rel.: October 15.

**Wedding Breakfast.** *Ernest Borgnine* as a Bronx cab-driver who has been saving all his life to buy his own hack, and *Bette Davis* as his wife who wants to blow the money on a big white wedding for daughter *Debbie Reynolds.* A portrait of a family, life's down-to-earth problems, and beautifully underplayed sentiment. Moving, sometimes amusing. Rest of cast: *Barry Fitzgerald, Rod Taylor, Robert Simon, Madge Kennedy, Dorothy Stickney, Carol Veazie, Joan Camden, Ray Stricklyn, Jay Adler, Dan Tobin, Paul Denton, Augusta Merighi.* Dir.: Richard Brooks. Pro.: Sam Zimbalist. (M-G-M). Rel.: August 20. (M.)

**The Werewolf.** Poor *Steven Ritch,* experimented upon by unscrupulous scientists, becomes the creature of the title. Rest of cast: *Don Megowan, Joyce Holden, Kim Charney, Eleanore Tanin, Harry Lauter, Larry J. Blake, Ken Christy, James Gavin, S. John Launer, George M. Lynn, George Cisar, Don C. Harvey, Ford Stevens, Marjorie Stapp, Jean Charney, Jean Harvey.* Dir.: Fred F. Sears.: Pro.: Sam Katzman. (Columbia) Rel.: Aug. 13.

**Whistling Hills.** *Johnny Mack Brown* solves the series of stage robberies that are marked by the appearance of a weird rider and the sound of a silver whistle. Rest of cast: *Jimmy Ellison, Noel Neill, Lee Roberts, Stan Jolley, Marshall Reed, Lane Bradford, Pamela Duncan, Bud Osborne.* Dir. Derwin Abrahams. Pro.: Vincent M. Fennelly: (A.A.-Assoc.) Rel.: Oct. 1.

**Wings of Eagles.** Typical John Ford film mixing sentiment and slapstick humour in the story of an American pioneer aviator who overcame paralysis. Cast: *John Wayne, Dan Dailey, Maureen O'Hara, Ward Bond, Ken Curtis, Edmund Lowe, Kenneth Tobey, James Todd, Barry Kelley, Sig Ruman, Henry O'Neill, Willis Bouchey, Dorothy Jordan, Peter Oritz, Louis Jean Heydt, Tige Andrews, Dan Borzage, William Tracy, Harlan Warde, Jack Pennick, Bill Henry, Alberto Morin, Mimi Gibson, Evelyn Rudie, Charles Trowbridge, Mae Marsh.* Dir.: John Ford. Pro.: Chas. Schnee. (M-G-M). Rel.: May 27. (M.).

**Wiretapper.** *Bill Williams* in the true story about the way a race-track crook became a gangster, double-crossed his boss and then found salvation when he heard Billy Graham. Rest of cast: *Georgia Lee, Douglas Kennedy, Phil Tead, Stanley Clements, Ric Roman, Richard Benedict, Paul Picerni, Steve Conte, Melinda Plowman, Art Gilmore, Howard Wendell, Dorothy Kennedy, Barbara Hudson, Evangeline Carmichael.* Dir.: Dick Ross. Pro.: Rodney Nelson. (            ) Rel.: January 28.

**Women Without Men.** *Beverly Michaels,* rather unfairly mixed up in an assault case (defending her honour) gets a prison sentence and breaks out of jail to keep a Christmas Eve tryst with her lover, who also breaks out (of hospital) to get there on time. Rest of cast: *Joan Rice, Thora Hird, Paul Carpenter, Avril Angers, Ralph Michael, April Olrich, Sheila Burrell, John Welsh, Valerie White, Maurice Kaufmann, David Lodge, Eugene Deckers, Gordon Jackson, Hermione Baddeley, Olwen Brookes, Betty Cooper, Doris Gilmore, Fanny Carby, Yvonne Manners, Peter Welsh, Oscar Nation, Katherine Feliaz, Michael Golden, Anthony Miles, Mark Kingston, Verne Morgan, Chas. Saynor, Bill Shine, Muriel Young.* Dir.: Elmo Williams. Pro.: Anthony Hinds. (Ex.) Rel.: Sept. 24.

**John Wayne in THE WINGS OF EAGLES—M-G-M.**

**World Without End.** About a group of space-ship scientists who smash through the "time barrier" and re-land on earth in the year of after-atomic destruction, 2508! Cast: *Hugh Marlowe, Nancy Gates, Nelson Leigh, Rod Taylor, Shawn Smith, Lisa Montell, Christopher Dark, Booth Colman, Everett Glass, Stanley Fraser.* Dir.: Edward Bernds. Pro.: Richard Heermance. (A.A.-Assoc.) Rel.: July 30.

**Written on the Wind.** The tangled lives and loves of an oil-rich family. Cast: *Rock Hudson, Lauren Bacall, Robert Stack, Dorothy Malone, Robert Keith, Grant Williams, Harry Shannon.* Dir.: Douglas Sirk. Pro.: Albert Zugsmith. (U.I.) Rel.: Oct. 29. (T.)

**The Wrong Man.** Hitchcock film, of less suspense than usual, based on the true story of a New York musician erroneously arrested, bailed and finally released after an abortive trial on a charge of armed robbery. Cast: *Henry Fonda, Vera Miles, Anthony Quayle, Harold J. Stone, Charles Cooper, John Heldabrand, Esther Minciotti, Doreen Lang, Laurinda Barrett, Norma Connolly, Nehemiah Persoff, Lola D'Annunzio, Kippy Campbell, Robert Essen, Richard Robbins, Dayton Lummis, Francis Reid, Peggy Webber.* Dir.: Alfred Hitchcock. Pro.: Herbert Coleman. (Warner.) Rel.: March 10.

X **X The Unknown.** A mysterious explosion on a lonely Scots moor, the bottomless, horror-filled chasm it leaves behind—the earth once more in danger from the horrors of space. Cast: *Dean Jagger, Edward Chapman, Leo McKern, William Lucas, John Harvey, Peter Hammond, Michael Ripper, Anthony Newley, Ian MacNaughton, Kenneth Cope, Edwin Richfield, Jameson Clark, Jane Aird, Fraser Hines, Michael Brook, Neil Hallet, Norman Macowan, Marianne Brauns.* Dir.: Leslie Norman. Pro.: Anthony Hinds. (Hammer) Rel.: Nov. 4.

Y **Yield to the Night.** The last few weeks in the life of a condemned murderess, related with cool, documentary thoroughness and without any hysterical undertones or false pity; and related by some excellent direction and fine performances, not the least being that of *Diana Dors* as the girl who has killed and can't feel sorry for her crime. A first-class British film. Rest of cast: *Yvonne Mitchell, Michael Craig, Marie Ney, Geoffrey Keen, Liam Redmond, Olga Lindo, Joan Miller, Marjorie Rhodes, Molly Urquhart, Mary Mackenzie, Harry Locke, Michael Ripper, Joyce Blair, Charles Clay, Athene Seyler, Peggy Livesey, Mona Washbourne, Alex Finter, Marianne Stone, Mercia Shaw, Charles Lloyd Pack, Dandy Nichols, John Charlesworth, Frank Hawkins.* Dir.: J. Lee Thompson. Pro.: Kenneth Harper. (Assoc.) Rel.: Sept. 9.

**You Can't Run Away From It.** Light-hearted musical about a father who, to save his daughter from being rushed into marriage by a man after her money, arranges that she shall be kidnapped. Cast: *June Allyson, Jack Lemmon, Charles Bickford, Paul Gilbert, Jim Backus, Stubby Kaye, Henny Youngman, Allyn Joslyn, Jacques Scott, Walter Baldwin, Byron Foulger, Richard Cutting, Howard McNear, Elvia Allman, Louise Beavers, Raymond Greenleaf, Edwin Chandler, Jack Albertson, Queenie Smith, William Forrest, Frank Sully, Dub Taylor, Steve Benton, Bill Walker, Herb Vigran, Larry Blake.* Dir. & Pro.: Dick Powell. (Columbia) Rel.: Nov. 5. (C. & T.)

**You Pay Your Money.** Private Eye *Hugh McDermot* involved in the case of the books which could lead to Holy War. Rest of cast: *Jane Hylton, Honor Blackman, Hugh Moxey, Ivan Samson, Ferdy Mayne, Shirley Deane, Gerard Heinz, Peter Swanwick, Basil Dignam, Fred Griffiths, Ben Williams, Elsie Wagstaff, Vincent Holman, Mark Daly.* Dir.: Maclean Rogers. Pro.: W. G. Chalmers. (Butchers.) Rel.: April 29.

**The Young Stranger.** Sincere and thoughtfu story about the relationship between parents and children and how easily it can be strengthened or lost. Cast: *James MacArthur, Kim Hunter, James Daly, James Gregory, Whit Bissell, Jeff Silver, Jack Mullaney, Eddie Ryder, Jean Corbett, Charles Davis, Marian Seldes, Terry Kelman, Edith Evanson, Tom Pittman, Howard Price.* Dir.: John Frankenheimer. Pro.: Stuart Miller. (R.K.O.). Rel.: June 24.

Z **Zanzabuku.** The documentary story of Lewis Cotlow's expedition into the darkest Congo jungles; the people, fauna and backgrounds of the Uganda plains, the Kilimanjaro slopes and Tanganyika highlands. Pro.: Lewis Cotlow. (Republic.) Rel.: Oct. 8. (T.)

**Zarak.** Highly coloured story of the North-West Frontier of the Kipling period, with *Victor Mature* as a bold, bad bandit, *Michael Wilding* as the pukka sahib who pursues him and *Anita Ekberg* the curvaceous cutie who is Mature's father's slave and the cause of all the trouble. Rest of cast: *Bonar Colleano, Finlay Currie, Bernard Miles, Eunice Gayson, Peter Illing, Eddie Byrne, Frederick Valk, Eric Pohlmann, Andre Morell, Geoffrey Keen, Harold Goodwin, Alec Mango, Patrick McGoohan, Oscar Quitak, George Margo, Arnold Marle, Yana.* Dir.: Terence Young. Pro.: Phil C. Samuel. (Warwick-Columbia.) Rel.: February 11.

# AWARDS

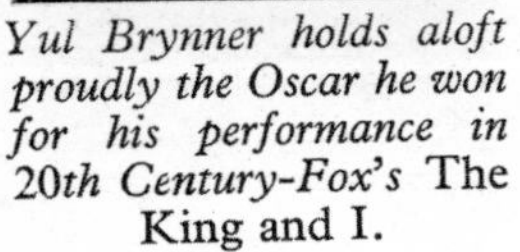

*Yul Brynner holds aloft proudly the Oscar he won for his performance in 20th Century-Fox's* The King and I.

*Ingrid Bergman smiles happily the morning after being announced as this year's Oscar winner for her performance in Fox's* Anastasia.

In March last the *American Academy of Motion Picture Arts and Sciences* announced the following annual awards, the now famous "Oscars":—

**BEST MOTION PICTURE:** "Around the World in 80 Days," Michael Todd Co., United Artists; Michael Todd, Producer. **BEST PERFORMANCE BY AN ACTOR:** Yul Brynner in "The King and I," 20th Century-Fox. **BEST PERFORMANCE BY AN ACTRESS:** Ingrid Bergman in "Anastasia," 20th Century-Fox. **BEST ACHIEVEMENT IN DIRECTING:** George Stevens, for "Giant," Giant Production, Warner Brothers. **BEST PERFORMANCE BY A SUPPORTING ACTOR:** Anthony Quinn in "Lust for Life," M-G-M. **BEST PERFORMANCE BY A SUPPORTING ACTRESS:** Dorothy Malone in "Written on the Wind," Universal-International. **BEST ACHIEVEMENTS IN WRITING: MOTION PICTURE STORY:** Robert Rich, for "The Brave One," King Brothers, RKO Radio. **SCREENPLAY:** James Poe, John Farrow and S. J. Perelman, for "Around the World in 80 Days," Michael Todd Co., United Artists. **STORY AND SCREENPLAY:** Albert Lamorisse, for "The Red Balloon," Films Montsouris, Lopert Films Distributing Corp. (French). **BEST CINEMATOGRAPHY, BLACK-AND-WHITE FILM:** Joseph Ruttenberg, for "Somebody Up There Likes Me," M-G-M. **BEST CINEMATOGRAPHY, COLOUR FILM:** Lionel Lindon, for "Around the World in 80 Days," Michael Todd Co., United Artists. **BEST ART DIRECTION, BLACK-AND-WHITE FILM:** Cedric Gibbons and Malcolm F. Brown, for "Somebody Up There Likes Me," M-G-M. **BEST ART DIRECTION, COLOUR FILM:** Lyle R. Wheeler and John De Cuir, for "The King and I," 20th Century-Fox. **OUTSTANDING ACHIEVEMENT IN MUSIC, BEST SCORING OF A MUSICAL:** Alfred Newman and Ken Darby for "The King and I," 20th Century-Fox. **ACHIEVEMENT IN DOCUMENTARY PRODUCTION, SHORT SUBJECTS:** "The True Story of the Civil War," Camera Eye Pictures; Louis Clyde Stoumen, Producer. **FEATURES:** "The Silent World," Filmad-F.S.J.Y.C.—Columbia. **BEST SOUND RECORDING:** "The King and I," 20th Century-Fox Studio Sound Department; Carl Faulkner, Sound Director. **BEST SPECIAL EFFECTS:** "The Ten Commandments," Motion Picture Associates, Paramount, John P. Fulton. **BEST SHORT SUBJECTS, CARTOONS** (1,000 feet or less): "Mister Magoo's Puddle Jumper," U.P.A., Columbia; Stephen Bosustow, Producer. **ONE-REEL:** "Crashing the Water Barrier," Warner Brothers; Konstantin Kalser, Producer. **TWO-REEL:** "The Bespoke Overcoat," Romulus, George K. Arthur. Producer. **BEST FOREIGN LANGUAGE FILM:** Italy's "La Strada."

## THE BRITISH FILM ACADEMY

During the previous month (February) the *British Academy* had announced its own awards as follows:—

**BEST FILM FROM ANY SOURCE, BRITISH OR FOREIGN:** "Gervaise" (France). **BEST BRITISH FILM:** "Reach for the Sky." **UNITED NATIONS AWARD** for the best film illustrating one or more of the principles of the United Nations Charter: "Race for Life" (France). **BEST DOCUMENTARY FILM:** "On the Bowery" (U.S.A.). **SPECIAL AWARD** for work lying outside the feature and documentary fields: "The Red Balloon" (France). **BEST ANIMATED FILM:** "Gerald McBoing Boing on Planet Moo" (U.S.A.). **BEST BRITISH SCREENPLAY:** "The Man Who Never Was," Nigel Balchin. **BEST PERFORMANCE BY A BRITISH ACTOR:** Peter Finch in "A Town Like Alice." **BEST PERFORMANCE BY A BRITISH ACTRESS:** Virginia McKenna in "A Town Like Alice." **BEST PERFORMANCE BY A FOREIGN ACTOR:** Francois Perier in "Gervaise." **BEST PERFORMANCE BY A FOREIGN ACTRESS:** Anna Magnani in "The Rose Tattoo." **MOST PROMISING NEWCOMER TO FILMS:** Eli Wallach in "Baby Doll."

Previous to both these polls, in which the films and performances are voted for from the artistic viewpoint, came the always interesting results of the American trade paper "Motion Picture Herald's" annual poll. Here the voting, by cinema managers and cinema owners, is from the purely commercial angle: being for those stars who in their opinion and experience attracted most money into the box-office during the year under review. The American choice was as follows:—

(1) **William Holden**
(2) **John Wayne**
(3) **James Stewart**
(4) **Burt Lancaster**
(5) **Glenn Ford**
(6) **Martin & Lewis**
(7) **Gary Cooper**
(8) **Marilyn Monroe**
(9) **Kim Novak**
(10) **Frank Sinatra**

The British exhibitors and owners have their own "M.P.H." poll, which this year resulted in the following results:—

**BRITISH STARS** who have appeared in films made in Britain:—

(1) **Kenneth More**
(2) **Jack Hawkins**
(3) **Dirk Bogarde**
(4) **Virginia McKenna**
(5) **Norman Wisdom**
(6) **Anthony Steel**
(7) **Peter Finch**
(8) **Alec Guinness**
(9) **John Gregson**
(10) **John Mills**

**INTERNATIONAL STARS** who have appeared in any films:—

(1) **Kenneth More**
(2) **James Stewart**
(3) **Burt Lancaster**
(4) **Audie Murphy**
(5) **Jeff Chandler**
(6) **Doris Day**
(7) **Danny Kaye**
(8) **Martin & Lewis**
(9) **Frank Sinatra**
(10) **Robert Mitchum**

**WESTERN STARS:—**

(1) **James Stewart**
(2) **John Wayne**
(3) **Audie Murphy**
(4) **Jeff Chandler**
(5) **Kirk Douglas**
(6) **Randolph Scott**
(7) **Robert Mitchum**
(8) **Joel McCrea**
(9) **Frank Sinatra**
(10) **Glenn Ford**

In America, according to the "M.P.H.," the following films made the most money—and were therefore commercially the most successful—of all those presented during the past year:—

**The Bad Seed, Bus Stop, Carousel, The Conqueror, The Eddy Duchin Story, Giant, Guys and Dolls, High Society, The King and I, I'll Cry Tomorrow, The Man in the Grey Flannel Suit, The Man Who Knew Too Much, The Man With the Golden Arm, Moby Dick, Picnic, Rebel Without a Cause, The Rose Tattoo, The Searchers, To Catch a Thief, Trapeze,** and **War and Peace**—a pretty significant list.

Here in Britain the same source indicated that within the same period the top four money-makers were **Reach for the Sky, Private's Progress, A Town Like Alice** and **Trapeze**, in that order, with **The Baby and the Battleship, The Bad Seed, Cockleshell Heroes, It's Great To Be Young, Sailor Beware** and **The Searchers** all coming closely along behind. And though it had no major circuit booking, Fox's **The King and I** was among the year's best.

(*Above*) : Frankenstein Junior. PETER CUSHING played Baron Victor Franken-
ein, son of the wicked old Baron F., in *Warners'* British-made THE CURSE
F FRANKENSTEIN, a real chiller-thriller which accentuated all the horrors
by presenting them in full gorycolour !

(*Below*) : The age-and-youth team of FRED ASTAIRE and AUDREY HEPBURN proved a great success in *Paramount's* FUNNY FACE, a quite outstanding musical including some daring and fascinating experiments in colour.

(*Left*) : JEFF CHANDLER gave one of his best performances in the *United Artists* film DRANGO, as a military governor from the Northern Army who at the end of the American Civil War takes charge of a war-ravaged Southern town and by his integrity gradually wins over most of the, at first, greatly resentful inhabitants.

(*Below*) : SHEREE NORTH and JEFFREY HUNTER in *Fox's* THE WAY TO THE GOLD.

(*Above*) : Fear : JACK HAWKINS played a new-boy fire assessor who meets an old girl-friend and through her becomes involved in a murder and some pretty desperate adventures in *Columbia's* British production FORTUNE IS A WOMAN.

Little Tim Hovey shocks grown-ups JOHN FORSYTHE, MAUREEN O'HARA and FRANK FAYLEN in this scene from the *Universal-International* comedy EVERYTHING BUT THE TRUTH.

A romantic moment for co-stars TONY CURTIS and MARTHA HYER in *Universal-International's* MISTER CORY, a drama about a gambler who crashes his way into high society.

A

One of the many spectacular scenes from the *Warwick-Columbia* film ZARAK, an unabashed melodrama of love, hate and battle along India's turbulent North West frontiers in the 19th century. ANITA EKBERG *inset A* as the seductive dancer loved by both outlaw ZARAK (VICTOR MATURE *inset B*) and MICHAEL WILDING.

B

A tense moment for British racing driver ANTHONY STEEL as his passenger, a crook (STANLEY BAKER) using the race to get across the border and away from a murder charge, points a pistol and suggests they get a move-on, to the consternation of Steel's girl friend ODILE VERSOIS. A scene from the *J. Arthur Rank* motor-racing thriller CHECKPOINT.

'oneymooner JUNE THORBURN looks quizzically :ross at husband JOHN GREGSON to see if he els the same rather damp, depressed way about iings as she does, in this scene from the *J. rthur Rank* maritime comedy TRUE AS A 'URTLE. But skipper CECIL PARKER is bviously enjoying every minute of it.

THE SECRET PLACE was a most effective British crime melodrama about the planning, carrying through and sorry aftermath of a robbery ; seen against an authentic East End background. Here crook RONALD LEWIS persuades a girl friend BELINDA LEE to help him, while DAVID MCCALLUM and STEPHEN GWYNN look on.

OHN MILLS as Mike Halloran, a tough Scotland Yard detective ho becomes a little less tough when he tells BARBARA BATES iat he loves her. A scene from the excellent British whodunnit TOWN ON TRIAL.

Two well known stage comics, TED RAY and ROBERTSON HARE were in the cast of the *Associated British* comedy MY WIFE'S FAMILY, which also starred RONALD SHINER and GRETA GYNT.

Debonair DAVID NIVEN, whose more recent films have included THE SILKEN AFFAIR for *Associated British* and the Todd AO film ROUND THE WORLD IN EIGHTY DAYS.

# THE *Foreign* FILM

TO say that more of the ordinary, average moviegoers have been watching foreign language films this year than ever before is a pretty safe statement to make. For the first time since the talkies began nine foreign films (admittedly eight were French) have had major general releases through one or other of our largest circuits, while a number of others had quite a wide release at specially selected localities through the same circuits.

This should make me happy, for I have always fervently believed in a truly international cinema. But there is, I am afraid, to fall back on an old adage, a fly in the ointment! All the films were very easy to appreciate: the thrillers *Every Second Counts* and *Gas Oil*, the musicals *Mam'selle Pigalle* and *Folies Bergere* and the Fernandel comedy *The Dressmaker*. Only *The Red Balloon*, Albert Lamorisse's exquisite poem in celluloid, was to a greater extent more truly nationally French in character.

The trouble about this increasing popularity here of foreign films is, as I see it, that a trend has begun to develop by which the Italian and, more especially, French producers, anxious to reap the larger rewards that wider international releases can bring them, are shying away from truly national style, story and treatment in favour of the sort of thing which can be done better in, say, America. I may, of course, be unduly pessimistic about this, but I can't help feeling that France is at present sending us less truly *French* films (by which I mean wonderful movies like *La Traversee de Paris—Pig Across Paris*—and *Gervaise*) and more films of wider, more popular appeal, like *Mam'selle Pigalle* and *Folies Bergere*.

In any case France has continued the domination of our foreign language cinemas which has existed for many years. Well over half our imported films came across the Channel, with Italy—as usual—a pretty good second. After that,

*(Above) One of the most completely delightful French films of the year was Albert Lamorisse's exquisite 30-minute poem in celluloid* The Red Balloon, *which related the adventures of a small boy and a large red balloon against a background of blue-grey Montmartre. The boy was played by M. Lamorisse's small son. This film deservedly won the 1956 Golden Palm at Cannes and the Gold Medal Grand Prix of the French Cinema for that year. And over here it won a circuit general release.*

*(Below) Another outstanding French film was Rene Clement's* Gervaise *which, adapted from Zola's novel, " L'Assommoir ", told the story of a young girl's struggles against her environment, the Paris slums of 1860. Maria Schell (seen in the background) gave a beautiful performance in the title role. Also in this scene, (r. to l.) the lodger, the daughter and the husband : Armand Mestral, Patrice Catineaud and Francois Perier.*

*Right) Of vintage French quality was Claude Autant-Lara's* La Traversee de Paris *(Pig Across Paris), an ironic comedy about the German Occupation that had serious and even bitter undertones. Jean Gabin and Bourvil, as artist and black marketeer runner, were superb in this story of the hilarious efforts to smuggle the parts of a " black " pig across Paris from killer to seller during the blackout.*

Seeing her portrait in a German film magazine, director Henry Koster was so impressed that he asked Fraulein ELISABETH MUELLER to take a trip to Hollywood. Already a veteran of some thirty films in her native land, Miss Mueller said " Yes " and the result was her part in *M-G-M's* THE POWER AND THE PRIZE.

Californian GEORGE NADER is now one of *Universal-International's* brightest male stars. Spanish speaking, much-travelled, six-foot-odd Nader's more recent films have included JOE BUTTERFLY and FOUR GIRLS IN TOWN.

There are now many nations with quite large film industries of whose product we see nothing at all. Yet surely *some* of this product must be worth seeing?

My ideal, of course, would be a small cinema showing a succession of films from all over the world, changing them at weekly intervals. How one could overcome the enormous —and costly—problem of sub-titling such a succession of movies I don't know, but I feel sure a way around this snag could be found if we all thought hard enough.

I've left myself very little space in which to discuss the actual films. However, you'll find my comments about many of them in the captions to the pictures in this feature, also in the thumbnail critiques on a later page.

Actually it wouldn't be difficult to choose the best of the foreign films within the period we are considering. I regard Albert Lamorisse's *The Red Balloon* as a masterpiece of the cinema; imaginative, poetical, technically outstanding and completely artistic from conception to cutting. After that comes Rene Clement's *Gervaise*, which had a wonderful sense of period and a great deal of the character of the original Zola story upon which it was based. And third I'd be inclined to place another French film, Autant-Lara's

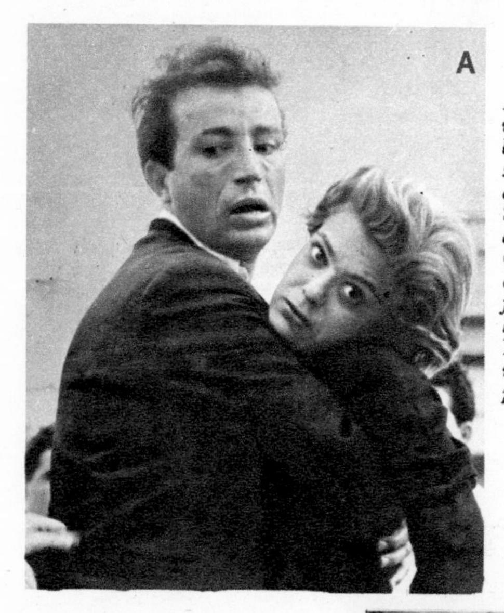

A

*Both the Greek films shown here were interesting for their unusual backgrounds, their simplicity of style and the outstanding performances of their feminine stars. In* Stella (A) *Melina Mercouri (seen dying in the arms of her lover, Georges Foundas), as the girl who cannot resist men, was memorable for the sheer force and poetry of her performance. And in* Girl In Black (B) *it was Ellei Lambetti who showed equally remarkable power in her performance.*

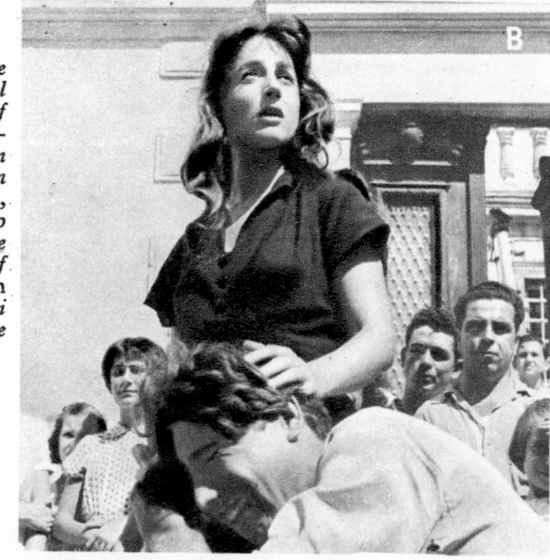

B

(*Left*) *Typical Martine Carol pose in the lavish historical film* Mistress du Barry, *in which she played the famous lady of French history.*

(*Below*) *Typical of the more sexy kind of French film import was* Desired (*La Foire aux Femmes*) *which presented Etchika Choureau as the virginal heroine who is seduced by the man who saves her from forcible seduction at the hands of another, while he himself is desired physically and frantically both by his female boss (seen here looking askance at the scene of love) and a charming lady visitor from Paris.*

(*Above*) *An unusual, German, film was* Is Anna Anderson Anastasia? *which dealt in careful documented fashion with the actual claim of a living woman to be the only survivor of the* 1918 *massacre of the last of the Russian Tsars and his family. Lilli Palmer gave a moving performance in the title role.*

In *Fox's* THE GIRL CAN'T HELP IT glamorous JAYNE MANSFIELD proved herself a real screen discovery. In this gay, witty little comedy with rock-'n-roll trimmings she showed she had a fine sense of comedy.

*La Traversee de Paris*, which, of vintage quality, reminded one of the best movies that France made before the war. This story of the efforts of two oddly assorted characters (played beautifully by Jean Gabin and, more especially, Bourvil) to smuggle a slaughtered pig across Occupied Paris during the blackout had a great deal of rather macabre humour and also more serious, even bitter undertones.

Of all the Italian films, *Il Bidone*, *The Swindlers*, with its Italo-American cast (stars included Broderick Crawford and Richard Basehart) stood out. It was directed by Frederico Fellini, who has previously impressed.

Among the other French films we saw were several good, simple comedies like those starring Fernandel, the highly immoral but highly diverting *Lock Up the Spoons*, the usual quota of sex films like . . . *And Woman Was Created* (which was little more than a detailed tour by hubby Roger Vadim of wife Brigitte Bardot's many, curvaceous and often uncovered charms) and *Desired*, and a whole series of violent, very tough, death-filled gangster pieces including *Chnouf* and *Touchez Pas au Grisbi*. After this one could even turn with relief to the sad results of lust as revealed in Marcel Carne's careful picturisation of the Zola story *Therese Raquin* !

Most of the Italian films were gay. *Scandal in Sorrento* with Sophia Loren and de Sica was highly diverting, as was *The Bigamist*, again with de Sica.

But of all these films one that still stands out in my memory is one that wasn't new at all. Made way back in 1937, it was shown here for the first time this year : Marcel Pagnol's *Harvest*. A story of the loneliest regions of sun-drenched Provence, it had everything (including the cinematic faults) that one might expect from Pagnol and, in addition, it had a more subdued, more serious (and some thought more brilliant) Fernandel in the cast.

*(Right) The year has also been a most successful one for glamorous Italian star Sophia Loren, who is now making films in America as well as her native country. At least part of the reason for this success was her gay and charming performance in* Scandal in Sorrento*—a continuation of the " Bread, Love and Dreams " series of films—in which she co-starred with Vittorio de Sica and (in the background) Antonio Cifariello.*

*(Above) Curd Jergens and Jean Servais in Yves Ciampi's steamy story of crime in a small, run-down African republic,* The Heroes are Tired.

*(Below) Marina Vlady played the girl who had her own ideas of revenging the death of her lover at the hands of two escaped criminals in Robert Rossein's oddly poetical yet violent and uneven* The Wicked Go To Hell.

*(Below) The Japanese town of Nagasaki, which will always be associated with the evils of the atom bomb, formed the rather novel background of Yves Ciampi's* Typhoon Over Nagasaki. *Actually a triangle story, it was of the struggle for the affections of engineer Jean Marais between Japanese mistress Keiko Kishi and his former girl-friend Danielle Darrieux, who after a long interval arrives from France ready to carry on where they had left off.*

*(Left) Wickedly comic, terribly immoral and wonderfully amusing was Carlo Rim's* Lock Up the Spoons, *the story of a 103-year-old rascal whose end is enlivened by a series of stories told by his crooked friends. Here is the old man (Yves Robert) talking with two of them : Eddie Constantine and Noel-Noel.*

Scots-born, British star DEBORAH KERR has in the past few years, since her first film MAJOR BARBARA in 1940, established herself as one of the leading screen actresses in Hollywood. Her more recent pictures have included FROM HERE TO ETERNITY (for *Columbia*), THE KING AND I (for *Fox*), and TEA AND SYMPATHY (for *M-G-M*).

# THE FOREIGN FILM

**Details of those foreign language movies first shown here during the year.**

**. . . And Woman Was Created.** A cinematic "poem" by director Roger Vadim in visual praise of wife *Brigitte Bardot's* provocative contours. She plays an 18-year-old orphan in St. Tropez who works at the bookstall and, taking three lovers, sends the rest of the local males mad with desire. Rest of cast: *Curd Jurgens, Christian Marquand, Georges Poujouly, Jean Louis Trintignant, Jane Marken, Mary Glory, Jacques Siron, Isabelle Corey, Jean Lefebvre, Philippe Grenier.* Dir.: Roger Vadim. Pro.: Raoul Levy. (Ucil-Cocinor-Miracle.) First shown at the Cameo-Royal in March, 1957. Gen. Rel.: June 17, 1957.

**The Aristocrats.** *Pierre Fresnay* as the dignified but out-of-touch head of a provincial aristocratic family who has to suffer the loss of his son before he realises the truth. Rest of cast: *Brigitte Auber, Jacques Dacqmine, Georges Descrieres, Alain Quercy, Francois Guerin.* Dir.: Denys de la Patelliere. (Curzon). First shown at the Curzon in June, 1957.

**Attila the Hun.** Italian—English-dubbed—historical drama based on the story of the so-called Scourge of God, who left a bloodstained trail through the then known world but was turned back miraculously at the gates of Rome. Cast: *Anthony Quinn, Sophia Loren, Henri Vidal, Irene Papas, Ettore Manni, Claude Laydu, Colette Regis, George Brehat.* Dir.: Pietro Francisci. (Lux-Archway.) First shown at the Queen's, Bayswater, in February, 1957.

**The Bigamist.** Noisy, laughable Italian satirical comedy highlighted by *Vittorio de Sica's* performance as a great but forgetful lawyer who likes his clients to plead guilty—even when innocent—in order that he can fully develop his performance in court! Rest of cast: *Marcello Mastroianni, Franca Valeri, Giovanna Ralli, Marisa Merlini, Ave Ninchi, Memmo Carotenuto, Guglielmo Inglese.* Dir.: Luciano Emmer. (Curzon.) First shown at the Curzon in October, 1956.

**Casanova.** Gay, fast-moving adventures of the great lover; with wit, wonderful stamina and a great sense of humour he races from bed to bed and from arms to arms. Cast: *Gabriele Ferzetti, Corinne Calvet, Irene Galter, Nadia Gray, Mara Lane, Marina Vlady.* Dir.: Steno. (Gala.) First shown at the Cinephone in April, 1957.

**Chnouf.** French gangster film. A rough, tough and brutal exposure of the drug traffic, with an explosive, deadly climax. Cast: *Jean Gabin, Lino Ventura, Albert Remy, Marcel Dalio, Pierre Louis, Alain Nobis, Armontel, Michel Jourdan, Francois Patrice, Magali Noel, Lila Kedrova, Jacqueline Porel, Francoise Spira.* Dir.: Henri Decoin. Pro.: Paul Temps. (Gala.) First shown at the Cinephone in December, 1956.

**Cut-Throat.** French crime melodrama set against a background of the seaport of Marseilles. Cast: *Jean Servais, Madeleine Robinson, Jean Chevrier, Yves Denlaud, Michele Cordue, Claude Bertrand, Brainville, Micheline Gary, Henri San Juan, Janine Caire, Chambois.* First shown at the Paris-Pullman, Kensington, in April, 1957. (C. & E.)

**Death of a Cyclist.** A Spanish film which starts with a road accident in which a car runs down and kills a cyclist and then shows the evil effects this has on the lives of several people. Cast: *Lucia Bose, Alberro Closas, Otello Toso, Carlos Casaravilla.* Dir.: Juan A. Bardem. (Suevia-Mondial.) First shown at the Academy Cinema in June, 1956.

**Desired—La Foire aux Femmes.** A story of high-pressure passion, with lovely little *Etchika Choureau* dodging rape only to be seduced by her deliverer, who is desired in turn by his woman boss and a girl visitor from Paris. Rest of cast: *Dora Doll, Elisa Lamothe, Jean Danet, Alfred Adam, Rene Clermont, Juliette Faber, Germaine Sablon, Marie Louise Godart, Christine Langier, Claudine Bleuse.* Dir.: Jean Stelli. (Astarte.) First shown at the Paris-Pullman in November, 1956. (E.)

**Don Camillo's Last Round.** *Fernandel* again as that remarkable priest tussling with his great rival, the Communist Mayor, *Gino Cervi*. Rest of cast: *Claude Silvain, Leda Gloria, Gaston Rey, Umberto Spadaro, Memmo Carotenuto, Marco Tulli, Saro Urzi, Carlo Duse.* Dir.: Carmine Gallone. (Films de France.) First shown at the Paris-Pullman in September, 1956.

**Every Second Counts—Les Assassins du Dimanche.** First-rate suspense story about a car with damaged steering gear and the efforts to contact the driver before it actually breaks and causes an accident. Cast: *Barbara Laage, Dominique Wilms, Jean-Marc Thibault, Paul Frankeur, Michel Andre, Suzanne Cramer, Joachim Moch, Solange Certain, Georges Poujouly, Jacques Moulieres, Rosy Varte, Alone.* Dir.: Alex Joffe. Pro.: G. de La Grandiere. (Filmonde-British Lion.) First shown at Gaumont in September, 1956. Gen. Rel.: Oct. 21, 1956.

**Fernandel Joins the Army.** Fernandel getting the last ounce of humour out of the old cinematic situation of the misadventures of the raw recruit. Dir.: Rene le Henaff. (Mondial.) Floating Release.

**Fernandel the Dressmaker.** France's No. 1 screen comic inherits a fashion house and with it has plenty of happy fun—as does his screen wife *Suzy Delair*, a delightful co-star. Rest of cast: *Francoise Fabian*, and a host of gorgeous mannequins. (Miracle.) First shown at the Cameo-Poly in October, 1956. Gen Rel: Jan 6, 1956.

**Folies Bergere.** Slim little romance story of French star *Zizi Jeanmaire* and G.I. *Eddie Constantine*, seen against a colourful and lavish background of the show of the title. Rest of cast: *Nadia Gray, Yves Robert, Pierre Mondy, Jacques Castelot, Edith Georges, Serge Perrault, Nadine Tallier, Jeff Davis, Jacques Morel, Robert Pizani.* Dir.: Henri Decoin. Pro.: Wladimir Roitfeld. (Roitfeld-Films de France.) First shown at the Cameo-Royal in January, 1956. Gen. Rel: May 13, 1957.

**Forbidden Women.** The story of a group of (modern) Roman prostitutes: how some are killed, some reform and others just carry on with the dreary round. Cast: *Linda Darnell, Valentina Cortese, Lea Padovani, Giulietta Masina, Lilla Brignone, Anthony Quinn, Roberto Risso.* Dir.: G. Amato. (Supra.) First shown at the Paris-Pullman in March, 1957.

**Friends for Life.—Amici per la Pelle.** Touching little film about the friendship of two schoolboys in Rome. Dir.: Franco Rossi. (Contemporary.) First shown at the Academy cinema in April, 1957.

**Gas Oil.** French comedy-thriller with *Jean Gabin* as the good-natured truck driver driven to infuriated action by a gang of Paris gangsters. Rest of cast: *Jeanne Moreau, Ginette Leclerc, Camille Guérini, Marcel Bozzufi, Henri Crémieux, Albert Dinan, Bob Ingarao, Roger Hanin, Jean-Marie Rivière, Robert Dalban, Jean Marin, Lisette Lebon, Simone Berthier, Germaine Michel, Gaby Basset, Jacques Ferrière, Albert Michel, Guy Henri, Marcel Perès.* Pro.: Gilles Grangier. (Rank.) Gen. Rel.: March 18.

**Gervaise.** Brilliant Rene Clement film based on the Zola story "L'Assommoir"; a realistic, moving picture of Paris low-life a hundred years ago. And a beautiful performance in the title role by *Maria Schell*. Rest of cast: *Francois Perier, Suzy Delair, Mathilde Casadessus, Armand Mestral, Jacques Harden, Ariane Lancell, Jacques Hilling, Jany Holt, Florelle, Rachel Devirys, Christian Denhez, Patrice Catineaud, Michele Caillaud.* Dir.: René Clement. Pro.: Jean Darvey. (Agnes-Delahaye-Miracle.) First shown at the Cameo-Poly in December, 1956.

**A Girl in Black.** Lovely, wonderfully photographed Greek film about a writer and his friend and the girl he falls in love with on a small island, and so becomes involved in local feuds and, nearly, grim tragedy. Lovely performance by *Ellie Lambetti* as the girl. Rest of cast: *Dimitri Horn, George Foundas, Eleni Zafiriou, Stefanos Stratigos, Notis Pergialis.* Dir.: Michael Cacoyannis. (Curzon.) First shown at the Curzon in November, 1956.

**Raf Vallone and Roland Lesaffre, who impressed so much with his performance as the blackmailer in Marcel Carne's THERESE RAQUIN, the adaptation to the screen of Zola's story of lust and its tragic consequences.**

**The Grasshopper—La Cigale.** Beautifully sensitive and fine Russian screen adaptation of the Chekov story about a woman who only realises the true worth of her doctor husband when he is dying from overwork, trying to keep pace with her extravagances. Cast: *L. Tselikovskaya, S. Bondarchuk, V. Druzhnikov, V. Teterin.* Dir.: S. Samsonov. (Mosfilm-Contemporary.)

**Harvest—Regain.** Delightful 1937 Marcel Pagnol film, set in his beloved Provence and telling the story of the way that a dying village in the mountains is brought to life again when the last man takes unto himself as wife the ill-used mistress of a wandering tinker. Cast: *Fernandel, Orane Demazis, Gabriel Gabrio, Marguerite Moreno, E. Delmont, Milly Mathis, Blavette, Le Vigan, Henry Poupon, Odette Roger.* Dir.: Marcel Pagnol. (Academy.) First shown at the Academy in Oct., 1956.

**The Heroes are Tired.** Fascinating, wonderfully atmospheric film about a small free African Negro State where the whites are crooks and hangers-on, and where *Yves Montand*, fleeing with his boss's smuggled diamonds, faces the man who is sent to settle the matter—or him—ex-Luftwaffe fighter ace *Curd Jurgens*. Rest of cast: *Maria Felix, Jean Servais, Elizabeth Manet, Gérard Oury, Gert Froebe, Manolo Montez, Jean Werner.* Dir.: Yves Ciampi. Pro.: Raymond Froment. (Cila-Terra-Films de France.) First shown at Cameo-Poly in July, 1956.

**His Two Loves—Puccini.** Italian colour film based on the life of the famous composer, with some of his loveliest music sung by great artists, including *Gigli*. Rest of cast: *Gabriele Ferzetto, Marta Toren, Nadia Gray, Paolo Stoppa.* Dir.: Carmine Gallone. (Rizzoli-Films de France.) First shown at the Paris-Pullman in January, 1957.

**Is Anna Anderson Anastasia?** German film presenting in factual and sometimes documentary detail the story of the girl from a mental asylum who, it was claimed, was the sole survivor of the Romanoff massacre. Cast: *Lilli Palmer, Ivan Desny, Susanne von Almassy, Erika Danhoff, Berta Drews, Tilla Durieux, Margot Hielscher, Franciska Kinz, Ellen Schwiers, Adelheid Seeck, Alice Treff, Paul Bildt, Rudolf Fernau, Otto Graf, Reinhard Kolldehoff, Ernst Schroder.* Dir.: Falk Harnack. (Gala.) First shown at the Berkeley Cinema in February, 1957.

**Jackboot Mutiny.** Clear, documentary-style relation of the unsuccessful 1944 attempt to assassinate Hitler. Made in Germany. First shown at the Berkeley, June, 1956.

**La Traversee de Paris—Pig Across Paris.** Delightful French comedy with slightly bitter and satirical undertones, about the journey across Occupied Paris in the black-out by a black marketeer and his artist friend with four cases of pork. Cast: *Jean Gabin, Bourvil, Jeanette Batti, Louis deFunes, Monette Dinay.* Dir. and Pro.: Claude Autant-Lara. (Franco-London.) First shown at the Academy in February, 1957.

**Lady Chatterley's Lover.** Careful, commendable effort to bring to the screen D. H. Lawrence's long-banned story about the love of a lady, wife of a rich and impotent milord, for the rough but sex-appealing gamekeeper. An impossible task bravely attempted. Cast: *Danielle Darrieux, Leo Genn, Ernos Crisa, Berthe Tissen, Jeanine Crispin, Jean Murat, Gerard Sety, Jacqueline Noelle.* Dir.: Marc Allegret. Pro.: Gilbert Cohen-Seat. (Regie du Film-Orsay: Columbia.) First shown at the Curzon in July, 1956.

**Law of the Streets.** French film suggesting there's good in the worst of us by telling a story about a young lad escaped from a reformatory whose best friends are the worst citizens. Cast: *Raymond Pellegrin, Silvana Pampanini, Fernand Ledoux, Jean Louis Trintignant, Jean Gaven, Josette Arno, Mary Marquet, Jean-Marc Tennberg.* Dir.: Ralph Habib. (Columbia). First shown at Paris-Pullman in May, 1957.

**Le Defroque—The Renegade Priest.** *Pierre Fresnay* as the ex-priest whose courage and character inspire another young man to go into the Church and the tragedy their moral conflict brings about. A most unusual, difficult to discuss and controversial film, rooted firmly in religion. Rest of cast: *Nicole Stephane, Pierre Trabaud, Marcelle Geniat, G. Decomble.* Dir.: Leo Joannou. First shown at the Curzon in August, 1956.

**Letters from My Windmill.** Three-part French film based on stories by Alphonse Daudet. (A) The ghostly tale of "The Three Low Masses"; (B) the amusing, satirical tale of "The Elixir of

One of the glamorous young *Rank* starlets is ANNE HEYWOOD who has this year been in CHECKPOINT and DOCTOR AT LARGE and whose latest film is DANGEROUS EXILE.

Father Gaucher"; and (C) the story of the windmill which came to life again and made the Provence village gay—"The Secret of Master Cornille". Casts: (A) *Henri Vilbert, Daxely, Rene Sarvil, Yvonne Gamy, Keller, Viviane Mery, Clara Michel.* (B) *Rellys, Robert Vattier, Christian Lude, Fernand Sardou, Guy Alland, Joseph Riozet, Jean Toscane.* (C) *Roger Crouzet, Pierrette Bruno, Delmont, Arius, Luce Dassas, Breols.* Dir. and Pro.: Marcel Pagnol. (Curzon.) First shown at Curzon in Sept, 1956.

**Lock Up the Spoons.** Tremendously amusing, if highly immoral, French film about a 103-year-old crook whose demise is enlivened by the outrageous stories of his friends. Cast: *Eddie Constantine, Noel-Noel, Jean Richard, Yves Robert, Robert Dalban, Berval, Sylvie, Helena Manson, Juny Astor, Nelly Vignon, Lucien Baroux, Claude Borelli, Irene Alexis, Irene Tune.* Dir.: Carlo Rim. (Gaumont-Franco-Miracle.) First shown at the Cameo-Poly in March, 1957.

**The Lost Continent.** Fascinating documentary about an Italian expedition to Malaya, Bali and the Dyak headhunters of Borneo. Wonderfully photographed in colour; a Cannes Festival prizewinner. (Astra Cinematografica-Leonardo Bonzi-Miracle.) First shown at the Academy in April, 1957.

**The Lowest Crime.** That is, blackmail. *Magali Noel* is the girl who gets entangled in the nasty activities of a blackmailing network. *Leo Genn, Raymond Pellegrin, Georges Chamarat* are the bad lots. Rest of cast: *Noel Roquevert, Etcheverry, Degrave, Michèlle Lahaye, Madeleine Barbule, Huguette Montreal.* Dir.: Guy Lefranc. (Gala.) First shown at the Berkeley in September, 1956.

**Mademoiselle de Paris.** French musical lightly dealing with *haute couture* in Paris. Cast: *Giselle Pascal, Jean-Pierre Aumont, Jacqueline Francois, Jean Marchat, Jean Lara, Nadine Basile, Rene Blancard, Claudie Chatelan, Raymond Loyer.* Dir.: Walter Kapps. (Regent.) First shown at the Paris-Pullman in April, 1957. (E. & Cinepanoramic.)

**Mam'selle Pigalle.** Gay and sometimes quite crazy French comedy along conventional lines; amusing and as fresh as a daisy; with music, colour and delicious *Brigitte Bardot*, playing the daughter of a night club owner erroneously suspected of a plot to pass counterfeit cash. Rest of cast: *Jean Bretonniere, Françoise Fabian, Bernard Lancret, Raymond Bussieres, Mischa Auer, Dary Cowl.* Dir.: Michel J. Boisrond. (Films de France.) (C. & E.) First shown at the Leicester Square Theatre in Nov., 1956. Gen. Rel.: Nov. 26, 1956.

**Mam'selle Striptease.** Gay, light-hearted French comedy about a young girl who went into a strip-tease competition incognito and won both it and a handome young newspaper reporter. Cast: *Brigitte Bardot, Daniel Gelin, Robert Hirisch, Darry Cowl, Nadine Tallier, Jacques Dumesnil, Mischa Auer, Georges Chamarat, Anne Collette, Luciana Paoluzzi, Jacques Fervil, Jacques Jouanneau, Madeleine Barbulue, Yves-Marie Maurin.* Dir.: Marc Allegret. (Miracle.) First shown at the Cameo-Royal in October, 1956.

**Mistress du Barry.** Technicolored period romp with *Martine Carol* as the young lady of uncertain morals, who catches the eye and later complete attention of King Louis XV of France. Rest of cast: *Andre Luguet, Daniel Ivernel, Jean Paredes, Massimo Serato, Denis d'Ines, Gabrielle Dorziat, Melnatti, Isabelle Pia.* Dir. and Pro.: Christian-Jaque. (Films de France.) First shown at the Cameo-Royal in December, 1956.

**O La-la Cheri.** Very light and frothy French comedy farce about 19-year-old beauty *Dany Robin* coming from school to Paris and pestering police-inspector *Daniel Gelin* to take her to bed and to wed. Rest of cast: *Marie Daems, Tilda Thamar, Mary Marquet.* Song by *Catherine Sauvage.* Dir.: Gaspard-Huit. (Gala.) First shown at the Berkeley, July, 1956.

**Obsession.** The story of a woman married to a trapeze artist who suspects that her husband is guilty of the murder for which another member of the circus has been condemned to death. Exciting climax. Cast: *Michele Morgan, Raf Vallone, Jean Gaven, Marthe Mercadier, Olivier Hussenot, Robert Dalban, Albert Duvaleix, Jacques Castelot, Louis Seigner.* Dir.: Jean Delannoy. (Gala.) (T.) A 1957 French Film Festival film: first shown at the La Continentale in April, 1957.

**Oh! My Pa-Pa.** *Lilli Palmer* as a circus-owner's wife in a German (but English-dubbed) melodrama with a Big Top background. Rest of cast: *Karl Schoenboeck, Romy Schneider, Werner Hinz, Rudolf Vogel, Margarete Haagen, Ernest Waldow, Liesl Karlstadt, Kathe Haack, Lina Carstens, Charlotte Witthauer, Michl Lang, Claus Pohl, Claus Bieder Staedt, Tatjana Sais.* Dir.: Kurt Hoffman. Pro.: Eric Charell. (Assoc.) Gen. Rel.: Jan 14. 1957. (T.)

**Once Upon a Time.** Slim little French fairy tale, told in colour with a cast entirely made up of animals and birds, and with a dear little duckling as the hero. Dir.: Jean Tourane. Pro.: Piere Bochart. (Del Duca Films.) First shown at La Continentale in December, 1956. Gen. Rel.: March 4, 1957.

**The Parasites—M'sier La Caille.** Oddly sentimental and occasionally sadistically brutal little film about pimps, gangsters and prostitutes and their sordid lives behind the bright lights of Montmartre. Cast: *Jeanne Moreau, Philippe Lemaire, Roger Pierre, Robert Dalban.* Dir.: André Pergament. (Astarte.) First shown at the Paris-Pullman in July, 1956.

**Pepote—Mi Tio Jacinto.** Spanish film about the sad efforts of an old retired, and tipsy bullfighter to make a come-back, for the sake of his adoring small nephew. A notable, heart-warming performance as the small boy by *Pablito Calvo* (of "Marcelino" fame). Rest of cast: *Antonio Vico, Jose Marco Davo, Juan Calvo, Mariano Azana, Pastora Pena, Julio Sanjuan.* Dir.: Ladislav Vayda. Pro.: Vincenti Sempere. First shown at the Cameo-Poly in April, 1957.

**The Poisoner—Soupcons.** Conventional French whodunnit from the Maurice Dekobra novel "Poison at Plessis" The wealthy De Montenoy is killed—and there are plenty of suspects. Cast: *Anne Vernon, Frank Villard, Jacques Castelot, Dora Doll, Henri Vilbert, Serge Nadaud, Roland Lesaffre.* Dir.: Pierre Billon. Pro.: Ben Barkay. (Astarte.) First shown at the Paris-Pullman in March, 1957.

**The Red Balloon.** An exquisite little 35-minute French film; a fairy story about a little boy and a balloon and their charming adventures together. Brilliantly photographed against a grey-blue background of Montmartre. One of the most acutely sensitive, finely artistic films of this, last or any other year. Dir.: and Pro.: Albert Lamorisse, whose small son, Pascal, plays the boy. (Films de France.) First shown at the Odeon, Leicester Square, in October, 1956. Gen. Rel.: December 24.

**The Red Inn.** French comedy-thriller, actually made some time back but held up by censor troubles, with *Fernandel* as the dumb (by vows) monk trying to warn the guests of a lonely Inn that the owners intend to murder them for their possessions. Rest of cast: *Lud Germain, Carette, Francoise Rosay, Marie-Claire Olivia, A Vialla, Andre Cheff, N. Germon, D. D'yd, G Aslan, Caussimon.* Dir.: Claude Autant-Lara. (Cross-Channel). First shown at Berkeley, May, 1957.

**Roman Signorina—La Bella di Roma.** The somewhat vicarious romance of *Silvana Pampanini* and *Alberto Sordi* in Rome. Rest of cast: *Paolo Stoppa, Luisella Beghi, Lina Volonghi, Sergio Tofano, Betty Foa, Bice Valori, Ciccio Barbi, Gigi Reder, Francesco Patrizi, Mario Meniconi, Giulio Cali, Ettore Jannetti, Luciano Forniti, Carlo Picchiotti,* and with the participation of *Antonio Cifariello.* Dir.: Luigi Comencini. (Lux-Archway.) First shown at the Classic, Hendon, in 1957.

**Scandal in Sorrento.** Another film in the "Bread, Love and . . ." series. This time *Vittorio de Sica* comes back to his lovely birthplace—and immediately becomes involved with gorgeous fish-wife *Sophia Loren* and equally gorgeous but sexually more timid *Lea Padovani.* Colour, CinemaScoped backgrounds and grand, pleasant fun. Rest of cast: *Antonio Cifariello, Tina Pica, Mario Carotenuto, Joka Berretty.* Dir.: Dino Risi. (Gala.) (C. & E.) First shown at La Continentale in Feb., 1957.

**The Seventh Commandment.** Smooth, entertaining French comedy with *Edwige Feuillere* making a delightful bait for a duo of not-so-bad crooks and spoiling everything by falling in love with one of their victims. Rest of cast: *Jaques Dumesnil, Maurice Yeynac, Jacques Morel, Jeanne Fusir-Gir, Jean Lefevre.* Dir.: Raymond Bernard. (Regent). First shown at Cameo-Poly, May 1957.

**The Sign of Venus.** Lively Italian comedy with a streak of pathos running through it. *Franca Valeri* as the dreaming romantic whose boy-friends inevitably gravitate to her sexy cousin, *Sophia Loren.* Rest of cast: *Vittorio de Sica, Raf Vallone, Virgilio Riento, Tina Pica, Alberto Sordi, Peppino de Filippo.* Dir.: Dino Risi. (Titanus-Gala.) First shown at La Continentale in August, 1956.

**Smiles of a Summer's Night.** Ingmar Bergman's (Swedish) film which is a kind of English Restoration comedy, polished, refined and sophisticated and transferred to a Swedish background of about a hundred years ago. Beautifully acted, directed and photographed; erotic, sensual and always well worthy of its X cert. Cast: *Ulla Jacobsson, Eva Dahlbeck, Harriet Anderson, Margit Carlquist, Gunnar Bjornstrand, Jarl Kulle, Ake Fridell, Björn Bjelvenstam, Naima Wifstrand, Jullan Kindahl, Gull Natorp.* Dir.: Ingmar Bergman. (Svensk. Film industri-Intercontinental.) First shown at the Academy, London, in September, 1956.

**Stella.** Powerful, fascinating Greek film telling the story of a singer's hectic affair with a footballer, and what happens when he tries to change her. An outstanding performance by the star, *Melina Mercouri.* Rest of cast: *Georges Foundas, Aleko Alexandrakis, Sofia Vembo.* Dir.: Michael Cacoyamis. Pro.: Anis Nohra. (Intercontinental.) First shown at the Paris-Pullman in August, 1956.

**The Swindlers.** Brilliant, realistic and in the end bitterly ironic Italian film about three petty crooks, their vile swindles, their complete immorality. Finely directed; splendidly acted. Cast: *Broderick Crawford, Richard Basehart, Franco Fabrizi, Giulietta Masina, Giacomo Gabrielli, Alberto de Amicis, Mara Werlen, Lorella de Luca, Irene Cefaro, Sue Ellen Blake, Riccardo Garrone, Milo Manfredi, Mario Passante, Maria Zanoli, Sara Simoni.* Dir.: Federico Fellini. (Titanus.) First shown at the Cameo-Poly in November, 1956.

**Ten Days to Die.** G. W. Pabst's direction of the Remarque script of the M. A. Musmanno book reconstructing, from records and eye-witness accounts, the last ten days of the Hitler story, the horrid climax in the bunker in Berlin. Cast includes: *Albin Skoda, Oskar Werner, Lotte Tobisch, Willy Krause, Helga Kennedy-Dohrn, Erich Suckmann,* etc. Dir.: Pabst. Pro.: Carl Szokoll. (Intercontinental-Films de France.) First shown at Cameo-Poly, June, 1956.

**That Girl Elisa.** Bitterly tragic little French film about a girl who in her whole life has only four years of freedom, during which she knows life in a brothel and from there escapes to true love and life with a blind organist. Cast: *Dany Carrel, Serge Reggiani, Valentine Tessier, Marthe Mercadier, F. Sardou, Bernard Lajarrige, Georges Chamarat, Lysiane Rey, Michel Etcheverry.* Dir. and Pro.: Roger Richebe. (Regent.) First shown at the Cameo Royal in June, 1957.

**Therese Raquin.** Marcel Carne's adaptation of the Zola story about the lovers who had to pay the full price for their guilty passion after they had murdered the woman's husband. Strong, sombre. Cast: *Simone Signoret, Raf Vallone, Roland Lesaffre, Sylvie, Jacques Duby.* Dir.: Marcel Carne. (Astarte.) First shown at Paris-Pullman, June, 1956.

**Touchez Pas au Grisbi—Honour Among Thieves.** Almost frighteningly cool relation of a double-cross plot among some Parisian racketeers, with ace thief *Jean Gabin* losing a stolen fortune and his partner in a single, violent operation. Rest of cast: *Rene Dary, Jeanne Moreau, Dora Doll, Gaby Basset, Lino Ventura.* Dir.: Jacques Becker. Pro.: Robert Dorfmann. (Films de France.) First shown at the Academy in June, 1956.

**Two Acres of Land—Do Bigha Zamin.** Interesting, simple little Indian film about a tragic and always hopeless fight of a peasant to keep his two acres of land. Cast: *Balraj Sahni, Nirupa Roy, Rattan Kumar.* Dir.: Bimal Roy. (Films de France.) First shown at the Paris-Pullman in August, 1956.

**Typhoon Over Nagasaki.** Engineer *Jean Marais,* working in the atom-bomb town, is torn between his present Japanese mistress *Kishi Keiko* and the French girl, a former mistress (*Danielle Darrieux*) who suddenly arrives on the scene willing to take up where they left off. The choice is made for him by the arrival of a typhoon; and the ending to the story is tragic. Also in the cast: *Gert Frobe.* Dir.: Yves Ciampi. (Curzon.) A French Film Festival exhibit. First shown at the Curzon in May, 1957.

**Un Condamme a Mort S'est Echappe—A Condemned Prisoner Has Escaped.** The true story of André Devigny, condemned to death by the Germans and imprisoned in the Fort de Montluc in 1943, from where, long later, he escapes. Cast of complete unknowns. Dir. and Pro.: Robert Bresson. (Films de France.) A 1957 French Film Festival exhibit. First shown at the Academy, London, in June, 1957.

**The Wicked Go to Hell.** French actor Robert Rossein's first effort at film directing is an oddly but persistently poetical, yet brutal and violent picture about two wretched young criminals who escape from jail and murder an artist in a wayside shack, meeting their doom at his mistress-model's lovely but coldly revengeful hands. Cast: *Serge Reggiani, Henri Vidal, Marina Vlady, Robert Hossein, Jacques Duby, Robert Dalban, Marthe Mercadier.* Dir.: R. Rossein. Pro.: Jules Borkon. (Miracle.) First shown at the Cameo-Poly in August, 1956.

**Woman of Rome.** *Gina Lollobrigida* as the girl who goes down and then goes up, from the gutter to the cloister, so to speak. Emotional drama. Rest of cast: *Daniel Gelin, Franco Fabrizi, Raymond Pellgrin.* Dir.: Luigi Zampa. (Exclusive.) Generally Released May 20, 1957.

# Looking Forward

ɔ far in this volume you have been reading about, and ɔoking at scenes from films which, by the time you read ɩis, will already have been generally released. So much ·r the year that has gone. Now, I'm sure you will agree, is time to look ahead and the following pages are devoted · illustrating those films which will be released either ɹuring the latter part of 1957 or the earlier months of 1958.

A word of warning. Some of the films in this section ill already have been premiered. But none of them will have been generally released. And that is the important point. Indeed, many of these movies are either only just completed or are even still in production, so they are not likely to be seen for quite a while yet and it will be still longer before they get their general release.

Taking these points into consideration I think you'll find that this feature gives you a pretty good idea of the cinematic way ahead, the kind of movies you'll be seeing in your local cinemas during the coming year.

*Above) One of the biggest " searches " in years was taged by Otto Preminger when he decided to find a ɩew and unknown girl to play the leading role in ɩis United Artists film of G. B. Shaw's play* Saint Joan. *The choice fell on Jean Seberg, who s seen here arriving at the Palace of Chinon from ɩer own small village. Other parts in the film are ɔlayed by Richard Widmark (as the Dauphin), Richard Todd (Dunois), Anton Walbrook (Cauchon) John Gielgud (Warwick). Premiered in June,* Saint Joan *is due for general release later in the year.*

*(Below) One of the many spectacular scenes from* The Pride And The Passion, *an epic-scale movie made by Stanley Kramer for United Artists release. Stars are Sophia Loren (though now shown first, it was the first English-speaking film she made), Frank Sinatra (as a Spanish guerrilla Chieftain) and Cary Grant. It is a story of the fight against Napoleon's armies.*

*(Below) Premiered at the Astoria in July and unlikely it appears to have a general release for some time is the gargantuan, Oscar-winning Todd film based on the famous Jules Verne story* Around the World in 80 Days. *David Niven, left, is the man who sets off on this fantastic journey for a wager and he is accompanied on his travels by a faithful servant (played by Mexican comedian Cantinflas—right). In the centre, Charles Boyer.*

(*Left*) *A film which should be worth watc ing for is the United Artists' producti* The Bachelor Party. *This story of f young men and their adventures duri one hot New York night is made by t "Marty" team of author Paddy Chaefsk director Delbert Mann and the produci unit of Hecht-Hill-Lancaster. In tl scene, two of the bachelors : Philip Abb and Jack Warden.*

(*Right*) *Silk stockings. The lure of a pair of silk stockings and fragile lingerie is all Cyd Charisse needs to toss aside her Russian inhibitions for one of the most interpretative and lyrical musical numbers in M-G-M's* Silk Stockings, *in which she stars with Fred Astaire and Janis Paige. Miss Charisse emerges into a glowing and glamorous woman when she sheds her Commissar uniform to pull on her first pair of silk stockings which in turn lead to high heeled slippers, silken lingerie, a frothy petticoat and the evening gown which wins her the cynosure of all eyes in Paris—including those of Astaire. His heart goes along too. It was directed by Rouben Mamoulian, produced by Arthur Freed. And if it all sounds familiar let us hasten to admit that it's a new musical version of the old Garbo success "Ninotchka".*

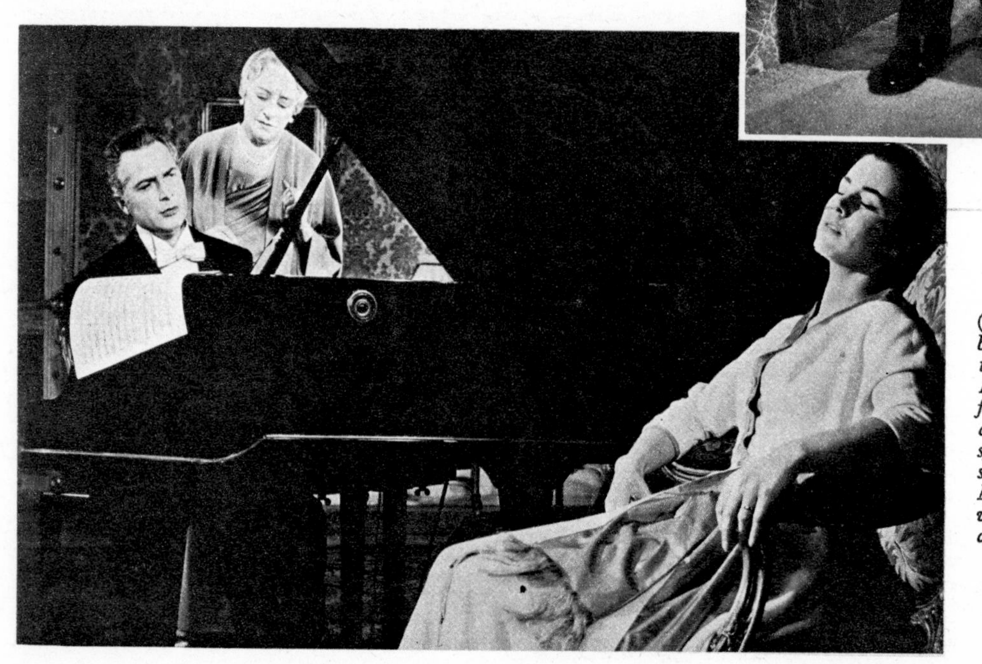

(*Left*) *While her aunt, Francoise Rosay betrays her deep concern, Rossano Brazz tries to soothe his emotionally ill wif Marianne Cook, with music in this scen from Universal-International's* Interlude *a dramatic story of love between a Europea symphony conductor and an American gir starring June Allyson, Brazzi, Miss Cook Miss Rosay and Keith Andes. The pictur was filmed in its entirety in CinemaScop and Technicolor in Germany and Austri*

*e of the forthcoming films which will be most eagerly ticipated is the new Charles Chaplin movie,* A King in w York, *the first film that Chaplin has made outside of nerica. A satirical story about exiled Royalty in the w World, it promises to be a highly controversial as well highly comic picture. In this scene Chaplin, as the King, es hard not to be aware of the flirtatious glances of Dawn ldams, his leading lady in the movie. The film is set for September premiere in London.*

*Above)* The Brave One *was made entirely in Mexico by roducers Frank and Maurice King and it presents British ad Michel Ray in one of the biggest juvenile roles in screen istory, as the peasant boy who adopts a bull calf as his pet, ears it to maturity, and then strives to save it from death the arena.*

*(Above) Kenneth More—seen here with Diane Cilento—as* The Admirable Crichton, *the perfect butler, in the Columbia British film based on the famous James Barrie classic about snobbery in strange places.*

*(Left) James Cagney, in clown make up, tells press agent Jim Backus that he's about to become a father. A scene from Universal-International's CinemaScope drama* Man Of a Thousand Faces, *life story of the late Lon Chaney. Co-starring with Cagney are Dorothy Malone and Jane Greer.*

(*Left*) *A magnificent film is Warners' story of American pioneer avia Charles A. Lindbergh and, more especially, his great aerial achievement crossing the Atlantic in his tiny, single-engined monoplane* The Spirit of S Louis. *James Stewart plays the intrepid aviator.*

(*Above*) *James Stewart plays a very differe kind of role in Universal-International* Night Passage, *a Western filmed in th Colorado Rockies. In this scene, Stewar who is a right-side-of-the-law investigator se his wrong-side-of-the-law brother Aud Murphy shot down by his side when at last th two get together.*

(*Right*) *Arriving in the outback township of Bungana with his young daughter in search of a job, swagman Macauley (Peter Finch) gets involved in a fight with a couple of toughs who want the job for themselves. Having dealt effectively with O'Neill, Macauley turns his attention to Christy. A scene from Ealing's* The Shiralee, *a realistic, tough and convincing picture of at least one aspect of Australian life. Ealing made this, the second of their M-G-M releases, entirely in Australia.*

(*Above*) *Silent Moment. Simon and Jean Scott (Tony Britton and Sylvia Sims) look silently at each other in the prison visiting room after Simon has been gaoled for smuggling in* The Birthday Present, *a British Lion production which co-stars Britton with Miss Sims. The story shows in dramatic terms the heartbreak and despair that a moment's lapse from honesty can bring a young happily married couple.*

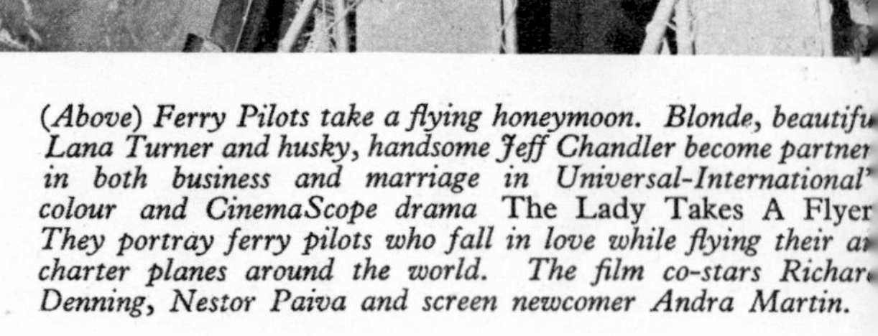

(*Above*) *Ferry Pilots take a flying honeymoon. Blonde, beautifu Lana Turner and husky, handsome Jeff Chandler become partner in both business and marriage in Universal-International' colour and CinemaScope drama* The Lady Takes A Flyer *They portray ferry pilots who fall in love while flying their ai charter planes around the world. The film co-stars Richar Denning, Nestor Paiva and screen newcomer Andra Martin.*

(*Left*) *Moviegoers with pleasant memories of the comedy co-starring team of Spencer Tracy and Katharine Hepburn will look forward eagerly to their new 20th Century-Fox comedy,* His Other Woman *based on a successful American stage comedy.*

*Right) Legend of Raintree . . . is heard by Eva Marie Saint and Iontgomery Clift during picnic for Pedee Academy's Class of* 1859 *this scene from M-G-M's* Raintree Country, *based on the best lling novel by Russ Lockridge, Jr. It is the first picture to be lmed with the new M-G-M Camera 65 and stars Montgomery lift, Elizabeth Taylor and Eva Marie Saint with a large, dis-nguished supporting cast. Edward Dmytryck is director.*

(*Left*) *Peter Finch as the notorious bushranger Captain Starlight in the Pinewood Australian production* Robbery Under Arms. *A story of life and adventures in the bush and goldfields of the 1850's, the film also stars Maureen Swanson, Ronald Lewis, Jill Ireland and David McCallum.*

*Right) Two hundred years ago Britain was invaded for the last time. A year earlier the Dauphin mysteri-usly disappeared from Paris. Were these events connected? The new J. Arthur Rank Organisation film,* Dangerous Exile, *blends historical fact with intriguing legend and presents a possible solution to one of the world's strangest mysteries. Louis Jourdan co-stars opposite Belinda Lee and the cast includes Keith Mitchell, Terence Longdon, Anne Heywood, Martita Hunt and Finlay Currie. In this scene from the film Dylan (Brian Rawlinson) realises that Patient (Finlay Currie) is a spy.*

(*Above*) *Three's a crowd . . . Arrival of Rhonda Fleming brings to a crucial pitch the conflict between Stewart Granger, centre, and Steve Rowland, as his embittered son. A scene from M-G-M's* Gun Glory, *unusual outdoor action story of a man of the Early West, a man whose reputation as a killer brings violence to a peaceful valley. Stewart Granger and Rhonda Fleming star, with Chill Wills and Steve Rowland also heading the cast. Filmed in CinemaScope and colour on vast Western locations, the picture was directed by Roy Rowland, produced by Nicholas Nayfack and based on the novel by Philip Yordan.*

*(Left) Due for London premiere in the autumn is Cecil B. de Mi great Paramount biblical epic,* The Ten Commandments. *Said to de Mille's greatest screen spectacle yet, it has an enormous cast. T scene shows the wrath of Moses (played by Charlton Heston) as comes upon the people worshipping the Golden Calf. On the left can seen Yvonne de Carlo (playing the wife of Moses) and right on the e of the picture John Derek (as Joshua) and Lilia (Debra Paget).*

*(Above) Moment between brother and sister : Elizabeth Newton (Wen Hiller) comforts weary brother Peter (Rock Hudson) upon his return fr a man hunt in the hills of Kenya in M-G-M's* Something of Valu *adapted from the Robert C. Ruark best selling novel about the Mau-M troubles, starring Rock Hudson, Dana Wynter, Wendy Hiller, Sidn Poitier and Juano Hernandez.*

*(Right) Patrick McGoohan and Stanley Baker as rival drivers in the J. Arthur Rank production* Hell Drivers, *the story of the men who drive the big lorries. Others in the cast include Herbert Lom, William Hartnell, Jill Ireland and Peggy Cummins.*

*(Below) Paul Ford has a few—loud—words to say to Marlon Brando in this scene from M-G-M's screen adaptation of the extremely successful stage musical* The Teahouse of the August Moon, *which amusingly showed something of the problems of the Americans stationed in Japan.*

*(Right) The Butler and the Boss. June Allyson is a scatterbrain socialite who hires suave down-and-out David Niven as her butler in Universal-International's Colour and Cinema-Scope re-make of the* 1957 *comedy hit,* My Man Godfrey. *Martha Hyer plays Miss Allyson's sister in the film —and her scheming rival for Niven's affections. Gorgeous Eva Gabor co-stars as a wealthy Continental socialite.*

*(Left) But we must eat . . . says Lise (Anna Gaylor) as she shows Jim (Tony Wright) and Dave (Stephen Boyd) the food she has bought with the 500 francs she took from Dave's pockets. A scene from Daniel M. Angel's new production for the Rank Organisation* Seven Thunders, *which also stars James Robertson Justice, and Kathleen Harrison. Directed by Hugo Fregonese, Rupert Croft Cooke's exciting story of German occupied Marseilles is scripted by John Baines.*

*(Above) Due for late summer or early autumn general release (premiere was at the end of July in London) was Darryl F. Zanuck's* Island In the Sun, *filmed largely on location in the West Indies and telling an Alec Waugh story of murder and jealousy there. Among the stars are Joan Collins and Stephen Boyd (seen here taking tea in the sun), James Mason, Joan Fontaine, Harry Belafonte and Michael Rennie.*

*(Above) The contrast is complete. The mistress (Sylvia Sims), the wife (Yvonne Mitchell) and the husband (Anthony Quayle) as they appear together in the Associated British production* The Woman in the Dressing Gown, *the story of a marriage which goes wrong.*

*(Below) Eleanor Parker steals her aunt's supply of liquor while in the " hussy " aspect of her triple personality, a scene from* Lizzie, *a Bryna production for M-G-M, which is a psychological drama about a woman with three conflicting personalities. Eleanor Parker and Richard Boone are co-starred in a cast which also includes Joan Blondell, Hugo Haas and Ric Roman. The film was produced by Jerry Bresler, directed by Hugo Haas, from a screen play by Mel Dinelli, based on a book by Shirley Jackson.*

*(Above) 20th Century-Fox's* The Three Faces of Eve *is claimed to be based on a true medical case history, that of a young woman who developed three completely different and quite separate personalities. Playing this girl, Eve White, is promising screen newcomer Joanne Woodward, shown here with David Wayne.*

(*Above*) *Burt Lancaster and Kirk Douglas play two of the Old West's most famous characters, Wyatt Earp and Doc Holliday, in Paramount's large scale Western* Gunfight at O.K. Corral, *which is mainly concerned with the duo's efforts to wipe out the nefarious Clanton gang in* 1870-82.

(*Above*) *Carl Schaffner (Rod Steiger) is frozen out by the local Mexican villagers. With cases and the dog Dolores he staggers from hotel to bar and cafe—only to have doors shut in his face. Scene from* Across The Bridge, *an adaptation of a story by Graham Greene, depicting the downfall of an international financier who seeks asylum in Mexico. Cast also includes Marla Landi and David Knight.*

(*Right*) *One of the most important aspects of* 20th *Century-Fox's* Bernadine *is that it brings back to the screen after a very, far too long an interval, that great star of the early talkies, Janet Gaynor, seen here with Dean Jagger.*

(*Above*) Tarzan and the Lost Safari, *the new jungle adventure released by M-G-M, is the first in the ever-popular Edgar Rice Burroughs series to be made in colour and for the wide screen. It stars Gordon Scott as the jungle lord (his second performance in the role under his Tarzan contract), Robert Beatty, as the renegade white hunter who opposes him, and Yolande Donlan, Betta St. John, Wilfred Hyde White, George Coulouris and Peter Arne as a party of socialites whose plane crashlands in African jungle terrain and who make their way back to civilisation through hostile native territory with the invaluable aid of Tarzan and Cheta, played by Jo Jo the chimpanzee.*

(*Right*) *Universal-International's* Pylon *is a triangle story set against a background of an air circus of the early thirties with Robert Stack, Jack Carson and Dorothy Malone (seen here) as the aviators and Rock Hudson (shown talking to Miss Malone) as the reporter who gets tied up with them.*

*(Above) Though premiered in the Spring at the Plaza, where it had a long and successful run, and subsequently shown with acclaim at the Cannes Festival, Herbert Wilcox's* The Yangtse Incident *is not due for general release until the Autumn. Here is Richard Todd as Lieut-Commander John Kerans, who was in command of the frigate " Amethyst " when it made its dramatic dash by night past the threatening guns of the Communist batteries—one of the most thrilling of the several exciting sequences in this film based on the facts of the 1949 front-page news story.*

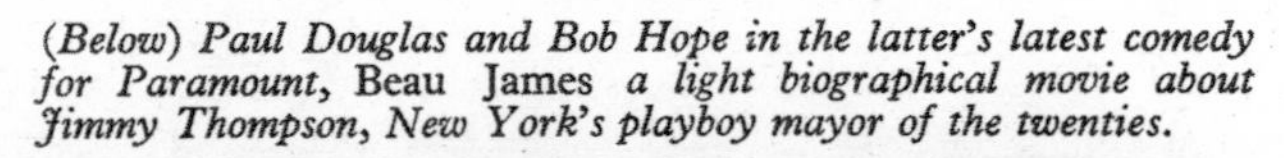

*(Below) Paul Douglas and Bob Hope in the latter's latest comedy for Paramount,* Beau James *a light biographical movie about Jimmy Thompson, New York's playboy mayor of the twenties.*

*(Above) Corporal Allison (Robert Mitchum) gets steadily more drunk on the Saki (rice wine) he has stolen from the Japanese food stores. And Sister Angela (Deborah Kerr) gets steadily more apprehensive as he begins to make advances to her. A scene from the 20th Century-Fox CinemaScope picture* Heaven Knows, Mr. Allison *starring Deborah Kerr and Robert Mitchum, directed by John Huston and based on the piquant situation of a nun and a marine thrown together on a deserted Pacific island.*

*(Above) Laurence Olivier and Marilyn Monroe in Warners' British production* The Prince and the Showgirl, *based on the play " The Sleeping Prince " in which Olivier already had enjoyed a big success during its London season, when wife Vivien Leigh played the part now taken by Miss Monroe.*

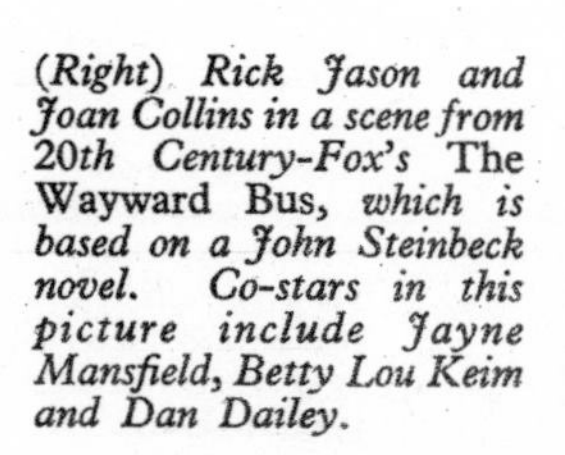

*(Right) Rick Jason and Joan Collins in a scene from 20th Century-Fox's* The Wayward Bus, *which is based on a John Steinbeck novel. Co-stars in this picture include Jayne Mansfield, Betty Lou Keim and Dan Dailey.*

*(Above) Gary Cooper and Audrey Hepburn in a scene from the Associated British film* Love in the Afternoon, *made largely in France and also starring Maurice Chevalier. It is a light and sophisticated comedy.*

*(Above) Anna Neagle returns to nursing uniform in* No Time for Tears, *the Associated British production set in a children's hospital and co-starring Sylvia Sims, George Baker and Anthony Quayle.*

*(Right) Heading the cast of M-G-M's musical* Les Girls *are, from left : Taina Elg, Kay Kendall, Mitzi Gaynor and Gene Kelly. The film, with songs by Cole Porter, is a gay, tune-filled musical set in France, Spain and England. Gene Kelly, Mitzi Gaynor, Kay Kendall, Taina Elg, Jacques Bergerac and Leslie Phillips head the cast.*

*(Above) The Columbia-Warwick film* Fire Down Below *is the story of two partners, Robert Mitchum and Jack Lemmon, who do a little legitimate and some illegitimate business with their old freighter among the islands of the Caribbean, and of the girl Irene (Rita Hayworth) who comes into their lives and takes both of their hearts.*

*(Right) Suzanne (Barbara Laage) and Mike (Gene Kelly) have trouble finding transportation in their pursuit of their missing children, and are forced to accept a lift from a French policeman, although Suzanne's tight skirt wasn't designed for motorcycle riding !* The Happy Road, *which also stars 11-year-old Bobby Clark, 10-year-old Brigitte Fossey, features Michael Redgrave. Filmed entirely in France, this comedy tells how two youngsters hitch-hike their way to Paris to find their parents. Kelly also produced and co-directed.*

*(Right) Captain Prothero (Trevor Howard) listens to Mario (Pedro Armendariz) a member of the engine room staff, who is trying to get the job of First Engineer in this scene from* Manuela, *Ivan Foxwell's British Lion production also starring Elsa Matinelli. Directed by Guy Hamilton from the novel by William Woods, it was filmed largely on location in Spain.*

*(Above) King Vidor's vast, epic-scale* War and Peace, *after a long run at the Plaza in the early Spring, is due for a number of pre-release playings this summer, to be followed by a general release in the autumn. This scene is typical of the many in the latter, more spectacular half of the film, which was a generally successful screen adaptation of the famous Tolstoy story. Stars include Henry Fonda, Audrey Hepburn.*

*(Below) Patricia Neal and Andy Griffiths in the new Elia Kazan production for Warners',* A Face in the Crowd.

*(Below) Island Mishap. In this scene from M-G-M's* The Little Hut, *Ava Gardner and David Niven are inspecting a blister on the foot of Stewart Granger. The film is the screen adaptation of the long-running stage success about two men and a girl wrecked on a desert island and their unconventional manner of solving an obvious problem.*

*(Above) Eva Marie Saint, Anthony Franciosa and Lloyd Nolan in 20th Century-Fox's screen adaptation of the Michael Gazzo stage play* A Hatful of Rain, *which also stars Don Murray (who you may recall as making a hit in his first film, the same company's* Bus Stop*). It's the story of a young man who gets "hooked" by dope pedlars and his struggles to get away from them.*

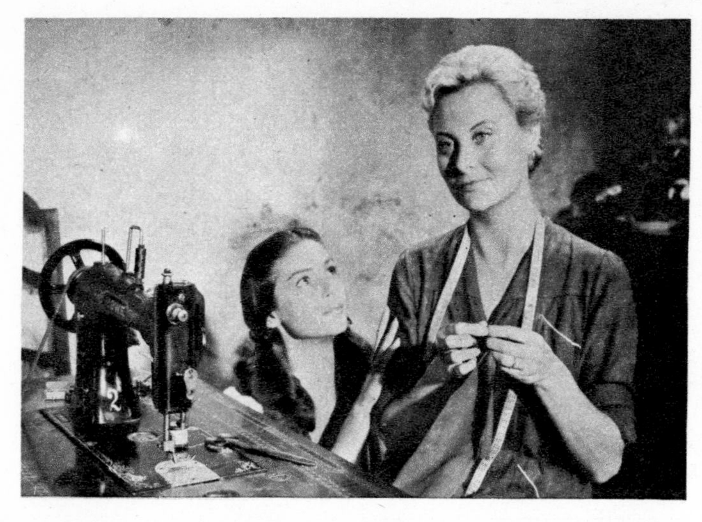

*(Above) Pier Angeli talks over her girlish doubts and hopes with older sister Michele Morgan in this scene from M-G-M's* The Vintage, *a dramatic love story filmed in France, with a cast also including Mel Ferrer, John Kerr, Leif Erickson and Theodore Bikel.*

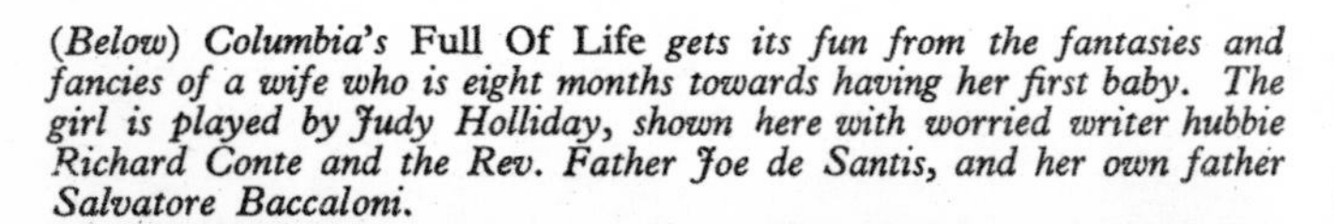

*(Below) Columbia's* Full Of Life *gets its fun from the fantasies and fancies of a wife who is eight months towards having her first baby. The girl is played by Judy Holliday, shown here with worried writer hubbie Richard Conte and the Rev. Father Joe de Santis, and her own father Salvatore Baccaloni.*

*(Above) Joan Crawford and Heather Sears in the Columbia British film* The Story of Esther Costello.

*(Below) Charles (Thorley Walters) learns that Deb (Adrienne Corri) is to do a further series of TV programmes, whilst Bill (Richard Wattis) wonders what will happen when he realises she has to go to New York. A scene from* Second Fiddle, *a British Lion release also starring Lisa Gastoni.*

*(Above) Belinda Lee as Julia, the girl behind the counter who is thinking of emigrating to Canada, and John Gregson as the roadman with the roving eye, in Emeric Pressburger's first film without partner Powell,* Miracle In Soho, *made for the J. Arthur Rank Organisation.*

*(Left) Wendy Hiller, the late Katie Johnson and Nigel Patrick in the Columbia British comedy* How To Murder a Rich Uncle.

*(Above) Deborah Kerr is surprised at schoolboy John Kerr's display of affection in this scene from M-G-M's film of the play,* Tea and Sympathy *which treads dangerous ground in telling its story of a lonely, understanding housemaster's wife, a misunderstood schoolboy and an insensitive schoolmaster (Leif Erickson), all recreating their original roles in one of the biggest successes and most talked about plays in the history of Broadway.*

*(Above) Eleanor Parker, bored with the quiet life as a doctor's wife, quarrels bitterly with her husband, Bill Travers. Set in Hong Kong, against the colourful background of international society, M-G-M's* The Seventh Sin *has an all-star cast headed by Eleanor Parker, British star Bill Travers, George Sanders, Jean Pierre Aumont and Francoise Rosay. David Lewis produced and Ronald Neame directed from Karl Tunberg's adaptation of the W. Somerset Maugham novel " The Painted Veil ".*

*(Right) A dramatic scene from M-G-M's* Man On Fire, *with Bing Crosby (on steps) battling Richard Eastham and E. G. Marshall as they stop him after he has tried to board a plane with his young son. At left Mary Fickett, who plays Crosby's divorced wife, is restraining the boy, portrayed by Malcolm Brodrick. Custody of the boy has been awarded to his mother and Crosby has been trying to kidnap him and take him out of the country.* Man On Fire *starring Bing Crosby, was produced for M-G-M by Sol C. Siegel. Also heading the cast are Inger Stevens, Mary Fickett, Malcolm Brodrick, Richard Eastham and E. G. Marshall.*

*(Below) Escaped from San Quentin, the fugitive (left) turns angrily on his brother who has helped him escape. The dual role of the brothers being played by Jack Palance. With all location scenes filmed inside California's famed San Quentin Prison, M-G-M's* House of Numbers *is an exciting story of suspense and passion. The film will introduce M-G-M's new discovery, Barbara Lang.*

*(Above) Cary Grant and Deborah Kerr in a scene from the Jerry Wald production of Leo McCarey's* An Affair to Remember, *released by 20th Century-Fox.*

*(Below) Frankie Vaughan sings one of his popular Rock'n-Roll numbers from his first film, the Associated-British production* These Dangerous Years.

*(Above) Rod Steiger is one of the stars in another of the new R.K.O. Radio films,* Run Of the Arrow. *This is a story about a Southerner who is so disgusted at the outcome of the American Civil War that he joins forces with the Redskins in order to fight on against the hated Yankees. And he marries a girl of the tribe, Yellow Moccasin (Sarita Montiel, shown here with Billy Miller, who plays the little mute boy they adopt as their son).*

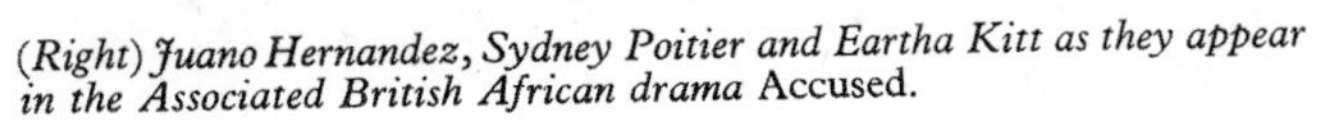

*(Right) Juano Hernandez, Sydney Poitier and Eartha Kitt as they appear in the Associated British African drama* Accused.

*(Above) France's Martine Carol accepted her first role in an American-made picture in M-G-M's* Action For the Tiger, *in which one of her co-stars is Van Johnson.*

*(Below) The innocent little girl from the country, Jean Simmons, fixes the tie of her nighterie owner boss Paul Douglas in this scene from Joe Pasternak's happy atmosphered musical for M-G-M,* This Could Be the Night.

*(Above) Dirk Bogarde and Barbara Murray in the J. Arthur Rank film of the Hammond Innes' best-selling novel* Campbell's Kingdom.

*(Above) Jack Palance plays* The Lonely Man *in the Paramount Western of that title. He is in fact a father whose odd relationship with his son leads to the final tragedy. Also in this scene, Elaine Aiken.*

*(Left) After several excursions into dramas and thrillers, in Warners'* The Pajama Game *Doris Day returns to the kind of film which first brought her screen fame and fortune. The movie is based on the successful stage musical of the same title. With Miss Day, co-star John Raith.*

*(Below) American comic Red Skelton returns to the screen in R.K.O. Radio's comedy (with music)* Public Pigeon No. 1. *With him are Vivian Blaine, Allyn Joslyn and Benny Baker.*

*(Below) Somebody is about to have their head lopped off in this scene from Paramount's spectacular colour film* Omar Khayyam.

# INDEX

*Figures in Italics indicate illustrations*



Made and printed in Great Britain by L.T.A. Robinson Ltd., London, S.W.9